Gorges Uge

Wall Street's on Democracy

How Financial Markets Exacerbate Inequalities

Springer

Georges Ugeux
Rye, NY, USA

ISBN 978-3-031-29093-0   ISBN 978-3-031-29094-7   (eBook)
https://doi.org/10.1007/978-3-031-29094-7

This Springer imprint is published by the registered company Springer Nature Switzerland AG
The registered company address is: Gewerbestrasse 11, 6330 Cham, Switzerland

To the people, families, and communities who had their lives ruined by the abusive practices of capital market operatives.

Foreword

Jacques de la Rosiere
Former Governor of the Banque de France and Director General of the
International Monetary Fund.

The author is a Belgian-born financier of high caliber. He was Vice President, International and Economic Research at the New York Stock Exchange, which gives an idea of the reputation he has acquired in the United States. He was an investment banker, a commercial banker, a specialist in financial markets, a university professor....

I only mention this curriculum to point out to his readers that Georges Ugeux "knows what he is talking about" when he speaks on financial subjects.

But the author is not only a fine technician and connoisseur of financial markets. He has a very broad vision of the system that governs us. He has reflected on the doctrinal foundations of our paradigm. He has developed a very precise and documented conception of what has become one of the essential foundations of our society. Not for a moment does Georges Ugeux indulge in technicality for its own sake.

He explains in a simple and clear language the roots of our problems, the way they have evolved over the last decades, and the consequences—quite unheard of—that these developments have had on our society and on the very future of our democracy.

Throughout this book, the author reveals himself: he belongs to the—all too rare—species of humanists.

As such, he dares to pose the dilemma: "Are markets only neutral instruments that allow the financial settlement of our economies? Or are they powerful factors of anti-democratic transformation of our society?"

And, with frankness mixed with science, lucidity, and conviction, he chooses without ambiguity the second alternative of this dilemma.

Yes, finance is deeply altering our democratic values. Indeed, the way in which our financial system has evolved over the last 20 years has powerfully favored the rise of social inequalities.

This is a theme that is often sketched out but rarely developed and argued. Georges Ugeux shows in his book with remarkable objectivity and precision that the monetary and financial policies followed by the so-called "advanced" countries over the last 20 years have favored the unprecedented rise in stock market valuations for the benefit of a minority of the population (around 10%) while the mass of wage earners saw their incomes stagnate.

He shows, with an almost medical precision, that the fact that central banks bought trillions of financial securities favored the rise in the stock market value of these securities while interest rates were falling to zero.

In other words, monetary policy—which is a public responsibility—favored stockholders while penalizing saving households.

Our author, a profound humanist, does not accept the enormous distortion of the distribution of wealth that has occurred before our incredulous or unconscious eyes over the past 15 years.

His formulas—all supported by figures and illustrated with graphs—hit the nail on the head: "Since the end of the Second World War, financial resources have been privatized while the welfare states have sunk into debt," or again: "the financial markets are not neutral: they directly influence savings, pension and insurance schemes and the distribution of resources between savers and borrowers," or: "Convincing households to accumulate more and more debt is a way, in the long run, to ruin the poorest among them".

Georges Ugeux, with the precision of a watchmaker, shows the interactions between:

– Monetary policy and worsening social inequalities
– Financial innovation and its consequences on society

And, perhaps even more boldly, Georges Ugeux explains that this world of financial markets, which is difficult to understand because of its technical nature, is dominated by a doctrine, a culture, that of "Anglo-Saxon capitalism."

It is this culture that exalts the shareholder and promotes the—permanent—increase of dividends.

Georges Ugeux shows the limits of this oversimplified principle and makes us understand that in a financialized world, where central banks organize the rise in stock market values, the fate of the shareholder cannot be systematically aligned with stock market performance, insofar as an important—not to say sometimes essential—part of this performance is not due solely to the results of the companies, but in large part to the financialization of the system. The same questioning applies to the—absurd—remunerations of current executives that are strongly influenced by the monetary policy which has, in an arbitrary and artificial way, pushed up stock market evolutions.

In conclusion, one must read the wise recommendations of the author:

- It is a matter of reconciling the two enemy sisters: finance and democracy.
- Central banks should henceforth focus on their basic task: the stabilization of the currency and not the rise of the stock markets.
- A whole series of specific reforms must be undertaken:

  - On the regulation of financial markets and their actors.
  - Taking into account the individual responsibility of decision makers.
  - A more efficient regulation of fraud and abuse (of which the author gives a detailed description).
  - The rationalization of the calculation of the emoluments of top executives, which today reach extreme and artificial amounts.
  - The intelligent questioning of the over-simplifying thesis of the indefinite and systematic increase of dividends.

The author believes that this change of direction is possible provided that governments and public opinion (as well as the media) become aware of the importance and urgency of such a policy. He also points out, with figures, that this need to reshuffle the deck requires a normalization of our tax system through an adequate contribution to corporate income tax by large companies (a significant number of which escape normal taxation).

A book full of facts and observations, a book that is both a cry of alarm (at a certain level, inequality kills democracy) and a coherent, precise, and optimistic vision of what must be done.

J. de Larosière

Without equality there can be no democracy.
Eleanor Roosevelt, October 12, 1944
No one pretends that democracy is perfect or all-wise. Indeed, it has been said
that democracy is the worst form of Government except for all those other forms
that have been tried from time to time...
Winston S. Churchill, November 11, 1947

Acknowledgments

This book is the result of a long journey that brought me in 1996 to the New York Stock Exchange, at Richard A. Grasso, its Chairman, and CEO's invitation. He trusted me to launch the International Division and oversee the Research Department, as Group Executive Vice President.

The opportunity to teach International Banking and Finance at Columbia Law School was a great learning process (nothing is better to learn than teaching). My colleagues Katharina Pistor and Kathryn Judge were a great encouragement in this endeavor. Agreed on the theme of inequality.

Emily Abrons has been a diligent and thoughtful editor of the manuscript for which I am very grateful.

To those whose time together has been curtailed, my gratitude for your patience and understanding.

Contents

About the Authors

Georges Ugeux is Chairman of Galileo Global Advisors LLC, which he founded to offer independent advice on international strategy, finance, and capital raising. Prior to founding Galileo, he was Group Executive Vice President, International and Research, at the New York Stock Exchange, where he built and managed the Exchange's International Group. He is a Lecturer on International Banking and Finance at Columbia Law School.

Ugeux published several books in France, Belgium, China, and the United States focusing on the various aspects of the financial regulation of banking and finance, including its human and societal impacts. His book *International Financial Regulation* is considered as a reference. He is regularly called to speak or comment on international financial matters.

Ugeux, a dual American and Belgian national, began his career at Société Générale de Banque (now BNP Paribas Fortis) before becoming Managing Director of Morgan Stanley's Mergers and Acquisitions and Corporate Finance departments in London. He became Group Finance Director at Société Générale de Belgique, the leading Belgian diversified industrial and financial conglomerate. Subsequently, he became the President of Kidder, Peabody International, owned at the time by General Electric, where he ultimately led the firm's global origination efforts. He was a member of the European Executive Council of General Electric.

Ugeux lectured at the University of Louvain and the College of Europe and served as a Special Advisor to the Program on International Financial Systems at Harvard Law School.

Jacques de Larosière, Former Managing Director, IMF was the Managing Director of the International Monetary Fund between 1978 and 1987. After beginning his career as a member of the Inspectorate General of Finances, he became Director of the French Treasury, Governor of the Banque de France, President of the European Bank for Reconstruction and Development, and President of the European Savings Institute and of the think tank EUROFI. He is currently Advisor to BNP Paribas's Chairman.

Jacques de Larosière, a former student of the ENA, graduated from the IEP (Institut d'Etudes Politiques of Paris). He is a member of the Académie des Sciences Morales et Politiques of the Institut de France. He authored a dozen books, the most recent on *50 Years of Financial Crises* and *Putting an End to the Reign of Financial Illusion: For Real Growth*, published in Paris at Editions Odile Jacob.

Introduction: Wall Street's Denial

Too weak the markets and society becomes unproductive, too weak a democratic community and society tends toward crony capitalism, too weak the state and society turns fearful and apathetic. Conversely, too much market and society becomes inequitable, too much community and society becomes static, and too much state and society becomes authoritarian. A balance is essential. (*Raguram Raja, the Third Pillar*[1])

---

[1] https://www.penguinrandomhouse.com/books/566369/the-third-pillar-by-raghuram-rajan/

© The Author(s), under exclusive license to Springer Nature Switzerland AG 2023
G. Ugeux, *Wall Street's Assault on Democracy*, https://doi.org/10.1007/978-3-031-29094-7_1

2022: The Year When the Veil of the Temple Was Torn

On November 24, 2020, in the midst of the second phase of lockdown, the Dow Jones Industrial Average (DJIA) surpassed 30,000 points to the delight and delirium of Wall Street. Since its brutal fall in March 2020, the index had risen by more than 100%, seemingly unaffected by the structural consequences of a pandemic that had rocked the planet.

By 2022, the convergence of the pandemic crisis, the surge of inflation, the explosion of sovereign debt, the misguided monetary policy of central banks, and the Chinese economic and financial downfall created the perfect storm that Wall Street chose to ignore.

The Pandemic Crisis

Faced with the invasion of SARS-CoV-2 (severe acute respiratory syndrome coronavirus 2), public authorities took drastic budgetary measures whose consequences did not reach their target. Already financially weakened before the coronavirus crisis, nations worldwide developed stimulus programs that exploded their budget deficits and consequently their indebtedness. If this capital had found its economic destination, such a financial imbalance would have been acceptable. Most of it, however, went to the financial markets. It was too much, too soon. Combined with the record low and sometimes negative interest rates of central banks, whose balance sheets exploded by $9 trillion, it created a financial inflation that will inevitably unravel.

It would be unfair, however, not to recognize the benefit of hindsight in the cost-benefit analysis of a decision that was taken under extreme circumstances.

© The Author(s), under exclusive license to Springer Nature Switzerland AG 2023
G. Ugeux, *Wall Street's Assault on Democracy*, https://doi.org/10.1007/978-3-031-29094-7_2

As Jerome Powell, the Federal Reserve Chair, stated in April 2020: "We are deploying these lending powers to an unprecedented extent…We will continue to use these powers forcefully, proactively, and aggressively until we are confident that we are solidly on the road to recovery." Couldn't a gradual approach have produced better results?

During the heat of the COVID crisis, media trumpets heightened public anxiety and forced the political class to focus on the evolution, the figures, and the actors of the sanitary crisis. Their tone and discourse have distilled fear and paralyzed households, schools, and businesses. Even the most serious among them bear responsibility for considering only the virus without putting it into perspective with other economic and societal factors, creating a dynamic of fear-based paralysis. It proved toxic and anxiogenic.

And Then There Was War

Russia's invasion of Ukraine was prepared as early as the summer of 2021. One-hundred thousand troops were on the Ukrainian border by year-end. President Biden warned the world of an imminent invasion on January 19, 2022. It was not until the end of March that Wall Street started to realize the seriousness of the threats to Europe and the world.

Blind to the most serious geopolitical threat since World War II, Wall Street did not look at the long-term consequences of a conflict involving a country, Russia, which has as many nuclear warheads as the United States.

For the first time, Europe is at war again and relies on the United States for its defense. The shadow of a nuclear war is looming.

The Energy Crisis

At the core of the economic consequences of this war lies the profound disruption of the energy markets. The dependency of Europe on Russian oil and gas was driven by the antinuclear lobby in Germany.[1] The country turned its back on nuclear energy and, as late as January 2022, closed its last nuclear plants. The war exposed the continent's vulnerability to political tension with Russia, while countries like France were immune to those pressures, having developed nuclear energy to represent half their consumption.

---

[1] https://www.cleanenergywire.org/factsheets/history-behind-germanys-nuclear-phase-out

Yet the war is not the main source of the increase of oil and gas prices. Both prices doubled, but only one-fifth of the increase happened after the start of the war in Ukraine. Western oil companies, partly under pressure from investors and environmental activists, are drilling fewer wells than they did before the pandemic to restrain the increase in supply.[2]

While oil prices have returned to where they were back in 2019, the gas prices remain at record levels and threaten European energy stability. Immediately the OPEC (Organization of Petroleum Exporting Countries) countries and Russia decided to reduce the oil production by two million barrels a day.[3]

It was the first, but not the only, source of inflation spreading across the world. The main impact was on the consumers, who saw the price at the pump double and saw other energy costs explode. As usual, those who were most affected were low-income households.

But All Is Not Lost for Everybody

The major energy groups were summoned to testify by the Energy Committee of the US Congress yet denied their role in this increase of energy prices. The increase of their profits and their denial of the benefit they derive from the energy crisis is yet another demonstration of their abdication of responsibility for the impact of those profits on the cost increase for customers. The tumult of war and climate breakdown has proved lucrative for the world's leading oil and gas companies, with financial records showing 28 of the largest producers made close to $100 billion in combined profits in just the first three months of 2022. In 2021, Exxon raked in $8.8 billion, also a near threefold increase.[4]

The TotalEnergies, the French oil major, refused to stop its oil activities in Russia, in line with the ambiguous attitude of the French government. Saudi Arabia refused to increase its oil supply, while its oil company Saudi Aramco doubled its profits in 2022 to $48 billion.[5]

---

[2] https://www.nytimes.com/2022/02/02/business/economy/oil-price.html

[3] https://www.nytimes.com/live/2022/10/05/business/economy-news-inflation-stocks#opec-russia-oil-output

[4] https://www.theguardian.com/business/2022/may/13/oil-gas-producers-first-quarter-2022-profits

[5] https://www.statista.com/chart/27887/big-oil-sees-profits-increase/?utm_source=Statista+Newsletters&utm_campaign=839a9c0582-ll_InfographTicker_daily_COM_PM_KW28_2022_Fr_COPY&utm_medium=email&utm_term=0_662f7ed75e-839a9c0582-336414038

The Looming Sovereign Debt Crisis

Ever since the glorious decade of the nineties, sovereign debt has been exploding.

Global public debt levels were already elevated before the COVID-19 pandemic. The crisis is adding to spending needs as countries seek to mitigate the health and economic effects of the pandemic, while fiscal revenues are falling due to lower economic activity. This has pushed debt levels to new heights, close to 100% of the GDP globally.[6]

Global government debt is set to rise 9.5% in 2022 to a record $71.6 trillion, driven by the United States, Japan, and China. It was $50.5 trillion in 2020.[7] Yet this only applies to those countries that have the luxury to access capital markets to fund their budget deficits. We cannot ignore the dramatic situation of emerging markets whose situation has been worsened by the recent developments of the world economy.

The fiscal deficits were driven by two main factors in the United States: the increase of military expenses and the tax complacency toward large companies. The balance was paid by a set of taxes affecting the public social insurance, consumption tax, and social insurance tax. As interest rates increase, their impact on budget deficits will profoundly destabilize public finance.

Globalization led to a fierce tax competition that provoked a reduction of corporate taxes from 40% to 20%. Short of corporate tax income, governments increased consumption tax and personal income tax as well as borrowed their budgetary shortfall.[8] New sovereign borrowing is expected to reach $10.4 trillion in 2022, almost a third above the average prior to the COVID-19 pandemic. Global sovereign debt is expected to climb by 9.5% to a record $71.6 trillion in 2022.[9]

Central Banks Lose Control of Inflation

After a decade of accommodative monetary policies, central banks lost their economic compass and failed to predict, let alone contain, the inflation eruption in 2022. However, we need to be honest: While they were in charge of

[6] https://www.imf.org/en/Topics/sovereign-debt

[7] https://www.janushenderson.com/en-gb/investor/jh-sovereign-debt-index/#:~:text=The%20 Sovereign%20Debt%20Index%20is,and%20the%20risks%20it%20presents

[8] https://www.imf.org/en/Publications/Policy-Papers/Issues/2019/03/08/Corporate-Taxation-in-the-Global-Economy-46650

[9] https://www.cnbc.com/2022/04/06/global-government-debt-set-to-soar-to-record-71-trillion-this--year-research.html

managing inflation, central banks were not the only factor that explains this unexpected resurgence.

"The leading central banks appear to have lost control of consumers' inflation expectations, and the costs could be high. If wage increases accelerate over the next quarter, monetary policymakers will be obliged to respond firmly by raising interest rates sharply, or else lose even more credibility," according to Sir Howard Davies, former Deputy Governor of the Bank of England.[10]

The monetary policy was the source of one of the greatest inequalities in the history of capital markets: Central banks expropriated savings to favor borrowers. They might not have done it intentionally, but they could not ignore that this was the direct consequence of their policies. They did it through an "alternative monetary policy" known as quantitative easing (QE). In the last ten years, the balance sheet of the US, European, and Japanese central banks collectively increased sixfold to reach $25 trillion.

It was the central banks who came to the rescue of sovereign borrowers during the pandemic by subscribing to their debt to the tune of $6 trillion in the space of six weeks at the end of March 2020—an amount equivalent to the ten years of quantitative easing spent to revive the economy after the Lehman crisis.

There was no chance that this capital could be used productively, since the monetary transmission mechanism takes months or years.[11] Deprived of interest on bonds due to the lowering of interest rates by these same central banks, investors rushed to the stock market. The rush to equities was responsible for the sharpest increase in history of the stock indices.

Central banks can only affect one dimension of the economy through monetary policy: the demand for assets. At a time when supply was already reduced because of the sanitary policies of governments, central banks amplified the demand for goods and services, provoking rather than containing inflation. In 2021, the signs of a growing inflation were ignored by central banks, who continued to heat the imbalance between supply and demand. Already by April 2021, US inflation had reached 4.5%, the highest level since the infamous year 2008.[12] By year-end, it had reached 7%. A double-digit inflation now seems unavoidable.

---

[10] https://www.project-syndicate.org/commentary/central-banks-losing-control-of-inflation-expectations-by-howard-davies-2022-01

[11] https://www.bostonfed.org/publications/research-department-working-paper/2006/the-monetary-transmission-mechanism.aspx

[12] https://www.bbc.com/news/business-57090421

European Central Bank (ECB) President Christine Lagarde explained at the end of October 2021 that "Rising energy prices, the recovery in demand and supply bottlenecks are currently pushing up inflation…We continue to foresee inflation in the medium term remaining below our two percent target."[13]

As for the Bank of Japan (BOJ), it continues its accommodative monetary policy but reduces its purchase of Japan Government Bonds (JGB) despite the plunge of the value of the Japanese Yen.[14]

The Chinese Economy in Financial Demise

While all this was happening, little attention was being paid to the situation in China.

Evergrande, the largest real estate developer in China, was approaching bankruptcy. Its stock price dropped by 95%. Its bond prices dropped 90% to yield over 25% while its rating was reduced to B. Importantly, 1.6 million Chinese households are still awaiting the delivery of their apartments from Evergrande.

What could have rescued Evergrande and its $305 billion in debt would have been a recovery of the Chinese economy. President Xi Jinping's zero-COVID policy brought China's large cities to a standstill. President Xi Jinping's increasingly ideological campaign to rid China of the Omicron variant of COVID-19 is threatening to throttle economic growth this year.[15]

China is experiencing its most serious financial and economic demise. China's response to crisis has a common root: swagger and hubris in public, an obsession with control in private, and dubious results.[16]

China's banks face mortgage losses of $350 billion in a worst-case scenario, as confidence plunges in the nation's property market and authorities struggle to contain deepening turmoil.

In the wake of some of the most challenging economic conditions in decades, China's middle class is demonstrating a level of defiance that has arguably never been seen before in the country's modern history.[17]

---

[13] https://www.ecb.europa.eu/press/pressconf/2021/html/ecb.is211028~939f22970b.en.html

[14] https://www.boj.or.jp/en/announcements/release_2022/rel220423a.htm

[15] https://www.economist.com/finance-and-economics/2022/05/07/chinas-erratic-policies-are-terrifying-investors

[16] https://www.economist.com/weeklyedition/2022-04-16

[17] https://www.asiamarkets.com/china-evergrande-social-unrest/

2023 or the Year Depositors Were Favored with Public Money: SVB, FRB, and Credit Suisse

If we needed the demonstration that the authorities are too afraid of a financial crisis to apply their own rules and, instead, use public money, 2023 demonstrates the inability of those authorities to apply their own rules.

The Mismanagement of Silicon Valley Bank

It started with Silicon Valley Bank: its management had exceeded its deposit collection and invested that $200 billion surplus deposits into long-term securities: 10-to-20-year US Treasuries. By doing so they breached the golden rule of duration. Not invest short-term deposits in long-term assets. They did it when US Treasuries were still offering low yields. It was their way of creating the illusion of positive carry. Inflation and an increase of interest rates in 2022 would ruin this policy.

Furthermore, those $200 billion were not intended to be treated as disposable assets. While these bonds were classified as marketable securities while it was obvious that if interest rates were to increase, SVB would only have one option: sell US Treasuries at a loss. And so, they did. They were the only US bank who hid the long-term horizon of their US Treasury investments.

Under US banking regulations, deposits are guaranteed by the Federal Reserve up to $250,000 per depositor. That was not the case for SVB whose retail accounts only represented $30 billion. The balance would be subject to a haircut… Except that the Federal Reserve, turning its back to its own rules, decided to guarantee the extra $200 billion, using taxpayer guarantee to cover uninsured corporate deposits.

© The Author(s), under exclusive license to Springer Nature Switzerland AG 2023
G. Ugeux, *Wall Street's Assault on Democracy*, https://doi.org/10.1007/978-3-031-29094-7_3

The Federal Reserve renounced the protection of its own rules. It used public money to protect large depositors. It ignored the signals of mismanagement of SVB. Public money would be once more used to protect wealthy depositors.

The Contagion of First Republic Bank

One of the consequences of the guarantee of deposits of SVB was to leave another medium-sized bank, First Republic Bank, in difficulty. The fact that SVB deposits were guaranteed by the Fed was indirectly reducing the robustness of the deposits of FRB. FRB depositors transferred their deposits to SVB. And then, there was an FRB crisis.

In the context of the time, the entire sector of medium-sized banks became fragile. How to solve the problem?

The White House and the Federal Reserve managed a coup: JP Morgan Chase would take over FRB. That had no sense for JPM, and it would require public money to obtain the agreement of the Board of JP Morgan. Once again, the public sector extended public support to a large bank to have it rescue a weaker bank with public money support.

It is only because the FRB extended a deposit guarantee to SVB that depositors of FRB had to be helped. Once again, this extended to the totality of deposits, against all rules and regulations.

The Credit Suisse Saga

Totally independent from those two cases, but in a troubled banking climate, rumors started to emerge on the robustness of Credit Suisse, the second largest Swiss bank and an institution classified by the authorities a "Systemic Important Financial institution" (SIFI).

Switzerland decided to use emergency measures to fast-track the takeover by UBS of Credit Suisse, as the banks and their regulators rush to seal a merger deal before markets open. Under Swiss rules, UBS would typically have to give shareholders six weeks to consult on the acquisition, which would combine Switzerland's two biggest lenders.

The amount of deposit short fall was CHF 50 billion for $1 trillion. The Banque Nationale Suisse extended CHF 75 billion in guarantee. There was no urgency, no major risk, yet rather than acting according to the BIS rules, Switzerland uses public money to "save" Credit Suisse.

Needless to say, the market share of a combined UBS and Credit Suisse would explode to at least 40% with the next one at 7%: how will the Swiss Conseil d'État accept such a dominance of one single banking group? At the end, the Swiss Government decided.

The simple fact that no other solutions has been looked at seriously says it all: Credit Suisse is not in bankruptcy and its management has been restructuring the bank. The Swiss National Bank will be responsible for not pre-empting this situation that has of course nothing to do with banks in the US whose size is one thousandth of Credit Suisse.

The Three Cases Have a Common Thread

In the three cases, the authorities had been negligent, had not applied the rules and regulations established after the Great Financial Crisis to resolve financial crises, and favored large capital with public money. The consequences are clear: regulators are too weak to execute their own rules. The question is not the rules but their implementation. This leaves inequality in place.

The Disconnect with the Real Economy

On the one hand, the real economy had to face a brutal recession in 2020, characterized by an abysmal unemployment rate and household purchasing power at half-mast, which in turn led to a dizzying decline in corporate profits. Despite the recovery of 2021, the first quarter of 2022 saw a 1.4% decrease in the US GDP in the first quarter, followed by a 0.9% decrease in the second quarter.

The recession risks are spreading worldwide. A toxic mix of recession risks hangs over the world economy. American inflation, Europe's energy crisis, and China's Omicron outbreak threaten the world economy with a downturn.[1]

On the other hand, thanks to $100 trillion of growth in global debt since the global financial crisis (GFC) of 2008, stock market indices have soared to the top of the capitalization records, blithely ignoring the accumulation of threats to the economic, social, and financial stability of the planet, and thus the systemic risk that debt poses to the global economy.

Over the years, the actors of the financial markets (both public and private) have ignored any form of social and economic contribution to the smallest possible portion—only short-term enrichment counts.

Importantly, Wall Street, by ignoring these threats to society, the economy, inflation, and war, has become the puppet of gamification and in that sense has lost any relevance as a bellwether of the economy. This gamification has rendered it closer to a casino, where short-term supply and demand dominate fluctuations. Its price discovery has been irrational over the past ten years.

---

[1] https://www.economist.com/leaders/2022/04/09/a-toxic-mix-of-recession-risks-hangs-over-the-world-economy

© The Author(s), under exclusive license to Springer Nature Switzerland AG 2023
G. Ugeux, *Wall Street's Assault on Democracy*, https://doi.org/10.1007/978-3-031-29094-7_4

Inflation Rears Its Ugly Head

The inflation pressures started immediately after central banks injected $9 trillion into an economy that could not use it. The fundamental imbalance between supply and demand created by the lockdowns around the world has been increased by this injection, which pushed the demand beyond any reasonable possibility to use those massive monies in the real economy.

As early as May 2020, when it seemed no one else was paying attention, Larry Summers sent a clear message regarding these risks to President Joe Biden: "It is clear that inflation is the dominant economic problem as seen by the American people…significantly contributing to distrust in the institutions and to pessimism about the future. That is a terribly, terribly important thing at a time when our democratic institutions are being challenged."[2]

Fraud and Manipulation Are on the Rise

Beyond these vicissitudes, the years 2020–2022 were also the scene of manipulations and fraud on the part of companies.

The first bad news came from Germany, where German authorities gave massive support to **Wirecard**, the leading payment technology company, with fraud exceeding $3 billion. The scandal became known following an investigation by the Financial Times, which was then sued for publishing this information by the German regulator![3]

A few months later, **GameStop** drew attention to the maneuvers of some hedge funds that had massively shorted the company's shares, betting that it would go bankrupt. They were met with a protective response from an army of small buyers who sent the share price soaring and managed to put one of the funds that had taken on the company in jeopardy.[4]

At the beginning of 2021, it was **Greensill**'s turn to make the headlines, after abusing debt and investing unwisely in a British steel company owned by an Indian tycoon. Behind this failure, we find attempts to raise funds by the former British Prime Minister David Cameron, who had tried to bribe Her

---

[2] https://news.harvard.edu/gazette/story/2022/02/pandemic-only-partly-to-blame-for-record-inflation-says-lawrence-summers/

[3] https://www.ft.com/wirecard

[4] https://www.forbes.com/sites/jonathanponciano/2021/03/24/gamestop-crash-wipes-out-5-billion-reddit-fueled-surge/

Majesty's Treasury and the Crown Prince of Saudi Arabia. Several banks lost money.[5]

A few months later, another big scandal broke out surrounding the hedge fund **Archegos**, financed by a series of banks and whose collapse should cost Credit Suisse $5 billion, which had to increase its capital to restore its equity. The balance was distributed among the Nomura, Deutsche Bank, Morgan Stanley, Goldman Sachs, and UBS (Union Bank of Switzerland). It is the financing activity of hedge funds, called "prime brokerage," that allowed this over-indebtedness—without the banks to finance them, these funds could not exist. We will come back to this point.[6]

On the **cryptocurrency** side, the horizon is not clear either; Masayoshi Son; owner of the Japanese telecommunications firm SoftBank; Mark Zuckerberg, co-founder and CEO of Facebook; and Elon Musk, co-founder and CEO of Tesla, have all wandered into the world of digital currencies and failed.[7] The price of Bitcoin dropped from $68,000 to $17,000 in less than a year, confirming its substantive emptiness and its extreme volatility with a three-quarter decrease in value.

The last incarnation of toxic CEO hubris was Elon Musk's launch of a $44 billion offer on Twitter that is currently being investigated (once more) by the SEC and demonstrates the lack of professionalism of those who believe they are above the law and can do no wrong.[8]

These few situations illustrate my point: The so-called dark side of finance has not reduced its activities during the pandemic crisis. We would be naive to believe that reforms will not be fiercely opposed by the powerful lobby of the financial world, which, despite its constructive role, hides fraudulent, not to mention criminal, practices. Those who committed those frauds are still alive and well, and no criminal or civil pursuits against them as individuals are envisaged.

Wall Street Imposes Its Short-Term Vision

Little by little, the time horizon has become shorter: the generalization of quarterly results has led companies to focus on their immediate results and to abandon decisions that are essential to building a solid and robust industry.

[5] https://www.nytimes.com/2021/03/28/business/greensill-capital-collapse.html

[6] https://www.hedgeweek.com/2021/05/05/299729/archegos-collapse-shows-what-can-happen-when-leverage-misapplied

[7] https://gugeux.medium.com/masa%2D%2Dand-elon-the-crypto-influencers-2314a2924c8b

[8] https://www.washingtonpost.com/technology/2022/05/27/elon-sec-twitter/

Investors also publish their performance quarterly, favoring investments in companies based on their immediate results and short-term performance.

Within the financial world, hedge funds devote their activity to the search for "absolute" and maximum gain, without any interest in the companies in which it invests. Worse, once they have acquired a stake in the target company, some hedge funds function as activists and try to force its board of directors to adopt a short-term policy.

Executive compensation has become indecent. More than half of the country's 100 largest low-wage employers rigged pay rules in 2020 to give CEOs an average raise of 29% while their frontline employees made 2% less.[9] Two years after the start of the pandemic, the early data shows that CEO pay is back on the rise. In 2021, the median total direct compensation for companies included in the analysis increased to $14.3 million. This change from $12 million in 2020 would represent a near 20% increase should the trend persist.[10] Tied to the stock market price rather than to the results of their company, they encourage quarterly management at the expense of long-term management of the company. The typical compensation package for chief executives who run Standard & Poor's 500 companies soared 17.1% in 2021, to a median $14.5 million, according to data analyzed by Equilar for the Associated Press.

It is therefore to a change of perspective that this book calls the reader and our leaders, both business and political. It is a change of course that calls and awaits humanity, without which tomorrow will be worse than today. We will not solve the problems of energy transition and climate change with short-term policies. A long-term commitment is a necessity.

Sustainability is at the center of our concerns: It must be made a duty, and political, economic, and social leaders are its long-term guardians. It requires long-term investors rather than speculative funds.

Priority to the Shareholder: The Ideology That Creates Inequality

The ideology that excessively favors the shareholder has become a threat to democracy: It destroys jobs but creates wealth for the richest. Governments are part of the scheme. They do not dare to oppose the lobbies of big business and their shareholders, on whom they depend for their electoral campaigns.

---

[9] https://inequality.org/great-divide/pumped-up-ceo-pay-pandemic/

[10] https://corpgov.law.harvard.edu/2022/03/29/proxy-season-2022-early-trends-in-executive-compensation

Favoring shareholders to the detriment of employment, long-term investment, and the company as a social body is a dogma that comes from the United States. It is the very heart of Anglo-Saxon financial capitalism, which for decades has transformed the financial markets into a powerful machine threatening democracy.

Institutional investors possess increased power to push companies to increase their dividends and buy back shares to boost the stock price and therefore their return. These companies thus sacrifice long-term value to short-term gains, being themselves subject to the constraints of quarterly reporting.

Recently, voices have been heard from among major investors and companies for a broader consideration of social responsibility. This movement corresponds to values that are deeply rooted in European values but are not part of Anglo-Saxon financial capitalism. This year will have shown us that a new form of solidarity-based capitalism will have to replace the "all-for-the-shareholder" form of capitalism. This disruption will be the only way to prevent democracy from taking to the streets again.

So far, words have not been followed by actions.

Humanism Rather Than Populism

Financial markets have an essential economic purpose in allowing the financing of governments and companies. But the ecosystem has reached a size and influence that makes them more an instrument of enrichment than a tool for economic growth.

The attack by populists of both sides on capitalism and the financial markets themselves is inflammatory and sterile. They have the wrong target. Like any market, they reflect their participants, their objectives, and divergent interests, which by nature are self-centered. This book attempts to lift the veil on Wall Street and its global equivalents inspired by Anglo-Saxon financial ideology.

We will need to ask some tough questions and analyze the mechanisms that made this situation possible:

- How will policies reestablish a fair contribution from large companies to the public budget?
- How will central banks manage to reestablish equity between borrowers and investors?

- How will regulators oversee the need to avoid the abuse of financial innovation?
- How will executive compensation be based on performance rather than stock prices?
- How will financial communication and education reduce misinformation?
- How will corporations recreate a balance between profits and employment?
- How will we integrate long-term considerations in our policies?

If we want to reestablish a balance toward communities, it is those who participate in this drift, and not only the markets, that we must challenge. It is necessary to understand their objectives and the functioning of the markets that favor those interests. It is at this level that reforms are indispensable.

The risks to democracy posed by the various populisms, whether of the right or the left, rely on a unilateral ideology of the past. The "people" of these movements have nothing to do with the "demos" of democracy, which gave voice to all voters. Populism is influenced by racist, sexist, extremist, fascist, and in many cases autocratic ideologies. It is dominated by the pursuit of power.

The answer to the challenges created by the abuse of financial power is not populism but humanism. It is fundamental that finance, like economics and politics, puts the human being back at the center of our societies.

The Emergence of Plutocracy

The self-interest of financiers and markets, which our governments protect and nourish, has become intolerable and so unwieldy that their dark and malevolent side has burst into the open. The answer is not about patronizing or charitable actions. It is about fairness. It is about an inalienable right to justice. It is an ethical question. But in order to implement equity, it is necessary to dissect its components without getting lost in the labyrinth of technicality and logomachy in order to reveal its obvious requirement: a plutocratic world.

Each and every one of us is trying to free ourselves from these constraints in a way that is as clumsy as it is ineffective. Many households were abused by their bankers in 2008, mainly in the United States. Minimum wage earners were led to believe that they could afford a genuinely nice house despite their limited means. The lack of knowledge of personal finance management, and more generally of financial education, is a big part of this.

As Zachary Karabell has explained, "There's an emerging consensus in America today that the accumulation of vast wealth by a handful of individuals is untenable for our democracy. Balancing the other-worldly success of a few in contrast with the challenges many still face is one of the thornier dilemmas of a post-COVID-19 world where those gaps have grown ever wider. The recent analysis of the tax rates of the mega-rich—which showed that the 25 richest Americans, including Jeff Bezos and Warren Buffet, paid a paltry $13 billion in federal taxes on income and gains of $400 billion over a four-year period 2014 and 2018—is just the latest powerful example."[11]

The Cause Is Not Lost

There is no need to hope to undertake
  Nor to succeed to persevere (William of Orange-Nassau, known as the Taciturn)

All these mechanisms could give the impression that the cause is heard. Let us not waste time trying to destroy the Holy Alliance of big money, corporations, and governments. It is so powerful that we would be like Don Quixote if we tried to fight it! The unbalance between those who have and those who have not has become unbearable.

In half a century of working in the world of finance, I have seen how finance can change its perspective and care about people. As I am proposing strategic and financial partners to join the biggest platform to fight cancer in India, a country of 1.4 billion people, I can see the importance of finance as an impactful and purposeful tool. There is a way to democratize finance under three conditions: have the will, the courage, and the knowledge.

Revolutionary rhetoric will not do the trick if we do not elect politicians with integrity who are willing to refocus a confused debate. Let us take a closer look at the financial challenges of our time. We will find things we can do about them.

Let us never forget that market operators start from a viewpoint that is not wrong. Their clients are ignorant. The paths of this financial market reform are arduous and complex, but they are realistic. The time has come to demystify the role of financial markets.

A series of reforms will have to be put in place. There is no magic bullet—we will have to examine the role of the actors, the functioning of the financial

---

[11] https://time.com/6072132/americas-plutocrats-learn-past-generations/

markets, and the ideology that underlies them before we can specify the outline of reforms, without which the exacerbation of inequalities will only be perpetuated. Let us make no mistake, however: it is to a complete change of perspective and a redefinition of capital markets that this book invites the reader.

It Is Time to Tell the Truth

I started this book because, after half a century in the financial world, I have become increasingly convinced that financial markets, by exacerbating inequality, threaten democracy and have no other option than to reform, transform, and question themselves if they want to regain credibility and trust and avoid social unrest. Wall Street must reconnect with its economic and social purpose. I believe that the battle may be lost, but not the war. It is important to rebalance the economic and social relationship between markets, governments, and the population.

I developed a distinct understanding of the financial markets as a commercial banker, an investment banker, a manager of a public investment fund, and a corporate finance director, both in Europe and in the United States. Having managed the international and research division of the New York Stock Exchange at 11 Wall Street, I had the opportunity to experience the daily life of these markets both domestically and around the world. My international responsibilities have taken me to the four corners of the globe, and I have seen capital markets in action in widely different environments.

A strong academic interest enriched this practitioner's experience. I currently teach a seminar on the International Banking and Finance and a reading group on the Central Banking at Columbia University Law School in New York. These experiences have enriched my understanding of finance, by adding an academic and pedagogical dimension.

Given the devastating consequences of the law of silence and denial of the systemic risks, I only want to be a voice that questions the one-sided narratives of financial market participants. This book will identify the forces at play, their interests, and the various initiatives being taken inside capital markets to favor those interests rather than the common interest. It is not to destroy market economy but to outlaw market abuse by refusing to accept the exacerbation of inequalities.

This book will not be complacent. It will attempt to provide a vision and clarify the issues at stake in accessible language. It will also look at each and every mechanism that tweaks markets toward increased inequality and suggest reforms that could attenuate them.

I am inspired by a humanistic philosophy. I believe that without humanism our society is headed for ruin. The abuse of power is everywhere—we must first recognize it, track it down, and try to reform it.

Our democracy depends on it.

An Unsustainable Inequality

The imbalance of individual wealth has recently grown to create a profoundly inequitable society.

Democracy in such a society is not effective: Access to knowledge and education has become increasingly costly and is part of an elitist reproduction mechanism. For the first time, parents have been put in jail for corrupting the admission offices of major US universities.[1]

Access to quality, well-paid jobs are tainted by inequalities of all kinds. Inequalities such as these are the breeding grounds for populism, which, while offering no answers to these problems, makes people believe it will solve them. Have we really lost the sense of solidarity and humanism?

One of the drivers of this inequality is the enrichment of those who have access to the financial markets. As the saying goes, you only lend to the rich. It is compounded by the limits of access to credit: The 2008 Global Financial Crisis (GFC) has led to tighter lending conditions by the banks, depriving a generation of young families of access to home ownership. "Low-wealth families today face a crisis in both affordable homeownership and rental housing, but access to these assets is essential to building wealth and financial stability for renting or buying," explains Michael Calhoun, president of the Center for Responsible Lending, in a paper published by the Brookings Institute.[2]

---

[1] https://www.nytimes.com/2019/03/12/us/college-admissions-cheating-scandal.html

[2] https://www.brookings.edu/research/lessons-from-the-financial-crisis-the-central-importance-of-a-sustainable-affordable-and-inclusive-housing-market/

© The Author(s), under exclusive license to Springer Nature Switzerland AG 2023
G. Ugeux, *Wall Street's Assault on Democracy*, https://doi.org/10.1007/978-3-031-29094-7_5

Furthermore, housing determines affordable access to education. The proximity of one's home to the most sought-after schools often comes at an exorbitant cost.

The literature is full of books on savings management and access to financial markets. But when employment is erratic and stock values quadruple, as they have in the United States over the past decade, the odds are stacked against households. If we add the use of debt to acquire even more financial assets, we are faced with an inexorable wealth multiplier.

This phenomenon exploded when inflation erupted in 2021–2022. Mortgage rates' largest increases since 1987 make access to home ownership challenging.

30 Year Fixed Mortgage Rates
Mortgage News Daily

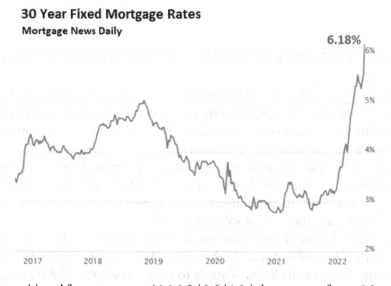

https://wolfstreet.com/2022/06/13/that-was-fast-30-year-fixed-mortgage-rate-spikes-to-6-18-10-yeartreasury-yield-to-3-43-home-sellers-face-new-reality/

The Excesses of Financial Markets Threaten Democracy

Finance is supposed to open the way to all ambitions. It allows one to purchase power, education, prestige, wealth, and even, for some, happiness. To acquire wealth, people steal, lie, cheat, rape, torture, and kill. This is often the origin of wars and terrorist conflicts behind which lie hidden economic and financial ambitions. Wasn't it the driving force behind the war unilaterally launched by the United States against Iraq? Isn't it at the core of the Russian aggression in Ukraine and the sanctions that followed?

The power of finance seems infinite. Faced with this inequality, individuals feel hopeless, threatened, and, in most cases, deprived of the basic necessities of life for themselves, their family, their community, their country, and their culture. Democracy comes from the Greek word Δημοκρατία: the power of the people. In financial matters, this power is seriously eroded.

Is this a war already lost by the people? Is democracy so venal and corrupt? The markets are at the heart of the capitalist system, and they support the economy and its growth. To reform them, we need to take a closer look at the abuses committed in their name. The most effective way to ensure the sustainability of complex systems is to blame them all together. It is urgent to identify their methods of fostering inequality in order to dismantle them.

The Stock Market Is Not an Economic or Political Barometer

Donald Trump's presidency will have been marked by his pretension to measure up to the vagaries of Wall Street. Despite a last-minute rebound, the financial markets have not been able to save his presidency that has been so favorable to the wealthy. Trump used every upward movement to justify his presidency while disavowing the downward movements.

The financial markets have often been designated as the barometer of the economy, imposing an ironclad rule on our societies and becoming the marker of political and economic success. It is a misunderstanding of what the markets represent and a folly to believe that being president of the United States is measured by the random fluctuations of the stock market indices. Since taking office, Joe Biden has not once alluded to the evolution of the financial markets.[3]

The pandemic crisis has worsened the precarious state of corporate and government finances with record levels of debt. It is against this backdrop of instability (the volatility so dear to traders) that the coronavirus crisis caused a spectacular fall in stock market prices followed by massive interventions by central banks, aggravating their structural imbalance. The size and suddenness of these injections were such that they could not be absorbed by the real economy, creating an artificial rise in stock prices. The rebound is a bubble financed by the taxpayer, who is more likely than not completely unaware.

---

[3] https://www.macrotrends.net/2482/sp500-performance-by-president

This disconnect between the so-called real economy and financial wealth has grown considerably. It casts doubt on the very mission of direct intermediation that is conducted by the capital markets.

Citizens Are Falling into the Debt Trap

Never has the use of leverage to increase wealth been more evident than in the last decade.

History demonstrates to no end that it is the poor who pay the bill for the overindebtedness of countries and corporations, which have not given any consideration to the rights of the taxpayer. At the 2012 State of the Union Address, Barack Obama announced a reform of financial regulation so that "if you are a big bank or financial institution, you're no longer allowed to make risky bets with your customers' deposits. You are required to write out a "living will" that details exactly how you'll pay the bills if you fail—because the rest of us are not bailing you out ever again." In 2020, it was taxpayers in various forms that mobilized four times the amount used in 2008.

The wealth accumulation in recent decades has been made possible by inciting the rich (companies, states, or individuals) to borrow to acquire assets at subsidized interest rates.

Investment banks and analysts were the first to blame companies for being underleveraged. Our world is waking up to a false surprise of monstrous debt, which exploded during the pandemic crisis but has been developing at a rapid pace for the past 10 years. In the developed countries, the mass of bonds issued on the capital markets exceeds the mass of credits granted by financial institutions. It is no longer the banks that dominate finance: it is the financial markets.

Modern Monetary Theory Is Political

Modern monetary theory (MMT) is all about hubris, so, as Dominic Pino writes in the *National Review*, "it may seem strange that so many economists are confident that "modern monetary theory" (MMT) is wrong. Paul Krugman has called it "Calvinball." Larry Summers likened it to fad diets. Noah Smith called it "a fringe ideology." Michael Strain wrote that it "sounded like lunacy."[4]

Faced with these dangers, distinguished economic minds have conceived of this modern monetary theory, which denies the risks of indebtedness on the

---

[4] https://www.nationalreview.com/magazine/2022/03/07/the-hubris-of-modern-monetary-theory/

pretext that sovereign debts cannot be repaid.[5] Populist discourse, which still dominates the extremes of the left and the right, has thrown itself on this theory—the debt must be cancelled. Do they even know that debts cannot be cancelled without the agreement of the lenders? Without this agreement, it is spoliation and leads to the ruin not only of investors in sovereign bonds but also of the populations of the issuing countries.

Strangely, I have had to defend my position to economists and professionals who deny the structural risks associated with government debt and the risks of inflating the balance sheets of central banks. I must confess that the Biden administration represents $6 trillion in spending that might need to be financed with public debt.

In 2022, the evangelists of MMT have become much quieter—the increase of interest rates will explode government's budget deficits and corporate debt costs.

We have seen this movie before. There is a widespread frustration with the performance of the economy. Traditional policy approaches are not delivering hoped-for results. A relatively unpopular president is loathed to an unusual extent by a frustrated opposition party that lost the previous presidential election while running a pillar of its establishment. And altered economic conditions have led to the development of new economic ideas that, according to former secretary of the Treasury Lawrence Summers, reflect a significant break with previous orthodoxy. The left's embrace of MMT is a recipe for disaster.[6]

Finance is perceived to be an enemy of the people, a predator that subjects them to a logic they do not understand. It must be said that financiers do not care. They do not care that their activity condemns an entire population to starvation. They do not care about the tens of millions of people who have fallen below the poverty line. The actions taken during 2020 privileged the wrong priorities while the world population was under house arrest. This is where the threat to democracy lies.

Hence, there is a feeling, both individual and collective, of hopeless dependence on capital markets and their beneficiaries, which sometimes reaches unsustainable proportions. Can finance be reconciled with democracy? Is this not a utopia? Can we, as Victor Hugo said in *Les Misérables*, *limit poverty without limiting wealth*?

It is tempting for the liberals to believe that they can have it all. It is a way to continue, as the Biden administration did, the 20 years of fiscal undiscipline.

---

[5] https://www.bloomberg.com/news/articles/2021-07-23/modern-monetary-theory-embrace-of-big-budget-deficits-doesn-t-mean-mmt-has-won

[6] https://www.hks.harvard.edu/centers/mrcbg/programs/growthpolicy/lefts-embrace-modern-monetary-theory-recipe-disaster

One only needs to say, as Olivier Blanchard, former Chief Economist of the IMF, did in April 2019, "…the current U.S. situation, in which safe interest rates are expected to remain below growth rates for a long time, is more the historical norm than the exception. If the future is like the past, this implies that debt rollovers, that is the issuance of debt without a later increase in taxes, may well be feasible. Put bluntly, public debt may have no fiscal cost."[7]

A Reminder of Previous Episodes

To understand the current situation, it is important to recall the context that has dominated the financial markets since the so-called Lehman Brothers crisis in 2008.

Attention was focused on strengthening the capital adequacy of banks, and central banks went from being firefighters to becoming gigantic accumulators of financial assets—a situation from which they are unable to exit.

So here we are, with our backs to the wall. Massive central bank intervention is a luxury of the rich countries. Emerging countries are on the brink of collapse and their ratings are threatened. These countries do not have access to the private capital market and depend on usurious financing. Never has the disparity between poor and rich countries been more striking.

Before and After 2008: A Classic Financial Crisis

The financial crisis that broke out in 2008 had a considerable impact. However, it was partial, not global. It was the financial sector that collapsed and only on two sides of the Atlantic. Eighty percent of the bank losses were in Europe and the United States. For the first time, a major financial crisis was not the result of macroeconomic disturbances. Finance was impaled and had only itself to blame. Regulators had neither the vision nor the competence to prevent this crisis.

The consequences have been dramatic for individuals, who are caught in the trap of financial institutions. We must face the facts: A financial bubble has developed and primarily serves the financial world.

In Davos, in January 2007, during a session on the future of finance, everything was contradictory. The financiers announced growth while the economy was beginning to weaken. After a rise of almost 100%, the stock market continued to hope for a bright future. In a debate with British Prime Minister Tony Blair,

---

[7] https://www.aeaweb.org/articles?id=10.1257/aer.109.4.1197

economist Noel Roubini sounded the alarm about debt. In other circles, the discourse of business leaders is worrying: The weakening of growth is indisputable. This disconnect between the markets and the economy is obvious to me. I predicted a financial crisis without being able to define its cause and tempo. At a time when risks had to be reduced, the banking system was proclaiming its good health. During the World Economic Forum, I realized that economists underestimate or ignore the financial risks contained in over-indebtedness.

This led to a crisis of confidence in financial services, which has not yet been fully restored. A wave of financial regulation around the world is trying to prevent the taxpayer from having to foot the bill for banking imbalances by regulating capital, liquidity, and leverage risks.

The Explosion of Debt Since the Global Financial Crisis of 2008

Recently, the pandemic of 2020 has demonstrated that the problem is broader: A global debt crisis awaits us. It has already started, and the Sri Lanka default is only the first of several countries that will default.[8]

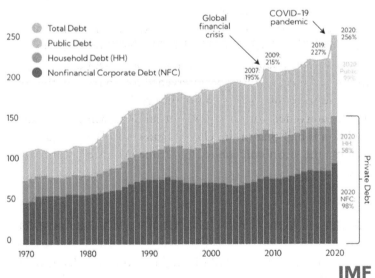

Historic highs
In 2020, global debt experienced the largest surge in 50 years.
(debt as a percent of GDP)

https://blogs.imf.org/2021/12/15/global-debt-reaches-a-record-226-trillion/

---

[8] https://www.economist.com/finance-and-economics/2022/04/16/sri-lankas-default-could-be-the-first-of-many

While banks were strengthened by global regulation after 2008, and some of the excesses of finance were tempered, little was done to ensure greater soundness in financial markets. And nothing has been done to temper the growth of debt.

Central banks embarked on an "alternative" monetary policy adventure that multiplied their balance sheets. Governments benefited from lower interest rates and borrowed massively, tripling their debt.

These QE (quantitative easing) operations will go down in economic history as the largest waste of capital. Not only governments but also corporations and wealthy individuals were able to borrow at or below zero interest rates, at the expense of savers—but they allowed for 10 years of stock market growth.

Confronted with an inflation that central banks were trying to stimulate but did not expect to explode, they now have to roll back these asset purchases and increased interest rates. It is probably the biggest failure of monetary policy since World War II.

The Year 2020: A Viral Tsunami

The year opened with enthusiasm, followed by a considerable drop in growth and a paradoxical question: How long can the financial markets continue to rise? It is sometimes forgotten that the stock market indexes rose 40% in 2019 and were slightly up until the fateful day of February 19, 2020. But since that fall, the S&P 500 has increased by 100%.

Central banks, already bloated from their operations of the previous 10 years, from which they have not exited (with the limited exception of the Federal Reserve), have relaunched into humongous asset buyback operations. In three months, the Federal Reserve intervened for $3 trillion, the equivalent of all the quantitative easing operations of the previous 10 years. The European Central Bank intervened for an equivalent amount while the GDP of the European Union is half that of the United States. The Bank of Japan, pushed by Abenomics, the economic policy of Prime Minister Shinzo Abe, followed course.

Wall Street at the Heart of Financial Capitalism

Wall Street has become the symbol of Anglo-Saxon capitalism, often called "financial capitalism." As the emblematic figure of the stock markets, this New York street refers not only to the stock market but to all of its players.

The stock market benefits from this generalization, but it also makes it a target for criticism that would be better directed at the authors of the abuses of power that abound throughout the world. If they stir up colossal capital, the stock exchanges are medium-sized enterprises. They are the epicenter that redistributes capital without owning it.

Stock exchanges are the crossroads of the equity market and various financial instruments, the fruits of financial innovation. They play an essential role in the valuation of companies and the fluidity of transactions. They have been considerably modernized. They are regulated. They are not to be blamed, even if abuses are sometimes committed and, in many cases, punished. They are the center of a system that is supposed to promote fairness among operators without ever really achieving it. It is the system that is at fault, even if the responsibility of its epicenter and of the rules it imposes cannot be totally dismissed.

The complexity of the stock markets makes them abstruse and incomprehensible for individuals, whether they participate or not. They can so easily be misled or cheated. The power of the citizen will come from information and education.

The Power of Financial Markets

To restore a balance between financial markets and democracy, we need to understand the mechanisms that favor institutions and the wealthy and exclude less fortunate citizens. They are infinitely more subtle than socialist, populist, or trade unionist slogans would have us believe, yet these slogans continue to populate populist discourse with a formidable effectiveness.

The triumphalist speeches of those who have a powerful interest in rising prices are no more effective. It is a Circus Maximus whose gladiators make no concessions. The market capitalization of American companies in 2019 represented as much as 200% of its gross domestic product (GDP) of the United States. This $50 trillion strike force gives considerable power to the holders of these assets. Can it be tempered? Or at least balanced in a more equitable way?

The financial markets are at the crossroads of financial forces with conflicting interests, but it is the players who take responsibility for what happens in them. They are the ones who have established the dominance of the financial markets and their rules. In a simple definition, their role is to put the investor and the issuer in direct contact, without the intermediation of a bank or an insurance company. They finance companies and governments and are essential to the functioning of the economy.

In recent years, economists who are not affiliated with governments, financial institutions, or special interests have undertaken research that leaves no doubt about the abuses that the markets have experienced.

The diagnosis of Raghuram Rajan, economist and former governor of the Reserve Bank of India, is clear: Markets and states leave the community behind.[9] French economist Thomas Piketty paints an apocalyptic picture of enrichment at the expense of people and says that COVID-19 reveals the violence of social injustice.[10]

Some leading actors such as Jean-Claude Trichet, former president of the European Central Bank, or Jacques de Larosière, former managing director of the International Monetary Fund (IMF), have the courage to enlighten us on the challenges they had to overcome in the face of political pressure and denial surrounding finance. These and many other authoritative voices challenge the official narrative. When French economists Patrick Artus and Marie-Paule Virard speak of capitalism's last chance, they are warning us. With prescience, Raghuram Rajan wrote a book on *Saving Capitalism from the Capitalists*.[11]

The IMF and the World Bank Sound the Alarm

Compared to pre-pandemic expectations, median debt in 2021 increased by about 17% of GDP in advanced economies, 12% in emerging economies, and 8% in low-income countries, as assessed by Geoffrey Okamoto, deputy managing director of the IMF. It is an alarming rise. With fewer resources and less capacity, low-income countries are particularly vulnerable—about half of them were already in or at high risk of debt distress prior to the 2020 crisis onslaught.[12]

Their denunciation of abuses invites us to explore the powers underlying this domination of democracy by the financial markets. It is legitimate and necessary. Yet it comes from economists who, albeit recognized in the United States, do not originate from there.

Still, financial markets have decided to ignore this potential systemic risk. They seem convinced that their risks are covered by governments and central

---

[9] Raghuram Rajan: the third pillar. How State and Markets Leave The Community Behind

    https://www.penguinrandomhouse.com/books/566369/the-third-pillar-by-raghuram-rajan/

[10] https://thehill.com/hilltv/rising/527587-thomas-piketty-says-pandemic-is-opportunity-to-address-income-inequality/

[11] https://press.princeton.edu/books/paperback/9780691121284/saving-capitalism-from-the-capitalists

[12] https://www.imf.org/en/News/Articles/2020/10/01/sp100120-resolving-global-debt-an-urgent-collective-eaction-cause

banks. While history could explain that belief, recent developments raise the question of the sustainability of finance.

It took an explosion of inflation and interest rates, a 2022 first semester negative growth, the prospect of a recession or stagflation, an energy and food crisis, and a war in Europe for Wall Street to finally wake up to the risks that had been accumulated during their euphoric decennia, to pay attention to and correct valuations that, particularly in the technology sectors, made absolutely no sense.

banks. While bankers could explain that belief, recent developments at the centre of the citadel in light of finance.

If it were an explosion of inflation, and interest rates above 20%, that then future growth, the prospect of a recession or stagflation, an energy and food crisis, and a war in Europe, for Wall Street to finally wake up to the risks that had been required during their euphoric decades, to pay attention to a fragile situation that, particularly in the technology sector, made them begin to sense.

Financial Accountability

As we become aware of this unbearable inequality, the question of responsibilities opens before us. The multiplicity of actors makes it difficult to assign responsibility. Who should absolve us for the excesses and abuses that are developing in the financial sphere?

The very nature of a complex system such as capital markets requires us to understand their functions and those who occupy them. The diversity of their interests must be balanced in a way that does not privilege one party over the other. To be able to judge the role played by the various operators in the financial markets, it is necessary to evaluate their responsibility and the authorities to which they are accountable.

However, what has happened over the past two decades is nothing less than the transformation of direct intermediation into an indirect one. In her remarkable book *Direct: The Rise of the Middleman Economy and the Power of Going to the Source*, Columbia Law School Professor Kathryn Judge explains that studies suggest that even if the middleman and intricate intermediation regimes create value, the middleman economy is one that too often enriches those middlemen at the expense of the people they are supposed to serve.[1] What is true of the supply chain is even more obvious in financial markets.

---

[1] https://www.harperbusiness.com/book/9780063041974/Direct-Kathryn-Judge/

G. Ugeux, *Wall Street's Assault on Democracy*, https://doi.org/10.1007/978-3-031-29094-7_6

To Whom Are Financiers Accountable?

For historical reasons, the regulation of capital markets has been organized around the institutions that focus on them: banks by central banks, security firms and stock exchanges by the market regulator, and investors by specific regulations that manage investment funds and hedge funds or pension funds.

As such, capital markets are not regulated. Banks, for instance, run capital market activities through their broker dealers, who are regulated by the market regulator while their banking activities are supervised by central banks. This inevitably creates risks of inconsistencies and makes capital markets subject to regulated and unregulated operators.

The consequence of this structure is a deficiency at two levels. First, the proliferation of activities subjects the heart of the financial system, the banks, to various supervisory authorities. In the United States, a major bank is subject to more than 20 government agencies. In Europe, banks are supervised by the European Central Bank, but their activities are the responsibility of three different authorities in addition to the national structures.

The second deficiency is in the markets themselves. If we take the equity market as an example, numerous players are regulated, but the market itself does not have a single regulator. The result is regulatory conflicts that allow large players to slip through the cracks. The vertical regulatory structure does not allow for regulation of the markets themselves. Horizontal regulation is a challenge that goes beyond interagency cooperation (and sometimes competition). It allows regulatory arbitrage and competitive advantages for the least regulated institutions.

One question that emerges is the nature of financiers' impact on wealth inequality, which was exacerbated during the pandemic crisis. Despite the deep recession around the world, capital markets had historically high and fast growth, favoring the owners of capital at a time when unemployment was looming. Should the main actors of the markets consider their societal impact, and in particular the fact that some of their behaviors and policies disenfranchise part of the population, in case of low-income households?

Do they have a conscience?

The Fragmentation of Authorities Facilitates Unaccountability

While the political world is structured and hierarchical, financial operators answer to diverse and fragmented authorities.

We are in Basel, on the premises of the Bank for International Settlements, which in 1999 brought together the major financial and banking players to take stock of the (in)famous "Y2K bug" and the risks of a financial explosion. The representative of a large international European bank raised the problem of fragmentation: We operate in a large number of countries and have received 126 requests from regulatory authorities around the world with different questionnaires. As it was impossible to answer these requests, we focused on the four most important authorities and sent these answers to the other institutions according to their location and field. A few months later, we spent New Year's Eve on the floor of the NYSE waiting for the blackout announced by the IT people. It was a damp squib that massively enriched the IT consultants.

This anecdote raises a more fundamental point: the lack of real coordination between the supervisory authorities, who often do the same investigations and research over and over again. In the European Union, the member states have refused to delegate decision-making powers to the regulatory authorities without referring to the European Commission, which is a political body. They do not have the same statutory powers as their American counterparts.[2]

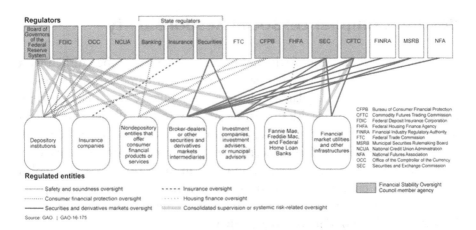

Of course, they consult each other, meet, and discuss the challenges of their activities, but what comes out of this cooperative process does not have the seal of authority, which remains national. While the Bank for International Settlements in Basel regulate banking, there is no equivalent authority for the financial markets. The International Organization of Securities Commissions

---

[2] https://www.gao.gov/products/gao-16-175

(IOSCO) seeks to establish stricter regulation of financial markets but does not have the authority to impose them. The United States, a major opponent of multilateral authorities, has never agreed to submit to its rules.

In Europe, the European Securities and Markets Authority (ESMA) plays an essential role but is limited by a decision-making structure that often leaves too much power to national regulators. The European Insurance and Occupational Pensions Authority (EIOPA) regulates large investors. Banking players are under the European Banking Authority (EBA).

In the United States, the stock market is itself subject to regulations stemming from the 1929 crisis, but the Securities and Exchange Act of 1934 only covers some of the financial players: the stock exchanges and the broker dealers. Hedge funds have succeeded in preventing the SEC (Securities and Exchange Commission) from supervising them but ultimately had to register with it, while banks are supervised by the Federal Reserve.

In many cases, governments are reluctant to delegate their decision powers, even to their own agencies. Attacks on the independence of central banks are constant. The first decision that authoritarian regimes usually take is to dismiss their governors.

Beyond Compliance: Social Responsibility

The fundamental question is whether market operators can be satisfied with compliance, a discipline that has grown in size and complexity in financial institutions and other regulated industries. Compliance is a tricky concept: Forbes' recent compliance risk study indicates that these challenges are coalescing around three major themes: cybersecurity, privacy, and environmental, social, and governance (ESG) concerns. These are the "riskiest risks," cited by more executives than any others. Meanwhile, an increasingly complex global regulatory and enforcement agenda—with authorities themselves adopting new technologies for monitoring and enforcement—has magnified the importance of appropriate corporate behavior.[3]

Beyond the specificities of the different financial professions, is there a societal responsibility? The answer to this question is far from obvious. Each of us and each institution has, beyond its individuality, a collective responsibility. A company's responsibility does not stop at its individual behavior and the enrichment of its shareholders. Compliance with regulations is not enough.

---

[3] https://www.forbes.com/sites/steveculp/2022/06/02/study-shows-major-headwinds-facing-compliance-functions/?sh=4511aff72066

The reaction of an entire generation of corporate leaders and governments who did not take climate risks seriously (or even denied them) has given rise to new criteria that investors have developed under the acronym ESG (environment, social, and governance). It is undoubtedly a tool of progress for responsible investors. This time, it is the aspiration of citizens that has fueled this fundamental movement: They wanted to ensure that their collective investments were not associated with the development of fossil fuel industries, child labor, chemical pollution, and other environmental harm. It is the social dimension that is increasingly scrutinized, and certain behaviors during the pandemic crisis will lead to revisions in corporate governance.

But resistance is fierce. The latest instance came from the Trump's administration. The new rule imposed by the Secretary of the Treasury, David Mnuchin, restricted the use of environmental, social, and governance considerations in making investment decisions. It was enacted at the end of July 2020 for federal pension funds—only financial risks and returns can be considered in the management of pension funds; "nonpecuniary objectives" cannot guide the investments of federal pension funds.

"In an uncertain world in which ESG matters more, not less, to strong corporate resilience and sustainable performance, promoting material ESG considerations in investment decision-making is good for the long-term retirement security of millions of American savers," assesses Cyrus Taraporevala, president and CEO of State Street Global Advisors.[4]

This example gives a sense of the responsibility of investors and the companies in which they invest. The traditional response of "this is not my role" is increasingly appearing as a denial of responsibility. Europe was the first to adopt these criteria. It is ahead of the United States and Asia in this area.

A new awareness seems to be emerging in the corporate world, and recent obligations to publish environmental information constitute a movement that can no longer be ignored. My fear is that the stranglehold of law firms will dilute these new obligations, as it has with other transparency measures.

A Coalition of Interests Facilitates Manipulation

Beyond their specific interests, the institutions that are part of the financial ecosystem have a common goal: the proper functioning of markets.

Finance cannot assert and abuse its power without the support of actors who benefit from what it provides and makes possible. It is at the center of a

---

[4] https://www.ft.com/content/81b267f4-414b-4c5a-b775-91c2f1a2f661

series of powerful networks. Whether through conferences or associations, the various components of the financial markets have the capacity to organize themselves to promote their collective interests, putting aside their competition.

Markets bring together investors, borrowers, and businesses. "Wall Street" has become the common name for these markets but also for those who participate in them in one capacity or another. It is additionally the meeting place for the ideology of the financial markets. The players meet around the world in search of the best opportunities.

As in all power structures, an army of satellite players clings to the most important players. Consultants, lawyers, accountants, lobbyists, and even the media are desperate to get a piece of the pie. They are not subject to any regulation.

Their multiplicity makes it impossible to blame one or the other actor alone for what are structural abuses of the markets. The question arises: "Are they all guilty?" It is by targeting the mechanisms that the necessary reforms can be identified. The complicity of the public sector solidifies a system whose humanism seems increasingly deficient. This is the challenge of an uncertain future.

The OECD recently published a paper on algorithmic collusion: The widespread usage of algorithms could also pose possible anticompetitive effects by making it easier for firms to achieve and sustain collusion without any formal agreement or human interaction.[5]

The Weakening of Democratic Control

In a system where markets are not regulated as such, but where regulation is aimed at the institutions that are part of them, it is almost impossible to exercise effective democratic control. In large capital markets where various categories of operators meet, the combination of regulations does not cover the whole. The fragmentation of control makes the regulation of the system itself ineffective.

This fundamental flaw explains the ease with which the various forces that grip the financial markets do so according to their own laws. If democracy is

---

[5] Algorithmic Collusion: Problems and Counter-Measures –
Note by A. Ezrachi & M.E. Stucke
Roundtable on Algorithms and Collusion
https://one.oecd.org/document/DAF/COMP/WD(2017)25/en/pdf

not to fall victim to these centrifugal forces, there must be regulation of the markets themselves and of all the participants. Many voices have been raised in this direction, but the difficulty of the task is considerable.

Abuse of rights and conflicts of interest in financial markets are commonplace. It would still be necessary for stock market regulation to be supported by common principles that would apply to all operators in the context of each activity. However, the core reason democratic control on capital markets is insufficient is financial education. What does the average citizen know about capital markets beyond the media headlines, often pushed by marketing and advertisement?

The Pillars: Issuers and Investors in Search of Growth and Profit

The heart of the financial markets is the meeting between issuers and investors. This is known as direct intermediation, where the same instrument is issued by the company or government and purchased by the investor without going through the balance sheet of a financial institution or any form of transformation. For companies, this is a crucial element of their financial stability. In fact, the bond markets make it possible to obtain fixed-rate debt as well as variations on this theme that the banking system is not able to provide. Given the amount of equity that banks must allocate to grant credit and the intermediation margin, it is financially strategic for companies not to depend solely on bank financing.

The same applies to the stock market where companies obtain equity financing. This is a dual role starting with the public offering of shares through an initial public offering (IPO), which is a one-off operation. Once the shares are listed, the most important role of the stock markets is to provide price discovery and liquidity to the shares throughout the life of the company.

G. Ugeux, *Wall Street's Assault on Democracy*, https://doi.org/10.1007/978-3-031-29094-7_7

Most firms plan to go to market in 2022

More than 80% of venture capital and private equity firms say they are planning to raise capital this year.

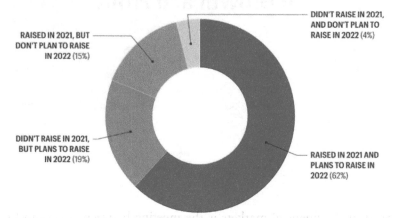

RAISED IN 2021, BUT DON'T PLAN TO RAISE IN 2022 (15%)

DIDN'T RAISE IN 2021, AND DON'T PLAN TO RAISE IN 2022 (4%)

DIDN'T RAISE IN 2021, BUT PLANS TO RAISE IN 2022 (19%)

RAISED IN 2021 AND PLANS TO RAISE IN 2022 (62%)

https://fortune.com/2022/03/02/private-equity-market-2022-charts/

Those wishes were not exhausted. The IPO market has known a virtual standstill, while investors were licking their wounds and valuations were becoming hazardous.

Companies Looking for Equity and Long-Term Financing

The primary player in the financial markets remains the companies that finance their investments and growth through share and bond issues. They are the backbone of the economy. They are the ones who generate productive jobs. They are the ones who provide goods and services. It is governments who can facilitate, not create economic growth. It is precisely because of this essential mission that their role cannot be limited to themselves but extends to society and its diversity as a whole.

If companies have access to private investors in the first phase of their existence, when they reach a certain size, they seek equity capital beyond the circle of their initial shareholders. Some of them will find private capital, others will be bought out, but many companies choose to finance themselves through the stock market.

The private and public equity market has grown considerably. New players such as venture capital companies, private equity funds, sovereign wealth funds, and pension funds have made equity financing of companies possible. Recently, a new form of stock market listing has developed: special purpose acquisition companies (SPACs). We will come back to the problems it raises in terms of shareholder protection and information.[1] The public market (the stock exchange) remains the main source of equity capital throughout the world. The slowdown could be more structural than occasional: regulators will ensure that the information available on SPACs is equivalent to regular IPOs (initial public offerings). It led to a virtual standstill of SPACs in 2022.

---

[1] https://clsbluesky.law.columbia.edu/2021/03/31/regulating-spacs-before-its-too-late/

© The Author(s), under exclusive license to Springer Nature Switzerland AG 2023
G. Ugeux, *Wall Street's Assault on Democracy*, https://doi.org/10.1007/978-3-031-29094-7_8

As expected, the SEC (Securities and Exchange Commission) had to move in in the name of investor protection. It did so in March 2022. The proposed new rules and amendments would require, among other things, additional disclosures about SPAC sponsors, conflicts of interest, and sources of dilution. They also would require additional disclosures regarding business combination transactions between SPACs and private operating companies, including disclosures relating to the fairness of these transactions. Further, the new rules would address issues relating to projections made by SPACs and their target companies, including the Private Securities Litigation Reform Act—a safe harbor for forward-looking statements and the use of projections in commission filings and in business combination transactions.[2]

The Challenges of the Listed Company

The public capital markets have been a decisive source of equity. They have, however, become increasingly complex: regulation after regulation has been imposed upon them to the point where large international companies, albeit

---

[2] https://www.sec.gov/news/press-release/2022-56

major players in the United States, have renounced their public listing in the United States.

This trend is leading to a change of landscape. Private capital markets, supported by institutional investors and private equity funds, are playing an increasingly critical role in equity financing.

Not Every Company Can Become Public

The regulatory approval process of the prospectus and the information provided by the companies is a tedious and costly process but one that is necessary to ensure that shareholders are properly informed.

The next step is to ensure that the company complies with the listing criteria that are set individually by the stock exchanges. The basis of these requirements is to ensure that the shares can reach a volume of transactions that allows for smooth trading. This includes shareholder criteria. The listing is usually accompanied by an issue of shares that will be widely sold to the public.

As costly and cumbersome as the IPO is, it is after the listing that the real work begins. The market authorities—Autorité des Marchés Financiers in France, the Financial Conduct Authority (FCA) in the UK, the Japan Financial Services Authority (JFSA), and the Securities and Exchange Commission in the United States—impose a series of transparency and compliance obligations.

The importance of ongoing relationships with investors in the form of events (road shows) or one-on-one meetings is essential, even if their content is limited to the issue prospectus or information published by the company. Any breach of these rules would lead to risks of insider trading, which weighed notably on Facebook's listing.

A publicly traded company must be accountable to its shareholders. This communication requires an investor relations department, often with the support of specialized firms, but above all a real commitment to this communication by the management and the investor relations department, whose role has grown as the needs have increased.

Governance of Listed Companies

The listing of a company on the stock exchange is one of the most fundamental transformations of its governance. It inevitably affects the culture of a company and its social fabric. Entrepreneurial or institutional shareholders generally own private companies. An agreement between them and the company's management sets the budgets and the long-term strategy.

In the case of an IPO, the governance rules of the country in which the company is established are imposed. It is as if the dialogue between the shareholders and the company were replaced by a triangular relationship in which, surreptitiously, a new interlocutor composed of institutional investors and private individuals was introduced into the management of the company. A few examples give an idea of this transformation:

- Quarterly financials give rise to public information that forces managers, whether they want to or not, to explain themselves on short-term developments. This change of horizon has both positive and negative effects. The greatest risk is the submission of long-term strategy to short-term considerations.
- Executive compensation is no longer based solely on the company's profitability but also on the performance of the share price. This leads to behaviors that are often justified by personal interest, sometimes as far as to backdate their options, like Steve Jobs, the co-founder of Apple.
- Transparency is good news, even if it sometimes has its drawbacks. How can we ensure that corporate communication is compatible with shareholder communication? It is not the same thing. The flow of information is corseted and often loses spontaneity.
- Shareholder communication is a heavy burden. I remember meetings with a large Japanese company we were advising on the communication of annual results at the time of the pandemic, where there were at least 50 participants. It has become the role of investor relation professionals and advisors and a vital component of corporate governance.

Access to International Capital

Having contributed to the listing of 256 non-US companies on the New York Stock Exchange, I have a broad enough idea of the needs and motivations of companies that decide to go public outside their own country.

- In the first phase, it was the privatizations of large public sector companies that fueled this activity. The development of markets outside the United States made it impossible to raise the capital necessary for these operations.

The vast majority of these privatizations took place on the New York Stock Exchange (NYSE). The consequence of this movement was to subject companies that were sometimes still majority state-owned to the rules of the US capital markets. While the stock exchange verified compliance with the listing criteria, the bulk of the work was subject to the exhaustive review of the SEC, the federal agency of the US government.

- The listing of a stock on the NYSE is a type of "seal of approval" that brings considerable value to the company's operations both in the United States and around the world. This event has often been the occasion of a spectacular financial marketing operation. Surprising as it may seem, it is an incentive that has allowed many companies to promote themselves or their products around the world. Alstom, for example, promoted its fast speed train with a life-size model that was to be followed a few years later by a Trans-European Express car. The German tech company SAP turned Wall Street into a volleyball court.

- The United States has used listings to subject foreign public companies to its Foreign Corrupt Practices Act (FCPA) as well as to the authority of the Office of Foreign Assets Control ("OFAC") of the US Department of the Treasury. This "Lex Americana" outreach might be questionable in law, but it is effective in practice:

A few weeks after the events of September 11, Deutsche Bank listed its shares on the New York Stock Exchange. On that day, the banks decided to favor transactions with Deutsche Bank, which suffered greatly in the attack, its headquarters having been destroyed. The board of directors and its chairman, Rolf Breuer, came by private bus to be able to leave quickly for a meeting of analysts at the Pierre Hotel. President Bush had decided to hold a Wall Street support event that day. When we left 11 Wall Street, the security services forbade us to go on the bus. There was only one solution: the subway. I took the Deutsche Bank executive committee and its CEO, Rolf Breuer, to the nearest station and used my subway pass to get them through one by one...

If this movement toward the United States has diminished considerably over the last decade, it is because the European markets—mainly the London Stock Exchange, Euronext (which was created by the merger of the Amsterdam, Brussels, and Paris stock exchanges), and the German stock exchange—have developed their ability to lead operations, such as the privatization of EDF, without having to call on American capital. The same is true of the Japanese market and the role of Hong Kong in the listing of Chinese companies.

The Chinese Dilemma

The scene is the Senate Office Building in Washington, D.C., in 1998. My NYSE colleague Sheila Bair, who would become the President of the Federal Deposit Insurance Corporation at the time of the 2008 crisis, and I are received by a senator anxious to block the listing of a Chinese company, China National Petroleum Company. The anti-Chinese lobby of the American Congress (financed by Taiwan) wants to stop this listing. To convince us, they show a video of the horrors perpetrated by the Sudanese government on the Christians in the south of the country. China is the main buyer of Sudanese oil, through the CNPC. A compromise will be found by Robert Hormats of Goldman Sachs by creating a subsidiary of CNPC, PetroChina, which does not integrate the activities with Sudan. The SEC could not have authorized this IPO if Congress had opposed it.

Listings of Chinese companies in the United States have become considerably politicized. While transparency obligations must be applied to all foreign companies listed on another market, the United States has taken measures, and recently by the United Kingdom as well, to prevent these listings from becoming a Trojan horse threatening the security of the host country.

Under the Trump administration, Chinese companies were in the news at all levels: the three major Chinese communications companies were forced to leave the NYSE because of their alleged links with the People's Liberation Army. Recently, Chinese authorities retaliated through a last-minute political intervention that prevented Alibaba's subsidiary ANT Financial from listing on the Hong Kong stock exchange. The last-minute intervention of the Chinese authorities at the time of the listing of the company Didi caused its stock price to fall by 25%. Threats that Chinese tech companies would be asked to leave US exchanges for "security reasons" have compounded the negative impact on Chinese companies. This is a far cry from President Jiang Zemin's reception during his 1997 visit to the New York Stock Exchange.

It was the first time that a Chinese President would ever visit New York, let alone its stock exchange, and Dick Grasso had invited the heads of the Wall Street Firms. The president indicated his interest to modernize Chinese capital markets and give Chinese Companies access to U.S. capital. A year later, we would visit him in Beijing, and he was noticing the increase of the stock prices since his visit while indicating that modernization would have to be progressive: "If we were deploying tractors for agriculture, we would have 100 million unemployed.

The year 2021 has seen a number of actions from the Chinese government that restrict the access of Chinese companies. It puts President Xi Jinping at the crossroads between prosperity and ideology.[3] The politicization of international capital markets is a source of concern. Using a listing as a sanction makes no economic sense and penalizes not only the company but also the investors.

The level of uncertainty created by the political interference is a deterrent to the diversity of investments. Since January 1, 2022, China has limited foreign ownership to 30%.

---

[3] https://gugeux.medium.com/china-xi-jinping-at-the-crossroads-of-prosperity-and-ideology-64866dd6a53c

Investors Look for Valuable Assets

The spectrum of investors ranges from individuals to pension funds and the whole kaleidoscope of channels through which they decide to invest their assets. The variety of their objectives is immense and ranges from altruism to short-term gains to value creation. It is this diversity that explains the very existence of financial markets. If all investors had the same objectives, there would be no market.

But above all, what is the investment horizon? Often subject to the publication of their quarterly accounts, many investors and capital managers cannot ignore their short-term performance. There is an ocean between a life insurance company and a hedge fund. Their purpose is fundamentally different. While this creates a robust capital market, the impact is divergent.

Investor Diversity and Market Fragmentation

The combination of the nature of these investors and their objectives is the main source of market liquidity.

The importance of *individual investors* has declined drastically in recent decades. This development creates a gap between the citizen and the individual investor. In most cases, they are entering the stock market to enhance their savings and secure additional resources, primarily a well-deserved retirement, which cannot be financed by state pensions.

Wealthier Americans also tend to have more money in stock. Families in the top 10% of income earners accounted for 70% of the dollar value of all stock holdings in 2019, with a median of $432,000 worth of stock per

© The Author(s), under exclusive license to Springer Nature Switzerland AG 2023
G. Ugeux, *Wall Street's Assault on Democracy*, https://doi.org/10.1007/978-3-031-29094-7_9

invested household. Meanwhile, the bottom 60% of income earners owned only 7% of all stocks that year. The median middle-class household invested in the stock market owned $15,000 worth of stock.[1]

Increasingly, the individual investor is looking for companies to pay attention to climate change, its societal role, or its governance. The individual investor is not in a position to promote these values directly but can express them through investments and asset managers. Voting rights are diluted in the company's decision-making by institutional investors. This explains the individual investor's distrust of large, listed companies whose appeasing rhetoric is not always confirmed by their actions.

The pandemic has seen a resurgence of interest from individuals, whose share of stock market volume has doubled. Contributing to this resurgence is a new generation of investors who are keen on using digital platforms that allow them to make transactions on a phone or a screen.

The decision by the popular trading application Robinhood to restrict the purchase of GameStop shares through its platform on January 28, 2021— when the stock price was still considerably elevated—contributed heavily to the price's sharp reversal. A brokerage that marketed itself as being accessible to small retail investors and promoting the democratization of finance and investing was suddenly suspending its service to those very investors at the most crucial time.[2]

Are those generations of market participants really investors, or are they nourishing the gamification of the capital markets?

Family groups are investors for life. Even within families, as generations pass, the number of shareholders increases and with it a loosening of the attachment to the family company. It is through the stock market that these families have often succeeded in obtaining liquidity, allowing the younger generations to sell their shares. They generally wish to continue managing the company. They have their own fragility as successions dilute the shareholding among a growing number of family shareholders, some of whom wish to sell their stake. The number of family offices ranges between 10,000 and 15,000 around the world.[3]

[1] https://usafacts.org/articles/what-percentage-of-americans-own-stock/
[2] https://internationalbanker.com/brokerage/gamestop-what-happened-and-what-it-means/
[3] https://www.famcap.com/2015/04/2015-4-29-10-family-investment-groupsand-what-they-invest-in/

Individual Investors

Institutional investors have a time horizon that oscillates between the short, medium, and long term. Hedge funds look for very short-term results. Venture capital funds are in the medium term (7–10 years), and insurance companies, pension funds, and other holding companies have a long-term investment horizon. Very often, the amount of their investment will be influenced by the liquidity of the stock so that they can sell in a few days without influencing the stock price.

A major exception is Berkshire Hathaway, an investment company created by Warren Buffet, whose shares have exploded from $7,000 to over $420,000 in 20 years. Except in unusual cases, it remains a shareholder in companies over a long period of time. But it is not the only one—many financial companies hold long-term stakes.

https://seekingalpha.com/article/4423498-berkshire-hathaway-versus-s-and-p-500-through-years

Private Equity Funds

The development of private equity funds goes in the same direction. Most of them have a duration of 7–10 years. They have to find a way to sell their participation in private companies with an annual profit that they estimate at 20%. This is why their exit often leads to a stock market listing, which is their best exit strategy. All too often, the founding shareholders have been taken in by the lark mirror that these funds hold out to them—the latter practice a management style that is solely a function of the profit obtained, even if it means leaving the company in debt in order to repay all or part of their purchase price.

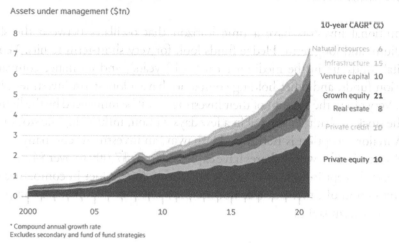

Private capital industry has exploded in size

Assets under management ($tn)

10-year CAGR* (%)

Natural resources 6
Infrastructure 15
Venture capital 10
Growth equity 21
Real estate 8
Private credit 10
Private equity 10

* Compound annual growth rate
Excludes secondary and fund of fund strategies

The vast majority of these funds, however, are genuine business developers and will, through the companies in which they hold a stake, enable innovation and development. Yet it should never be forgotten that few of them hold a stake for more than 10 years. Their horizon is therefore limited.

Mutual Funds and Investment Trusts

Mutual funds and investment trusts attract both retail and institutional investors. Most of them are long-term investors, but it is important that the stock market provides them with an exit door at any time in case of a hard blow or simply when they have decided to sell their shares. Specialized companies often manage their assets. Fund and asset management is a business that takes the form of private banks, fund managers, or investment portfolios. This industry has undergone developments that have concentrated in a few hands amounts that run into the trillions. There is no regulatory limit to this concentration. This is probably where societal values can seep in and exert their influence. Three American firms dominate the market: BlackRock, State Street, and Vanguard. The question is how they use their significant voting power. [4]

---

[4] https://blog.bizvibe.com/blog/top-investment-companies

Top 10 Investment Companies in the World 2020

Capital Group
5.2%
Bank of New York Mellon
5.5%
JPMorgan Chase
5.5%

Allianz
6.8%

State Street Global Advisors
9.1%

Fidelity Investments
9.3%

UBS Group
9.5%

BlackRock
21.6%

The Vanguard Group
18.0%

Charles Schwab Corporation
9.6%

Hedge Funds

In recent years, *hedge funds* have grown to significant sizes. The vast majority of them invest in listed shares. They are also short-term investors. The stock market is the heart of their activities. Their own shareholders are looking for short-term gains and their financing comes largely from banks. Hedge funds have gained a bad reputation since the Lehman crisis. It is important to distinguish between those who seek growth and those who seek immediate profit. It is interesting to note that their size is inversely proportional to their performance, while the assets under management are marginal.

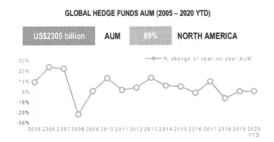

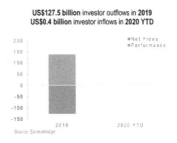

Insurance Companies

The most important segment of the institutional investors is by large the insurance companies, in particular the life insurance companies. Compared to hedge funds or private equity funds, they are, like mutual funds, subject to a series of rules and regulations that influences their access to investors (especially retail investors), their solvency, and their asset management.

In the United States, they represent more than 100% of the GDP. They are vulnerable to asset fluctuations that can affect their solvency ratio.[5]

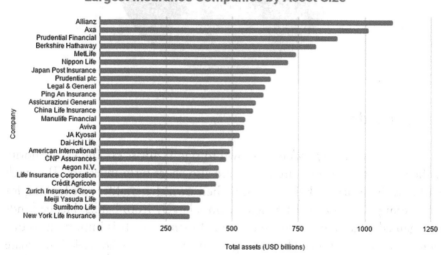

Largest Insurance Companies by Asset Size

Pension Funds

The importance of pension funds cannot be underestimated, but they also are a diverse universe, between corporate pension funds and government pension schemes and funds. They are largely invested in equity and bonds and represent a force in capital markets.[6]

[5] https://blog.bizvibe.com/blog/largest-insurance-companies
[6] https://www.statista.com/statistics/421220/global-pension-funds-assets/

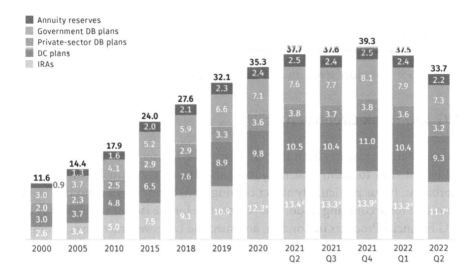

Governments as Shareholders, or the Double Language

"Do as I say, not as I do."

This expression applies perfectly to public sector shareholders. Indeed, it is the public authorities that set the rules of governance. When it comes to respecting them in companies where they are majority or largely minority shareholders, the tune changes.

In the best of cases, the state is a shareholder, to ensure that companies in strategic sectors behave in a way that does not jeopardize their policies. The slippage comes from a desire to control the economy through this shareholding, even if it is a minority one. The boards of directors of companies in which the state is a minority shareholder are often servile and reluctant to oppose maneuvers that favor the public interest but not the companies.

The ways governments function as shareholders and try to influence capital markets take quite different roads. Even within a specific country, the attitude of governments varies according to the ruling party and the robustness of the regulatory authorities.

The recent examples of the behavior of the US Treasury and some government agencies show that its intervention can be heavy handed and negatively affect other shareholders' rights. Since it generally occurs in the context of a rescue operation, however, the claims of the shareholders are not always legitimate.

It is difficult for governments to accept the limitation imposed by the rules of corporate governance when they oppose some political initiatives. The public shareholder believes that his rights are those of the state, not necessarily those of a shareholder, even an extraordinary one.

AIG and Hank Greenberg

The most abject case has been the attempt by the former managers and shareholders of AIG to claim that the profits the Treasury eventually made were exorbitant. It was particularly abject coming from Sandy Weill, who had been dismissed for accounting fraud, was responsible for the lack of transparency of AIG Financial Products in London, and sued the US government even though it saved the company.

As explained in *The New York Times* in 2013: "…such a move would almost certainly be widely seen as an audacious display of ingratitude. The action would also threaten to inflame tensions in Washington, where the company has become a byword for excessive risk-taking on Wall Street. Some government officials are already upset with the company for even seriously entertaining the lawsuit, people briefed on the matter said. The people, who spoke on the condition of anonymity, noted that without the bailout, A.I.G. shareholders would have fared far worse in bankruptcy."[7]

The Conservatorship of Fannie Mae and Freddy Mac

The US mortgage market is unique: Ninety percent of the mortgages are refinanced through agencies that take on the risk of defaulting on housing loans. The federal takeover of Fannie Mae and Freddie Mac in September 2008 consisted of the US Treasury placing into conservatorship the government-sponsored enterprises (GSEs) Federal National Mortgage Association (Fannie Mae) and Federal Home Loan Mortgage Corporation (Freddie Mac). Thirteen years later, both GSEs are still in conservatorship.

The mortgage crisis did indeed affect these two GSEs. It was up to the government to step in. However, there was ambiguity on how to assess the liabilities on the debt financing since it came from the government and as such had a rating of AAA. It was not a case of rescuing private, failing financial institutions like Lehman and AIG. The collision course was due to these events

---

[7] https://dealbook.nytimes.com/2013/01/07/rescued-by-a-bailout-a-i-g-may-sue-its-savior/

happening virtually the same month and putting millions of insured mortgage borrowers at risk.

Without entering into the details of the difficulty Treasury Paulson had to manage, including Congress receiving favors from the management of the GSEs, it is interesting to note that the conservatorship reduced the equity of the two institutions to negative while the Treasury was getting substantial dividends. Bondholders lost 80% of the value of their asset and sued the Federal Housing Finance Agency (FHFA). Discussions on a recapitalization and flotation of the agencies never came to any conclusion. After 13 years of failures, the FHFA described the situation as follows: "Fannie Mae and Freddie Mac are in conservatorship to preserve and conserve their assets and property and restore them to a sound financial condition so they can continue to fulfill their statutory mission of promoting liquidity and efficiency in the nation's housing finance markets."[8]

France and the Double Voting Rights

Varied examples of abuse of rights by government shareholders abound. You do not have to look far for the most surprising example in France: the Florange Law.

The law provides for the automatic granting of double voting rights to any shares held in a registered form by the same shareholder for at least two years (also known as "time-phased" voting or "loyalty shares"), provided that the company does not prohibit double voting rights in its bylaws. The act allows companies to amend their bylaws (with shareholder's approval) to opt out of this automatic granting of double voting rights and thus continue under the one-share, one-vote principle. The two-year holding period triggering the automatic acquisition of double voting rights started on April 1, 2014. As a consequence, double voting rights automatically applied on March 31, 2016. This meant French companies that had not already prohibited double voting rights in their bylaws then had to submit to such bylaw amendment.

The objective of the Florange Law was to encourage long-term shareholding by automatically attributing a double voting right to companies whose shares are admitted to trading on a regulated market and applies to all shares held in registered form by the same shareholder for at least two years. This double voting right may, however, be eliminated by adding a clause to the articles of association adopted by a two-thirds majority at an extraordinary general meeting.

[8] https://www.fhfa.gov/Conservatorship#:~:text=Fannie%20Mae%20and%20Freddie%20Mac%20are%20in%20conservatorship%20to%20preserve,the%20nation's%20housing%20finance%20market

The general meetings of companies such as Vinci, BNP Paribas, Crédit Agricole SA, Unibail-Rodamco, Capgemini, and L'Oréal have overwhelmingly approved the maintenance of the rule historically in force. The main beneficiaries of the law were the government itself and wealthy shareholders.

The authorities should be exemplary in terms of governance if they want to have the confidence and credibility to apply their own regulations. But they often prefer to use or abuse their political power. The Elysée and the Ministry of Finance are often the arbiters in France when they are playing the role of a mergers and acquisitions (M&A) department.

French-style capitalism, glaring examples of which include the recent LVMH-Tiffany and Veolia-Suez operations, is in fact a state capitalism in which the French Minister of Finance participates in disagreements between companies during M&A operations. As Jean Peyrelevade, a leading financier, writes in Les Echos, "the interests of shareholders still dominate French capitalism alone, and even by the selfish desire for power of this or that manager."[9]

Emerging Markets and State Ownership

In most emerging countries, the ownership of financial institutions is in the hands of the public sector. Of the 20 largest market capitalizations, six are from emerging and government-controlled markets, even though they are listed on the stock exchange. Five of them are Chinese, one is Russian.

Even though they accept the corporate governance rules of the markets they list on in theory, the majority ownership by the public sector leads to interventions that are far from considering the impact on minority shareholders. The Saudis, for instance, will not relinquish the governance of Saudi Aramco and decided it could not be listed on the London or the New York Stock Exchanges but only on the Saudi stock market. Needless to say, China's GDP is larger than the other six top emerging markets.[10]

Emerging 7: the top emerging markets

China	India	Brasil	Russia	Mexico	Indonesia	Turkey
GDP	GDP	GDP	GDP	GDP	GDP	GDP
$15.5tn	$3.2tn	$2.3tn	$1.8tn	$1.3tn	$1.2tn	$961bn

---

[9] https://www.lesechos.fr/@jean-peyrelevade
[10] https://www.ig.com/en/trading-strategies/how-to-invest-in-emerging-markets-191219

Sovereign Wealth Funds

Over the past decades, sovereign wealth funds became a key player in the equity markets. Their objectives were to retain the wealth they had accumulated, mostly from oil revenues, for future generations. Some of them are government pension funds.

The World's Biggest Sovereign Wealth Funds

Total assets of the biggest state-owned investment funds in the world (in billion U.S. dollars)

Government Pension Fund	1,122.1
China Investment Cooperation	1,045.7
Abu Dhabi Investment Authority	579.6
Hong Kong Monetary Authority Investment Portfolio	576.0
Kuwait Investment Authority	533.7
GIC Private Limited	453.2
Temasek Holdings	417.4
National Social Security Fund	372.1

As of January 2021
Source: SWF Institute

Sovereign Wealth Funds

Over the past decades, sovereign wealth funds became a key player in the capital markets. Their objectives were to invest the wealth they had accumulated mainly from oil revenues for future generations. Some of them are government pension funds.

The World's Biggest Sovereign Wealth Funds

The Operators in Search of Liquidity

The world of market operators is sometimes difficult to discern and is not characterized by its transparency. For the sake of simplicity, I will distinguish the operators whose job is to trade on behalf of investors, without forgetting that investors and issuers are the most important liquidity providers. Traders do not act with the objective of becoming shareholders, and they only remain owners of financial assets for a noticeably brief time. They are not investors. They are the powerful force behind liquidity and volatility.

Their role is therefore at the margin and precarious since their ownership of financial assets is only to ensure their ability to intervene in these markets.

Trading dominates the capital markets' short-term horizon. However, it is often the voice of traders that dominates the media debate. It is from them that journalists get information and find interpretations that they take as "the voice of the market," when in fact they are only opinions on the immediate state of the market.

Market Makers Between Volume and Investment

Market makers not only trade securities, but they also expose a buy-and-sell price for these same securities. In doing so, they assume a risk that requires them to allocate equity to this activity. To perform this function, they take on the risk of price fluctuations on the securities they hold. Market making can only be performed by accepting to own securities, even for a nanosecond. They are an essential cog in the wheel as far as they assume and correct the micro-fluctuations between buyers and sellers and are remunerated on the

G. Ugeux, *Wall Street's Assault on Democracy*, https://doi.org/10.1007/978-3-031-29094-7_10

margin between the purchase and sale price that they announce and negotiate. This is an activity that contributes to the liquidity of the market. It is legitimate and essential to the proper functioning of the equity and bond markets. These markets rely on the amount of equity capital allocated by each financial institution to this activity.

The growth of the markets concentrated these activities in the hands of specialized subsidiaries of large banks and a few investment banks like Goldman Sachs and Morgan Stanley. This concentration poses problems that are difficult to deal with, as their power raises the question of democracy. Even if it would be inappropriate to speak of collusion, the community of financial interests that they represent and their level of concentration make them an uncontrollable force. When a stock or a market is under pressure, they will often be the first to react and accentuate these fluctuations.

This is one of the sources of power, and sometimes of abuse of power or fraud. Regulatory authorities try to control and prevent market makers from favoring the management of their own account to the detriment of the companies and investors they are supposed to serve.

Algorithmic Trading: A Short-Term Mechanism

Why not entrust what human beings cannot do to computers or robots programmed to favor trading companies? It did not take long for computers to take over this activity, which are able to trade large amounts in microseconds.

The trading algorithm relies on a sophisticated economic and mathematical model to analyze the market and execute a predetermined investment strategy. The simplest example is the trading algorithm, whose function is to split orders for large amounts into smaller orders and to send them according to a precise timing to one or more carefully chosen platforms in order to optimize the execution conditions (purchase or sale price and transaction costs).

The most important operator on the stock markets is the computer: Sixty-five percent of the volumes traded in the United States are algorithmic. This does not mean that human beings are absent—they are the ones who set the parameters of the programs and capture, with artificial intelligence, the data for reading the market movements.

Contrary to the impression that this trading is neutral, it contains elements that are causes for concern:

- Despite the denials of high-frequency traders, this type of trading does not respect the principle of equal access to the markets: Only the best-endowed institutions and individuals manage to get ahead of the others.
- The power of computer systems in the big banks is so great that no one seems to have a comprehensive and detailed understanding of their mechanism.
- High-frequency trading has the major disadvantage of increasing market volatility by amplifying its pace.

This reinforces my conviction that short-term stock market movements are based on pure supply and demand logic, not on strategic considerations. The SEC (Securities and Exchange Commission) published a report in 2020 on Algo Trading.[1]

Brokers at the Service of the Investor

Those who used to be called stockbrokers have undergone an evolution that has practically transformed their function, which had originally been based on a personal relationship between the individual investor and a firm or a person they knew. The stockbroker knew their client's financial situation and advised them while conducting transactions on their behalf, either directly on the floor of the exchange or electronically.

This essential role is now often filled by financial institutions that are not exclusively dedicated to their investors. However, there are firms that have specialized in this investor service function—the private banks, whose clients must have sufficiently large assets to invest.

The brokers have considerably equipped themselves technologically, developing their consulting activities and adding analytic tools and a digital interface with their clients. But the domination of large institutions threatens their competitiveness because their size does not allow them to compete with financial institutions who are able to act both as market makers and as brokers for their clients.

Recently, however, the SEC took a closer look and introduced a new regulation that aims to prevent brokers from selling financial products (especially mutual funds) that pay them higher commissions, regardless of the quality of their management.

---

[1] https://www.sec.gov/files/Algo_Trading_Report_2020.pdf

The objective is to enhance the quality and transparency of retail investors' relationships with investment advisers and broker-dealers, bringing the legal requirements and mandated disclosures in line with reasonable investor expectations while preserving access (in terms of choice and cost) to a variety of investment services and products.[2]

Even inside the brokerage world, the interests of the client and the advisor can be divergent.

A new type of broker has appeared in the United States: Robinhood. Accessible from a simple cell phone, this application has become the darling of young people and has created (inexperienced) vocations of new investors. Even though the SEC recently investigated it, it has managed to attract 18 million users and trades at a market capitalization of $40 billion.[3] Robinhood's average customer is young and lacks investing knowledge. The average age is 31, according to the company, and half of its customers have never invested before.[4] The business model was too fragile, and the stock of Robinhood lost 90% of its value in 1 year while the company laid off one quarter of its staff.

[2] https://www.sec.gov/news/press-release/2019-89

[3] https://www.consumeraffairs.com/news/robin-hood-reportedly-faces-sec-probe-over-disclosure-practices 090320.html

[4] https://www.nytimes.com/2020/07/08/technology/robinhood-risky-trading.html

Banks at the Heart of Conflicts of Interest

Banks are everywhere and intervene in several capacities. Commercial banks and asset managers operate on the debt market and are borrowers. They operate in the equity market as market makers as well as brokers. They invest in bonds and advise issuers. In short, they are a nexus of conflicts of interest that has grown since the investment banks were taken over by the commercial banks.

Without them, however, the markets could not function, as they are the only ones who have the means to create liquidity, whether in bonds or shares.

The Crisis of 1929 Excluded Banks from Capital Markets

The role of commercial banks in capital markets has undergone major historical vicissitudes.

It all began when the markets collapsed in 1929. In four years, stocks lost half their value and only regained it after the war. Banks and their clients had accumulated stocks, and the fever of individual investors would lead to a stock market panic and three years of economic recession.

In 1933 and 1934, the Glass-Steagall Act excluded banks from trading and guaranteeing the investment of stocks. This led to the birth of merchant banks and investment banks. The House of Morgan was split into three entities: JP Morgan & Co. as a depository bank, Morgan Stanley for merchant and investment banking activities, and Morgan, Grenfell & Co. for certain activities outside the United States, in this case in London.

© The Author(s), under exclusive license to Springer Nature Switzerland AG 2023
G. Ugeux, *Wall Street's Assault on Democracy*, https://doi.org/10.1007/978-3-031-29094-7_11

The Glass-Steagall Act actually consisted of four provisions of the Banking Act of 1933, arguably the most important piece of US financial legislation to emerge from the Great Depression. This legislation also covered deposit insurance and other reforms designed to restore and maintain financial stability. One of the key provisions of the act called for a near-total separation of investment banking (the business) from fundraising (the bank). Companies licensed as commercial banks were thus excluded from market and securities operations, in particular the underwriting and trading of corporate debt, equity securities, and municipal revenue bonds.[1]

Why have no measures been taken to split up the banks of the European continent? The answer depends on the culture of each country. Germany allowed banks to control companies by being direct shareholders, to operate on the stock markets and to have the exclusive right to go public; they were an essential player in the financing of the Third Reich's war effort. The merchant banks in France, Lazard and Rothschild, were essentially limited to advisory activities, leaving the big banks to be active on the financial markets. In Italy, Mediobanca makes and breaks companies and governments. In Japan, it is securities companies like Nomura that operate primarily in capital markets, although large banks have entered that space over the past decade.

The End of the Glass-Steagall Act or the Return of the Universal Bank in the United States

The American banking sector was not happy with this exclusion by the Glass-Steagall Act and tried to change the act's regulations on securities activities. This separation between commercial and investment banking deprived them of important outlets. They found themselves confined to credit without being able to finance their clients through bonds.

In 2013, *The Economist* wrote that "Before the great crash of 2008, the universal banks swaggered around London, Hong Kong and New York. Barclays, Citigroup, Credit Suisse, Deutsche and UBS imagined they could be all things to investors in (almost) all corners of the globe. Five years on, in 2013, such ambitions will seem quaint as the American and European banks find themselves either shrinking further or increasingly marginalised."[2]

The Gramm-Leach-Bliley Act, also known as the Financial Services Modernization Act of 1999, is an American law that repealed the provisions

---

[1] https://www.federalreservehistory.org/essays/glass-steagall-act
[2] https://www.economist.com/news/2012/11/21/the-fall-of-the-universal-bank

of the Glass-Steagall Act. The legislation was proposed in the Senate by Phil Gramm and in the House by Jim Leach and Thomas J. Bliley, Jr. It was signed into law by President Bill Clinton on November 12, 1999.

Eight years later, the collapse of Lehman Brothers demonstrated that this repeal did not protect investment banks from disaster. Bear Stearns was bought by J.P. Morgan and Merrill Lynch by Bank of America. The circle was complete. Even Morgan Stanley and Goldman Sachs had to become bank holding companies to gain access to Federal Reserve funding.

The Domination of the Bond Market by the Banks

As soon as the Glass-Steagall Act was repealed, the banks, benefiting from the exclusive privilege of collecting deposits from individuals, naturally became institutions active on both the bond and credit markets. In general, they are driven to do so by the Bale III ratios, which require them to hold a significant portion of their balance sheet in liquid assets—Eurozone banks hold approximately one-third of their balance sheet in bonds.[3] The importance of this investment in bonds explains why they also dominate trading in sovereign and corporate bonds.

This remains the major difference between the American model and the others. Where US banks compete directly with the bond market for corporate financing, the European market is dominated by sovereign and bank bonds. Only large European nonbank and financial companies have access to the European bond market. This lack of disintermediation explains the size of European and Japanese banks in relation to GDP. They also constitute a power that creates an objective alliance between the banking sector and public issuers.

The European Commission has initiated a reform known as the Capital Markets Union to provide the European Union with a pan-European regulatory framework. It faces considerable challenges.

Banks as Prime Brokers at the Service of Hedge Funds

As we have seen previously, several crises have put a strain on the prime brokerage activity of the major banks. Prime brokers finance hedge funds that borrow a large percentage of their capital from banks. This leverage provides them with a higher return, but their financial structure does not allow them

---

[3] http://sdw.ecb.europa.eu/reports.do?node=10000028

to be financed on their own. They have to pledge the shares or bonds they hold to their prime brokers, allowing the bank to sell these assets when the fund defaults.

If they are doing their job well, they constantly monitor the hedge fund portfolio to ensure that it is sufficiently diverse to prevent any one asset from jeopardizing the fund itself. This explains the large losses suffered by banks in situations like GameStop, Archegos, or Greensill. As the *Financial Times* reported, "Credit Suisse plans to all but exit the prime brokerage business that left it with $5.1bn of losses this year, as new chair António Horta-Osorio unveiled a restructuring of the troubled lender."[4] He did not last and had to resign in 2021 for breaking COVID quarantine rules and using a private plane to attend the Wimbledon tennis championship.[5]

The fierce competition between these prime brokers explains why they sometimes go beyond reasonable limits. The recent scandals will certainly bring more discipline and sobriety to these activities, which will have to be supported by appropriate capital to avoid a speculative bubble.

It led to a situation that saw Credit Suisse in a substantial credit fall threatening its mere survival.

---

[4] https://www.ft.com/content/1f51d236-6f9c-4222-bc7e-9a5073696883

[5] https://www.bloomberg.com/news/articles/2022-01-17/credit-suisse-ousts-culture-fixing-boss-after-his-own-scandal

Are Public Authorities Complicit or Ignorant?

The year 2020 has highlighted the growing importance of the public sector in the capital markets. It was governments and government agencies that intervened massively and quickly to prevent a collapse of the system. Their interventions reached $16 trillion in the last 12 months, according to IMF (International Monetary Fund) statistics.[1]

The main underwriter of the debt created by these interventions has been the central banks, which have been at the forefront since the development of quantitative easing—sometimes known as "money printing."

How can we hope that the combination of government indebtedness and their financing by central banks at rates close to or below zero does not make the public authorities the accomplices of market forces, be they the banks they control, the large national and foreign investors, or the market makers who maintain explosive liquidity?

Governments and the Explosion of Sovereign Debt

The imposing mass of $71trillion of sovereign debt cannot be financed at market rates without the intervention of central banks. Governments have always called on lenders, either directly or through the issuance of debt securities or bonds. As needs have grown, these bonds have been the subject of a

---

[1] https://www.imf.org/en/News/Articles/2021/04/07/tr040721-transcript-of-the-april-2021-fiscal-monitor-press-briefing

G. Ugeux, *Wall Street's Assault on Democracy*, https://doi.org/10.1007/978-3-031-29094-7_12

market where investors have found an opportunity to buy and sell these desirable assets. Government debt has become one of the most unbalancing elements of financial stability because it has become non-redeemable. The risks associated with it are not restricted by regulators despite the potential systemic risks they carry. Banks and central banks are encouraged to buy sovereign bonds and hold them to maturity. This decision not to impose capital adequacy ratios for sovereign assets was adopted consciously and favors massive holdings of sovereign bonds in the balance sheet of the banks.

Is There a Limit to the Indebtedness of the United States?

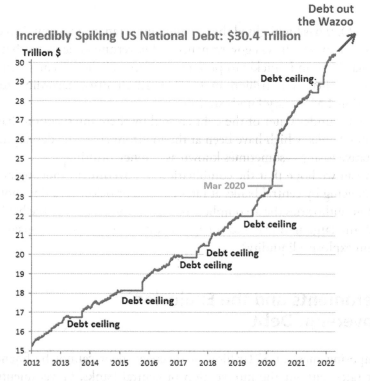

https://wolfstreet.com/2020/08/18/who-bought-the-gigantic-4-5-trillion-in-us-governmentdebt-added-in-the-past-12-months-everyone-but-china/

As the issuer of the world's reserve currency, the US Treasury has always considered that printing money has no limits. The current level of national debt amounts to $28 trillion, exceeding 100% of the country's gross domestic product (GDP).

To stimulate the economy during the year 2020, the United States injected more than $6 trillion in the form of loans or capital contributions into small- and medium-sized businesses to keep them out of bankruptcy while also attempting to rescue large, over-leveraged companies.

The Biden administration, surrounded by advocates of the monetary theory that denies the risks of government debt, does not seem to care. It projects $6 trillion in deficits over the next few years. The financing of the war in Ukraine increased these expenses, as will the reduction of taxes on energy products.

Treasury bills are held by foreign central banks, which are becoming wary of this unpredictable borrower and have not increased their investment as the debt load has grown. The share of foreign investors in the holding of US Treasuries has dropped from 35% to 25%. Confidence in the dollar and its supremacy is being undermined by the White House's tariff war and by the accelerated use of borrowing.

In the face of this mismanagement, the American taxpayer will soon be carrying $30 trillion in debt. The richest and most powerful country in the world is living at the expense of the entire planet willing to lend it capital. Its budget deficit in 2020 reached $3.1 trillion compared to $980 billion the year before. The year 2021 was only slightly better at $2.77 trillion. It decreased to $1 trillion in 2022. Can the United States play the sorcerer's apprentice forever? Cynical political and financial leaders claim that the rest of the world has no choice but to finance the country known allegorically as Uncle Sam.

Is Europe in Control of Its Indebtedness?

Europe has not followed the US policy of overindebtedness, even if the European Central Bank has conducted quantitative easing following the Federal Reserve. It had been confronted with a sovereign crisis in several member states, which led the European Commission and the European Council to take radical measures to control public deficits and approve annual budgets.

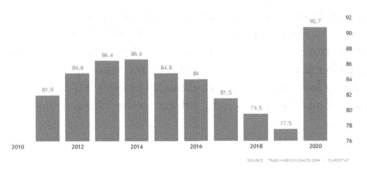

At the European Council in March 2005, the EU heads of state and government decided to revise the reform of the Stability and Growth Pact. According to the new version of the pact, member states must keep their deficits and public debt below the thresholds set at 3% and 60% of their GDP, respectively. However, the rules of the pact have been "relaxed" on several points: Member states will be able to escape an excessive deficit procedure if they are in a recession, whereas this exemption was previously granted only to states hit by a severe growth crisis (resulting in a loss of two points of GDP or more). Voices are now calling to reimpose this fiscal discipline.

Sovereign Debt Is Not European But National

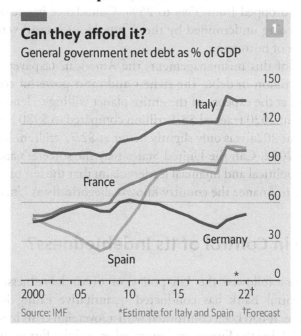

Can they afford it?
General government net debt as % of GDP
Source: IMF   *Estimate for Italy and Spain   †Forecast

This is where the risk of a default by one of the countries of the European Union exists. France and Italy have a sovereign debt of more than 1,300 billion euros each. The European recovery plan of 750 billion euros is an attempt to use the borrowing capacity of the European Union to redistribute resources to the member states most disadvantaged by the pandemic. It is therefore not a community loan that finances community projects but a direct funding of European member states projects, subject to the approval of the European Commission.

The recent widening of the spread between German Bonds and Italian government bonds reminds us that these discrepancies of fiscal discipline between the EU member states can cause serious disruption in the eurozone. This disruption increased as Mario Draghi, former ECB president, resigned as prime minister of the country.

The election of an extreme right government in September 2022 increases this risk: How responsible will Italy be under that regime?

The Japanese Mirage

With $13 trillion or 266% of the GDP, Japan is the world champion of the OECD (Organization of Economic Cooperation and Development) countries bearing public debt.

It is difficult to imagine how Japan will manage to get out of the debt trap. Their public debt represents 266% of its GDP, almost half of which is held by the Bank of Japan, with Japanese sovereign bonds representing 80% of the Bank of Japan's balance sheet—all this at zero interest rates.

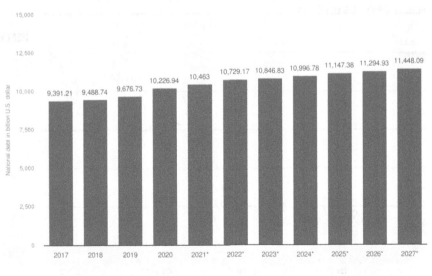

Japan: National debt from 2017 to 2027 (in billion U.S. dollar)

Source
IMF

Additional Information:
Japan; IMF

It is since the implementation of what has been called Abenomics that the explosion of public debt has reached stratospheric levels. Faced with a run on the yen caused by the 2008 sovereign crisis, Japan increased its debt and lowered its interest rates to revive the Japanese economy.

The term Abenomics refers to the combination of three "arrows" that are supposed to put the world's third largest economy back on the path to solid growth:

- Fiscal: This involves encouraging activity through massive economic support plans.
- Monetary: The Bank of Japan (BoJ) reformed its monetary policy in April 2013 to achieve a defined inflation target of 2% in about two years, via a technique known as "qualitative and quantitative easing."
- Reforming: Several structural projects have been launched to transform the system in depth and increase Japan's "growth potential."

Will the Kishida government be more effective than the preceding Suga one? The resistance of the Bank of Japan to increase interest rates has caused the Japanese Yen to plunge, fueling the fire of critics of the government.[2]

---

[2] https://www.dailyfx.com/forex/market_alert/2022/04/11/Japanese-Yen-Forecast-USDJPY-Surge--Persists-As-Bond-Yields-Hit-Fresh-Highs-JM.html

The Regulatory Authorities' Denial
of Sovereign Risks

There is a major risk associated with this explosion of public debt: the possibility of a government default. This is not bankruptcy (which is a commercial concept) but the impossibility of paying the interest and principal on these loans. The absence of bankruptcy, however, does not prevent a public debt crisis.

Countries with high debt vulnerabilities need to tackle them through a combination of fiscal policy adjustment and measures to restore growth. An IMF-supported program can facilitate that adjustment, but the IMF can only lend to a member if its debt is sustainable. There are cases where debt is unsustainable, even taking the adjustment efforts into account. If a member country enters into debt distress, only the country's government can decide whether to solve this by negotiating a debt restructuring with its creditors.[3]

One would be justified in considering that these public debt explosions represent a risk when they greatly exceed the growth of the economy. In order to encourage banks to subscribe to sovereign loans, a solution has to be found rather than deny the sovereign risk by not weighting it in the banks' balance sheets.

Asset holdings and loans are weighted under international agreements, the latest version of which is known as Basel III. This is to ensure that the risk of nonperforming assets and liabilities is covered by an adequate level of capital, liquidity, and leverage. In December 2017, sovereign borrowers and central banks converged to sacrifice their financial stability mission by letting states decide whether to make such a weighting.

Encompassing more than $30 trillion worldwide, the sovereign bond market is an important component of financial markets, not only because of its size but also because of its influence on interest rates and investor remuneration.

After the crisis, the Basel Committee initiated far-reaching reforms to address some of the major shortcomings of the precrisis regulatory framework. However, these reforms did little to change the regulatory treatment of sovereign risk exposures. The fragility of sovereign borrowers in various regions and jurisdictions since the financial crisis have served as a reminder that sovereign exposures are risky. The committee recognizes that these exposures, which play an important role in the banking system, financial markets, and

---

[3] https://www.imf.org/en/Topics/sovereign-debt

the broader economy, present risks at multiple levels. At this stage, the committee has not reached a consensus to update the regulatory treatment of sovereign risk exposures and has therefore decided not to consult on the ideas put forward.[4]

This denial of sovereign risk encourages banks to accumulate government or public sector debt without having to consider the risk of these assets. Consequently, Italian banks hold more than 150% of their equity in Italian Tesoro bonds, whose rating is one step away from losing its investment grade status and is in danger of falling into the "junk" category.

But the Basel III regulation has gone further: By imposing liquidity ratios, it has forced banks and insurance companies to hold a significant part of their balance sheets in sovereign bonds—hence the circle is complete.

This time bomb is bound to come back to haunt us when this risk, increased by the economic stimulus programs, explodes in the weakest countries. Any default by a major country will create a systemic crisis of gigantic proportions.

---

[4] https://www.bis.org/bcbs/publ/d425_fr.pdf

Central Banks to the Rescue of Financial Markets and Borrowers

Before opening this chapter, I would like to clarify a few points. Central banks are often caught between a rock and a hard place. In most cases, they have to integrate the difficult indebtedness of their governments. This is not only true in emerging markets—the dramatic explosion of sovereign debt has made central banks the largest individual owners of their countries' sovereign debt.

They justify these massive purchases as well as zero or negative interest rates by their monetary policies. Their justifications for (QE) quantitative easing operations have made them a nonindependent participant of capital markets.

Their recent failure to contain inflation is a result of their inability to focus on their primary duty. "The road to hell is paved with good intentions," said French existentialist philosopher Jean-Paul Sartre. The unintended consequences of their actions, as unintended as they might be, were predictable.

During the pandemic crisis, central banks became the main source of liquidity at a time when they could not be used. This provoked an explosion of equity markets, adding to the expropriation of savings at low interest rates and leading to an increase of wealth for the most fortunate.

On my watch, they have become a source of dislocation of wealth through capital markets. They are accountable for these "unintended but predictable" consequences.

© The Author(s), under exclusive license to Springer Nature Switzerland AG 2023
G. Ugeux, *Wall Street's Assault on Democracy*, https://doi.org/10.1007/978-3-031-29094-7_13

Central Banks Buy Back Government Bonds: A High-Risk Self-Financing Operation

With no exit strategy to sell their holdings of bonds issued by their governments, central banks have embarked on QE programs that have ballooned their balance sheets. In doing so, they objectively become an ally to government's overindebtedness.

Central banks, as guardians of monetary policy, have found themselves in the position of being the first holders of public debt. This "alternative" monetary policy does not hide the fact that this trend will weigh heavily on the financial markets.

Governments continue to overindebt themselves. They are trying to avoid paying the price of the risk they represent, and they drive interest rates down by selling an increasing part of this debt on the balance sheet of central banks.

The table below shows the extent to which central bank balance sheets are being inflated. While some people are not concerned by such inflation, I for one do not understand how a balance sheet can be allowed to reach such proportions in such a short period of time without exit strategy. As gold and banknotes in circulation are not scalable, the dependence of central banks is mutual and financed by the banks themselves.

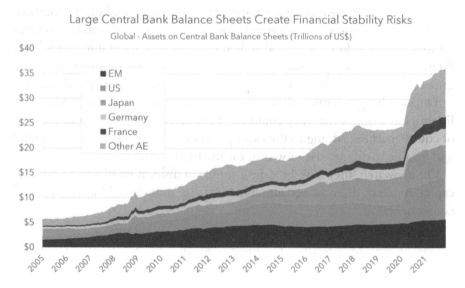

Large Central Bank Balance Sheets Create Financial Stability Risks

Global - Assets on Central Bank Balance Sheets (Trillions of US$)

https://www.conference-board.org/research/economy-strategy-finance-charts/Central-Banks-US-Feb2022

To avoid the worst-case scenario, central banks have turned into long-term lenders by collectively buying $8 trillion of capital in the first half of 2020—half of the bailout of the coronavirus crisis. The US Federal Reserve increased its balance sheet from $4 trillion to $8 trillion in a matter of weeks, a doubling that matches the three quantitative easing operations in the 10 years following the 2008 financial crisis.

But they have also crossed a line that threatens their credibility. Instead of providing liquidity to financial institutions to enable them to ensure the continuity of credit, they intervened directly by taking credit risks, and in some cases, the riskiest credit: junk bonds.

At the end of 2021, the inflation rate exploded in most countries; fueled by energy costs, it quickly spread to other aspects of the economy. Soon after, the risk of famine and the increase of food costs plunged the whole world into a risk of stagflation, or worse.[1]

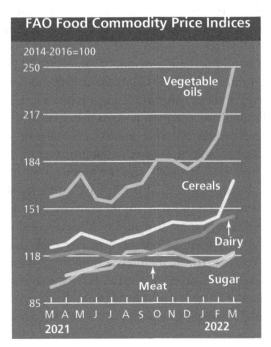

The President of the *Federal Reserve*, Jerome Powell, is a measured and courageous man. However, faced with COVID-19, the FED made the decision to print money in record time and in record amounts, rather than taking the

---

[1] https://www.weforum.org/agenda/2022/04/food-prices-fao-index-cereals-commodities-exports/

much more measured and courageous response of avoiding such an action. The scale and speed of the intervention give the impression that the FED believed the pandemic was a short-term crisis that had to be strangled. While the objective was to avoid a collapse of the economy, most of the $3 trillion was immediately rushed to Wall Street, creating a bubble that will make the inevitable next correction even more dramatic.

Confronted with a surge of inflation it had not seen coming, the Federal Reserve took the bull by the horns. It put an end to the purchase of assets within a few months and started increasing interest rates by 2.25% in a matter of three months.

The *European Central Bank (ECB)*, under Christine Lagarde, continued the policies of her predecessor Mario Draghi. Christine Lagarde and her team continue to believe that these purchases have no limits. "Has the ECB lost its ammunition? No, absolutely not," she said in September 2020. In the face of the economic crisis brought on by the COVID-19 pandemic, does the European Central Bank still have ammunition? While the FED was moving toward a reduction in Treasury bond buybacks,[2] the ECB hesitated to do so and continued its bond purchase program.[3] It waited until early July 2022 to increase its interest rates by 0.25%. Confronted with the war in Ukraine and dependent on energy and food imports, Europe is now particularly vulnerable.

One school of thought would even have us believe that public debt held by central banks could be erased. "This would be a violation of the European treaty, which strictly prohibits monetary financing of states. This rule is one of the fundamental pillars of the euro," said the president of the ECB.

These utopians forget that central banks have a balance sheet. Cancelling public debt would make it impossible for them to pay their depositors: central banks and financial institutions. It would be the Armageddon of finance. If governments claim that they do not have to pay back their debts, central banks will not be able to extricate themselves from this inflation of their assets. They will therefore continue to subscribe to new sovereign issues. It is perhaps useful to recall that the financing of central banks' balance sheets is essentially done through banks' short-term deposits.

---

[2] https://www.federalreserve.gov/newsevents/pressreleases/monetary20211103a1.htm

[3] https://apnews.com/article/coronavirus-pandemic-business-health-germany-europe-425dc836f121f62 09ec5c4920650854a

Should Central Banks Support the Financial Markets? For Whom Do Central Banks Work?

This question must be answered clearly if we want democratic control over these institutions, whose power far exceeds those of any government agency. Who are the main beneficiaries of this policy?

First and foremost, they allowed governments to borrow on terms that ignore the risks this indebtedness entails, and it is the central banks who make it possible by reducing short-term interest rates.

In the past few years, an essential change has taken place, which was confirmed in 2020: central banks have stepped outside the traditional boundaries of monetary policy and have set up a system that makes them dependent on banks.

Invited by Columbia University, Federal Reserve Vice-Chairman Stanley Fischer, former governor of the Bank of Israel, presented the way the Federal Reserve manages its communication:

> …there are very real limits to what even the most careful and deliberate communication strategy can do to temper market volatility. This is just the nature of the beast when dealing with speculative markets, and to suggest otherwise—to suggest that, say, "good communication" alone can create a completely smooth exit from a period of extraordinary policy accommodation —is to create an unrealistic expectation.[4]

In the debate that followed Fischer's speech, it appeared that the Federal Reserve's interest rate policy was driven by "market expectations." It is critical that the transparency of central banks does not allow the manipulation of their balance sheet by the financial markets and in particular by the banks.

Central Banks at the Service of the Capital Markets?

The massive liquidity injections by central banks in the form of QE fueled stock market prices to explode over the last 10 years. But the pandemic has shown that central banks inject liquidity that enriches shareholders even in times of recession and unemployment.

---

[4] https://sipa.columbia.edu/news/federal-reserve%E2%80%99s-fischer-discusses-central-bank-communication

The stock market should be off limits. Since 2012, the famous Wall Street "rally" has been built on sand. Starting in March 2020, governments took measures of unprecedented magnitude to try to curb the consequences of the virus. They shut down the economy, plain and simple, and tried to save it with $10 trillion in financial stimulus over three months, increasing their debt load to a pharaonic degree. The debts of the stimulus programs have ended up on the balance sheets of the central banks. The correlation seems increasingly obvious.

The arrogance of "market voices" has become unbearable. Having seen the index increase by 150% since the pandemic drop, they blame the central banks for no longer fueling prices that were astronomical and instead increasing interest rates to avoid yet another explosion of inflation. A decrease of 15% is no cause for worry after 10 years of a market increase of 400%.[5]

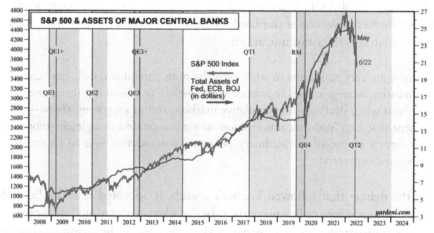

* Averages of daily figures for weeks ending Wednesday. Securities held by Fed include US Treasuries, Agency debt, and mortgage-backed securities.
Note: QE1 (11/25/08-3/31/10) = $1.24tn in mortgage securities; expanded (3/16/09-3/31/10) = $300bn in Treasuries. QE2 (11/3/10-6/30/11) = $600bn in Treasuries. QE3 (9/13/12-10/29/14) = $40bn/month in mortgage securities (open ended); expanded (12/12/12-10/1/14) = $45bn/month in Treasuries. QT1 (10/1/17-7/31/19) = balance sheet pared by $675bn. RM (11/1/19-3/15/20) = reserve management, $60bn/month in Treasury bills. QE4 (3/16/20-infinity). QT2 = balance sheet pared by $95 billion per month. Source: Federal Reserve Board.

Yardeni Research, Inc.
www.yardeni.com

To do this, central banks have invested in sovereign and, to a lesser degree, corporate bonds, artificially lowering long-term interest rates. The public sector has taken advantage of the savings by not providing the return on the risk that borrowing represents.

Increasing this risk further, central banks did not design their quantitative easing operations with a post-crisis exit route in mind. They are therefore

---

[5] https://www.yardeni.com/pub/peacockfedecbassets.pdf

unable to get rid of the $15 trillion ball and chain they have accumulated since 2008 and are thus dependent on government spending borrowing seemingly without limit. In March 2020, they have taken on several layers of debt in a desperate attempt to limit the damage caused by the coronavirus (over which they have no control), the drop in oil prices (which does not concern them), and, above all, the prospect of a serious economic recession.

By favoring borrowers to the detriment of investors, retirees, or life insurers, central banks have been responsible for one of the greatest inequalities of the last decennia. Additionally, they enriched shareholders. I am convinced that this was not intentional, and I would absolutely give central banks the benefit of the doubt, but it is urgent that they look at themselves and recognize their errors if they want to regain public confidence. They failed to recognize that their monetary policy would be responsible for one of the largest and fastest price increases in history when they were supposed to be custodians of inflation.

When the dust settles, a revision of their priorities should recreate independence from capital markets. The long-term markets are ahead of the game.

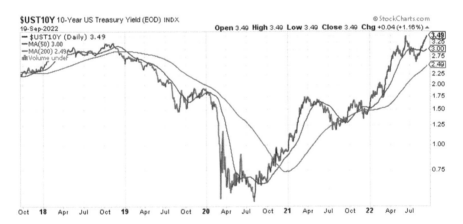

An Ecosystem at the Service of the Corporate World

A whole ecosystem is currently supporting capital markets, one that is complex and not at all transparent, where the balance of power has little to do with democracy. The combination of interests that meet in the lair of the markets seeks to favor companies, their managers, and their shareholders.

At the margin of the system is a series of "facilitators" who consolidate the system. Their apparent neutrality is contradicted by their actions. They too must question their role, which is increasingly called into question, not to mention directly flouted, by fraud, abuse, and conflicts of interest.

Law firms, audit firms, rating agencies, and the press, to name but four, are being directly financed by companies. Can they really be independent?

Law Firms or the Privatization of Financial Law

The evolution of the legal profession has led lawyers to take on responsibilities that do not belong to them. Their power over boards of directors and corporate executives has transformed their function from "speaking the law" to "doing the law." Supported by corporate compliance structures, they often appear as "kingmakers." This has led to a shameless increase in their remuneration, which, in the best firms, can reach $2,000 per hour. The largest law firm in the United States creates $7.5 million in profits per partner.

For perfectly objective reasons, the financialization of the world is based on laws and regulations. In a recent book by my colleague Katharina Pistor of Columbia Law School, she demonstrates how "large law firms are able to influence the law for the benefit of the wealthy and corporations. If their

G. Ugeux, *Wall Street's Assault on Democracy*, https://doi.org/10.1007/978-3-031-29094-7_14

clients don't like the law, these firms hijack it to the point of "privatizing" it to serve the clients' interests. Capital is created behind closed doors in private law firms, and this little-known fact is one of the main reasons for the widening wealth gap between those with capital and those without."[1]

The mechanism operates at three levels as follows:

- Lobbying governments: Law firms play a key role in the preparation of laws and regulations. They sometimes even approach members of parliament or ministers by proposing a bill they have drafted that is in line with their clients' interests. If there is one area where democracy can be influenced or even bought, it is in the drafting of laws and regulations. At the root of this influence is the difference in competence between law firms and parliamentarians or governments.
- Once the law has been passed, a second phase begins—that of influencing the regulators in the implementation of the rules and in the treatment of the cases concerned by this regulation. The drafting of rules for the application of important legislation is a highly technical task. It is not enough to implement a framework law; it is also necessary to consider all the regulations relating to this activity to avoid legal conflicts.
- In many cases, the influence of large law firms on courts and tribunals establishes a jurisprudence that can go against the rule of law and replace it with a private version. Here again, the competence gap is felt. A judge must be able to make decisions in a wide range of areas. In the face of a lawyer who has specialized in financial law, for example, an imbalance of competence arises.

Large corporations and the wealthy can afford to hire firms whose resources in terms of people and knowledge far exceed those of the executive, legislative, and judicial branches.

In financial matters, the pot of clay versus the pot of iron is particularly visible. The only way an individual can hope to be compensated for fraud or manipulation is to form a group of victims: These are the class actions. It will come as no surprise that European companies are opposed to this system, which places a burden of responsibility on them. However, the trend for class actions is set to continue, given the EU Directive on "representative actions

---

[1] Katarina Pistor: The Code of Capital: How the Law Creates Wealth and Inequality https://www.amazon.fr/gp/product/B07KM2FW65/ref=dbs_a_def_rwt_hsch_vapi_taft_p1_i0

for the protection of the collective interests of consumers," which EU member states must implement by the end of 2022.[2]

This does not mean that all hope is lost. The Dutch court forced the Shell group to reduce its CO_2 emissions. Other multinationals in the hydrocarbon sector are beginning their transition to renewable energy.[3]

Audit Firms and the Temptation of Complacency

The audit profession has undergone a chaotic evolution, notably because of fraud or inaccuracies. Often caught between their professional integrity and their dependence on commissions paid by companies, they navigate tumultuous waters. Once again, it is not to condemn but to take stock of a profession whose usefulness is indisputable and whose integrity is recognized in most cases.

Faced with exceptionally large clients, most audit firms play an essential and remarkable role. Recently, however, attention has been directed to situations that are as exceptional as they are problematic since the certification of financial accounts is an essential element of investor confidence.

The major stock market scandals have revealed flaws in the operation of external audit firms. Yet the certification of accounts is the very foundation of a company's credibility. This profession, too often considered as auxiliary, plays a role comparable to the rating of bonds.

It is the audited or rated company that pays the external auditor. It therefore has the upper hand in the scope of the audits. The following two historical cases have highlighted this importance a contrario.

Enron in Collusion with Arthur Andersen

The scene in front of the federal court in Houston on March 20, 2002, was somewhat unreal: Nearly 500 Arthur Andersen accountants, trading in their usual shirts and ties for black T-shirts emblazoned with "I am Arthur Andersen" in orange letters, marched for the dismissal of charges against their company. On March 14, spectacularly, Arthur Andersen had been charged with

---

[2] https://www.law.com/international-edition/2021/11/03/the-rise-class-actions-in-europe-will-london-remain-the-preferred-choice/?slreturn=20211005171841

[3] https://www.clearygottlieb.com/news-and-insights/publication-listing/dutch-court-orders-shell-to--reduce-emissions-in-first-climate-change-ruling-against-company#:~:text=In%20a%20groundbreaking%20judgment%20delivered,(compared%20to%202019%20levels)

obstruction of justice for having destroyed "tons of documents" relating to their client Enron.

The SEC (Securities and Exchange Commission) would have been satisfied with a record fine; the Justice Department settled for a fatal indictment. What constitutes the accusation against the most prestigious firm among the accounting firms, all American, that dominate the auditing of publicly traded companies? Too close to their client Enron, the auditors, one of whom was a partner on Enron's board, Arthur Andersen, sent an employee of his firm 26 boxes weighing 60 kilos and 24 boxes weighing 25 kilos full of documents. The auditors' instructions were clear: destroy everything. At the same time, the auditors in charge of the Enron case deleted their emails.

To avoid the partners' liabilities, the firm decided to liquidate itself.

Ernst & Young Does Not Check the Bank Statements of Wirecard

The riveting book *Money Men: A Hot Startup, A Billion Dollar Fraud, A Fight for the Truth, The story of a hot start up engaging in a billion-dollar fraught and the fight of a journalist*" written by the *Financial Times* journalist, David McCrum, exposed, at great risk, the collusion between the German authorities and the owners and managers of Wirecard.[4]

This case reveals the behavior of a company that has been spooked. As early as 2014, doubts appeared. When the *Financial Times* echoed this with supporting documents, the German market regulator BaFin initiated proceedings against the *Financial Times* for stock price manipulation.

Never since the Enron scandal has such a fraud looked so much like a Greek tragedy. All the characters of this book are there. A bunch of "senior executives," Markus Braun (now arrested), and Jan Marsalek (the fleeing bandit) coming from the porn and online gambling industry united to put together a scheme that would defraud the company by $1.9 billion. The various elements of the story include the collusion of the German regulator and authorities with the management, the weakness of the board of directors, a network of phantom companies in complacent jurisdiction, a nationalistic pride, a denial of the seriousness of the accusations by the German media, a lawsuit for insider trading of the most respected financial newspaper in the world, personal threats to the journalist and those who dared to take short positions, auditors' complacency, and, above, all hubris of toxic leadership.

---

[4] https://m.media-amazon.com/images/I/41+WeRxOVEL.jpg

In 2020, the company Wirecard desperately tried to resist the suspicion surrounding its accounts. This flagship company was the pride of Germany as a world leader in international payment methods. The company called in KPMG to audit its accounts in view of the suspicion surrounding Ernst & Young (EY), its appointed auditor. The bombshell burst on June 22: Wirecard admitted that a sum of 1.9 billion euros, although recorded on its balance sheet, "most probably" did not exist. The global auditing giant EY is now at the heart of the Wirecard affair. EY was responsible for auditing and validating the accounts of the German company now in bankruptcy. EY is now at the heart of the Wirecard affair, and the German shareholders' association SdK has filed a criminal complaint against one former and two current auditors of EY in Germany. According to the *Financial Times (FT)*, EY failed to request banking information from a bank where Wirecard claimed to hold up to one billion euros in cash.[5]

The collusion inside Deutschland GmbH was thus exposed. The whole of Germany was behind its golden child, and the investigations were all aborted until the truth was discovered outside of Germany. The ongoing investigations reveal total collusion with its auditing firm EY but above all negligence in the auditing of accounts. While the CEO is in jail, the real culprit and his cronies have fled to greener pastures.

Just months before the collapse, EY had vigorously defended the outsourced Asian business in internal meetings, according to documents seen by the *Financial Times*. This was despite a draft forensic audit commissioned by Wirecard's supervisory board that was unable to conclusively confirm that those operations existed.[6]

More recently, Ernst & Young refused to validate the accounts of a French company Solutions 30, and the management announced that it would take several months to obtain certification, causing it to lose 70% of its stock market value in one day in May 2021. In both cases, an activist hedge fund discovered the truth.

The auditors, Ernst & Young, at the highest level decided to ignore the results of audit reports of its own Wirecard auditors. It was in Singapore that some of their audit executives discovered the story—the mother of one of its top executives convinced her son to blow the whistle. Despite contrary evidence, they signed the accounts, contradicting the evidence uncovered by the *Financial Times*. The company refused a forensic audit by KPMG to dissipate

---

[5] https://www.zdnet.fr/actualites/scandale-wirecard-ey-dans-la-tourmente-39905899.htm
[6] https://www.ft.com/content/bcadbdcb-5cd7-487e-afdd-1e926831e9b7

the rumors of false accounting, and it took some guts for a minority of the board to force the investigation that became damning.

In July 2022, the *FT* announced that Wirecard forged client details to secure a 900-million-euro investment from SoftBank.[7]

The Media at the Service of the Financial Markets

The influence of the media in disseminating information likely to influence financial markets has become decisive. Long confined to specialized gazettes for rentiers, finance was invited to the level of essential subjects during the 2008 crisis. It remains a major topic of interest of medias in all forms.

In my contact with the press, I have always recognized the preparation of journalists in an unfamiliar field. But they are often forced to listen to the most powerful voices.

The various financial crises popularized financial information and have frequently been reduced to the level of news items without any reflection on the ins and outs of these developments. Journalists have often been content to relay the information that financiers and companies, and often political leaders, have wanted to have published.

Their biggest mistake has been to try to compete with unsubstantiated social media based on unverified information. They should have created a credible narrative separate from sensationalism. Their impact on financial markets has become toxic.

How Does the Control of Information Affect the Proper Functioning of Markets?

How can we prevent financial misinformation campaigns on social media?

We need to accept the fact that objective information is under threat: The spreading of fake news and the disrespect of facts and science are a major threat to our democracy. Financial markets fluctuate according to information, be it political, social, financial, or even international.

We are in a vicious circle: When economic news emerges, stock market commentators will turn to traders whose voice reflects the short-term reaction of the markets. What should be anecdotal opinion becomes "market opinion"

---

[7] https://www.ft.com/content/996c3c9b-c095-42c9-baf9-d07b1b319c9d

elevated to the status of Pythia. This short-circuiting influences public opinion and leaders who feel obliged to comment on what is only a small part of the picture. Moreover, behind the oracles of the market, there are considerable interests that seek to influence the debate.

Today, the role of information is incredibly important in the decision-making mechanisms of investors and market players. It is therefore necessary to study media's impact on the markets. Its influence is like Aesop's tongues, influencing them for better or worse. As in many other fields, has the media become news makers or news reporters?

But the media continues to be subservient to the powers of money and politics. Few media outlets have the means to be independent: Media ownership has also, over the past decades, become a matter of money, giving finance control over information. France has seen most of its press fall under the domination of financial groups. The control of information has been a key objective of the corporate world. Nothing has been done to limit concentration and ensure independence as media ownership changes hands.

Communication is replaced by the manipulation of information. This is not always the case, and journalists are proud of their independence. They have fought, sometimes courageously, to defend the truth or the facts. But financial necessities sometimes take precedence, which often lie behind the asymmetry of information. If the official version is suspect of subjectivity, the contrary information is not absent of various interests.

The dark side of this change in communications has become the advertising industry. Without any respect for privacy, they are assaulting the public with a multiplication of interruptions and uncontrolled messages. They are slowly but surely drifting into the world of the metaverse, an attempt to make people believe in virtual reality.

Trust will not be restored in media unless their narrative is authentic. By following the trend of "social" media, they have become part of a gigantic manipulation of public opinion.

The Single Mind of the Financial Markets

Unless they are very naive, journalists who cover the economy and finance know that political speeches or corporate communications are, by definition, subjective and even manipulative. Their role is therefore to take this information with a grain of salt.

At no time in the past decade, the media has considered that the accumulation of debt threatens financial stability, either on the side of corporations or on the side of sovereign borrowers. The IMF (International Monetary Fund), central banks, governments, and banks have engaged in laudatory communication while taking measures that threaten to exacerbate global indebtedness.

When the consequences of the extreme measures taken by public authorities appear in broad daylight, can we hope that the media will honestly ask themselves the question of their share of responsibility in the management of the crisis? Did they give in to sensationalism? Was their message balanced or one-sided?

This question goes far beyond the pandemic and finance. Faced with the rush of social media and the loss of advertising, the traditional media are understandably feeling helpless. The quality and balance of their analysis is their best protection. Wirecard and the Handelsblatt are a perfect illustration of this trend.

This sometimes-arduous journey of all the players, whether central or peripheral, must be part of the scrutiny we bring to bear on the financial market. The pursuit by each of the participants, whether private or public, creates an omertà that makes it difficult for the average citizen to pinpoint the culprits, and for good reason.

Attacking the system itself is essential. But a consensus must be built on the interconnections that make the capital markets a spider's web—one that is difficult to dismantle without losing the essential contribution of the financial markets to our economies.

It is therefore necessary to understand not only the stakeholders but what links them to each other and how they have managed to make financial markets work for them.

No One Size Fits All

The diversity of actors in financial markets makes the challenge to rebalance their individual interests enormous. Yet the liberal narrative that capital markets and their operators are toxic is political. Solving policy issues through politics in today's world misses the core of the argument.

From the plain vanilla transaction between an investor who buys shares of a company, capital markets have evolved into what is today called gamification. As reported in CNBC, in August 2021, the SEC announced that it is "stepping up its probe into so-called gamification and behavioral prompts used by online brokerages that encourage trading. SEC Chair Gary Gensler said new financial tech can mislead investors with rosy projections of profit without appropriate risk disclosures."[8]

The SEC often solicits public commentary before drafting new rules and regulations for Wall Street, meaning that the announcement could pose a headache for the industry's leaders. Most of the time, they represent their interests without any consideration for the environment or social consequences of their behavior.

---

[8] https://www.cnbc.com/2021/08/27/sec-steps-up-research-into-gamification-of-trading-with-online-brokers-gary-gensler-says.html

Financial Markets Operate in Their Own Interest

The purpose and mission of financial markets is to facilitate exchanges between investors and issuers. This is their raison d'être. Over time, this objective has been diverted to make the interests of financial market participants a new raison d'être. They do not make money by serving the markets; they drive the markets to make money for them.

This section attempts to trace the developments that led financial institutions to gradually turn their backs on this primary function and instead make finance an end in itself, for the benefit of some and to the detriment of others. The ecosystem of financial markets has gradually privileged particular interests to the detriment of the collective function.

How did they get there? By abandoning any purpose other than the search for enrichment for those who operate inside the system. They have achieved this through a combination of market fragmentation, weakening of regulation, and innovations with the sole objective of increasing their size, relegating any question of their social utility to the background.

Stock Markets in the Oven and in the Mill

In downtown Manhattan, 11 Wall Street is the home of the New York Stock Exchange. It is the largest stock exchange in the world. More than one billion shares are traded there everyday. It is this position that explains why "Wall Street" has become the symbol of the stock markets, that is, the markets for the shares of listed companies.

© The Author(s), under exclusive license to Springer Nature Switzerland AG 2023
G. Ugeux, *Wall Street's Assault on Democracy*, https://doi.org/10.1007/978-3-031-29094-7_15

Still dominated by the US stock exchanges, the equity exchanges are becoming increasingly diversified. This table ranks them by the market capitalization of their listed companies. The world exchanges market capitalization topped $90 trillion in 2021, doubling since the GFC.

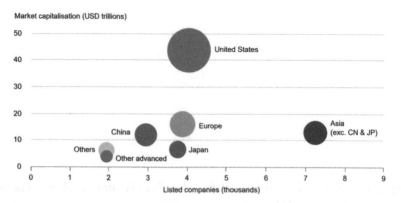

https://www.statista.com/statistics/270126/largest-stock-exchange-operators-by-marketcapitalization-of-listed

A Little History: From "Seat" Owners to a Public Company

In the early sixteenth century, Venice, Antwerp, Lyon, and Amsterdam were at the origin of fiduciary exchanges in a stock exchange form.

The Royal Exchange had been founded by English financier Thomas Gresham and Sir Richard Clough on the model of the Antwerp Bourse. It was opened by Elizabeth I of England in 1571. In 1801, it became the first regulated exchange, and the modern stock exchange is born.

The Paris Stock Exchange was created by a decree of the Council of State of King Louis XV on September 24, 1724. According to legend, a few decades later on May 17, 1792, 24 stockbrokers stood under a tree in front of 68 Wall Street and signed the "Buttonwood Agreement," establishing the New York Stock Exchange (NYSE).

Behind these exchanges were wealthy individuals and families, and they assumed the risks using their personal coffers. Subsequent members were co-opted based on their wealth.

This was the original stock exchange: a closed and confidential circle of stockbrokers with the privilege of a "seat" on the stock exchange and direct access to equity transactions. In the last 20 years, the stock exchange has taken a step forward: the listing of its own shares on its own stock market. This evolution has recently moved these institutions from a private cooperative form to that of joint stock companies that are increasingly listed on their own stock exchange.

Shareholder Transformation and Acquisitions

The United States

The first step was the establishment of a corporate structure for the exchanges, with shares held by stockbrokers and market makers. In most cases, the exchanges were nonprofit or cooperative corporations.

The shares of the exchanges were owned by domestic financial institutions. The exchanges have progressively privileged their financial profitability and their stock market price to the detriment of their economic role.

This was followed by the public listing of the stock exchanges themselves on their own market. They had to create from scratch a new governance structure and a dividend policy and pursue the level of growth required to enter new fields close to their primary activity.

However, the conversion to public companies came at a cost. Like other listed companies, stock exchanges had to focus on shareholder value, and sometimes they lost track of the fact that they are a utility and that their privileges are based on a purpose: to serve the public.

Europe

Europe has seen a wave of stock exchange acquisitions. The first was the creation, in September 2000, of the pan-European stock exchange Euronext (Paris, Brussels, and Amsterdam combined), followed by a wave of stock exchange acquisitions that continues to this day with Euronext's purchase of the Oslo Stock Exchange and, in 2020, their acquisition of Borsa Italiana after a competition between Paris and Frankfurt.

When Deutsche Boerse launched a bid for Euronext shares in 2005, the French establishment cried foul, sometimes unleashing anti-German instincts. Rather than enter into negotiations with Deutsche Boerse, Euronext's managers took refuge in the arms of the NYSE, supported in a great surge of European conviction by the French elite and its government.

As an advisor to Deutsche Boerse, I tried in vain to convince the French government (Thierry Breton was Minister of Finance) and Jean-François Théodore, the head of Euronext, to accept this merger, which would have created a European leader comparable to London. France appealed to the European Commission, which ruled that this was too large a market share for Europe. Our visit with Reto Francioni, the head of Deutsche Boerse, to see Commissioner McCreevy in Brussels was not welcome: the Commission had already made up its mind. This shortsightedness of the European anti-trust function has proved harmful to France and to Europe. It was the NYSE that bought Euronext and dismantled it.

A few years later, in 2011, Paris and Frankfurt attempted a friendly merger that was, once again, rejected by the European Commission's antitrust division. When the International Commodity Exchange (ICE) bought the NYSE in 2012, their goal was clearly to get their hands on the derivatives business that had been driving their growth. As planned, ICE was then to sell Euronext, but not without stripping it of its most valuable asset: derivatives, the fruit of the merger of the French (MATIF) and British (LIFFE) markets.

Frankfurt now dominates the European Union's stock market panorama since the United Kingdom is no longer a member. Deutsche Boerse has succeeded in bringing together the cash market, derivatives, clearing, and technology under its roof, which explains why its market value is 27 billion euros, compared to 7 billion for Euronext.

Euronext, which today combines Amsterdam, Brussels, Dublin, Lisbon, Oslo, and Paris, dominates Frankfurt in the cash market alone. The addition of Milan has further expanded the pan-European cash market by 4.3 billion euros. It was the Swiss exchange that was to take over the Spanish exchange in 2020.

The big loser has been the European Union, which, deprived of the London Stock Exchange because of Brexit, will have to reinvent itself. However, the dice is not yet cast, as stock market consolidation remains active. Even outside the European Union, the London Stock Exchange will continue to be a formidable competitor.

The better is sometimes the enemy of the good.

Asia

Four major players dominate the Asia capital markets: Japan, China, Hong Kong, and India. None of their exchanges is publicly listed.

Recently, the Shanghai Stock Exchange surpassed Tokyo, but the Japanese stock markets are a dominant player in Asia. The recent developments in China might affect that situation, since the Chinese authorities are taking measures that reduce the international importance of the Chinese capital markets. The Shanghai Stock Exchange index remained basically flat during 2021, while the Hang Seng Index in Hong Kong continued to lose value as a result of policy decisions.

However, their structures are drastically different.

Needless to say, the *Chinese exchanges* are under the strict control of the China Securities Regulatory Commission (CSRC) and are government owned. This raises serious questions regarding their integrity. The repatriation of Chinese listed companies abroad was not a business decision but rather a political move to control their domestic market. Yet, when one sees what happened to Evergrande, a real estate group close to bankruptcy, one can legitimately wonder whether the regulation is based on facts or power. Hong Kong is currently operating independently, but its future is uncertain. Taiwan is a vibrant exchange.

The *Japanese Exchanges* are the second largest after the United States. They follow the US model in a number of ways. The Japanese Financial Services Authority (JFSA) has a large responsibility to control the markets. They report back to the powerful Ministry of Finance. Their foray into the crypto exchanges and assets has, however, been particularly surprising. They serve the Japanese corporates efficiently but do not seem to have international ambitions.

The *Indian Exchanges* were handicapped by the various restrictions imposed on Indian companies to attract foreign capital. With a limited institutional investor base, they were striving for liquidity. Now that they have reached a critical mass of market capitalization, two main exchanges, the Bombay Stock Exchange and the National Stock Exchange, became fierce competitors. The Securities and Exchange Board of India (SEBI) is tightly controlled by the Finance Ministry and has not been allowed to rein in public sector banks and companies plagued by various forms of frauds and scandals. They are the host of large and successful Indian multinationals.

The Hong Kong Exchanges have been a major source of trading and listing of local and mainland China stocks and derivatives. Its future will be defined by the level of integrity that the People's Republic of China will leave to its legal status, independence of decision, and trading activities rather than trying to drive the activities to Shanghai. Key to this development will be the Hong Kong Dollar, whose convertibility compares to the limited Chinese Yuan.

The Valuation of Companies at the Heart of Stock Exchanges

What Is the Value of a Listed Company?

While there are many criteria that deserve our attention, the fact is that their value is generally based on the stock market price of the company's shares multiplied by the number of its shares. This is called the market capitalization. It is therefore the result of instantaneous transactions.

In order for a price to be established, there must be a buyer and a seller for the quantity of shares indicated. This may seem obvious, but if you read the headlines carefully, you will see that if the market goes down, investors get rid of their shares, and if it goes up, investors buy not a word from the counterparties who, by definition, see the situation differently. For a stock price to be established, there must be a buyer and a seller for the same number of shares. The same is true on the downside and on the upside.

The New York Stock Exchange probably has the most impressive price discovery mechanism. It is a sort of back and forth of orders that will search for a penny up or a penny down an equilibrium point. In most cases, the equilibrium between supply and demand at a certain price is satisfied as soon as the market opens.

When a company offers its shares for sale for the first time, which is the initial public offering (IPO), the mechanism becomes more complicated. In some cases, it will be necessary to wait for the indications of the lead manager of the operation to allow this equalization. Whether up or down, it might take several hours on the floor of the stock exchange before this equilibrium is found. The rule is an important protection for investors: they must all get the same price when buying or selling these shares. The role of the stock market is to ensure this fair treatment.

The equity markets are generally described as secondary markets. The primary market is the IPO of companies. Special Purpose Acquisition Companies (SPACs) are trading on the secondary market as any other company stock, subject to the same rules and regulations.

A company is worth more than its financial data and stock market ratios. If the accounts of companies provide essential information to measure the evolution of the company, it is not limited to its income statement and its balance sheet. It is an important player in the society in which it operates. The quality of its staff, its products, its sales network, the strength of its brand, its financial structure, and its governance are essential factors in this value. Above all, its reputation and the trust it inspires will influence the value of a company.

To be convinced of this, we need only look at the much-publicized evolution of Tesla's share price, which has fluctuated between 100 and 1000 times its earnings, while the average for automotive companies trade around 25 times the earnings.

Is value the result of supply and demand only, or is it based on intrinsic value? Value investors are often finding it difficult to relate to the current stock prices.

Price Fragmentation and Platform Abundance

The threat to what is known in the United States as the National Best Bid and Offer (NBBO) is the fragmentation of markets. A weakening of the exchanges in favor of electronic markets will reduce the importance of the NBBO price, which is subject to rules of transparency and fairness that technology alone does not provide.

How much credit can we give to the price of financial assets? The stock market price often represents a minority of the transactions conducted—the majority is done discreetly inside the banks' trading rooms, while others emerge on electronic platforms. There is a risk that the NBBO no longer represents the best market price and the best execution of an order to buy or sell securities. When there are a hundred different Bitcoin prices spread across a hundred different market maker platforms, which saint do we turn to?

Stock prices in 2021 were fueled by the glut of liquidity created by central banks. While the S&P 500 traded around 45 times earnings, the rate in 2021 dropped around 20 times in 2022.

Beware of Your Friends...

The main competitor of an exchange is its own members.

By appropriating trading volume for themselves, they saw off the branch on which they are sitting, confident in the representativeness of the financial markets. How do they manage to ensure the best possible execution in this jungle?

Exchanges can only survive if their members decide to trade through them. This creates a strong dependence of the exchanges on the big market operators, the big global banks. In recent years, many of them developed their "dark pools" or internalized their orders. One of them, called Turquoise, tried to replace the London Stock Exchange, which, in turn, ended up buying it.

It is always through brokers that orders must pass to reach the exchange. This can be a one-person firm or a giant like Merrill Lynch. The bulk of the orders are executed electronically.

The NYSE had proposed a system that met the need for anonymity, but the broker dealers were its shareholders. Institutional investors responded by creating their own "trading room." In doing so, even if they continue to transmit orders via brokers, they professionally manage the markets they know perfectly well. Why would they trust traders for orders when these traders are their competitors and are in a position to manipulate prices by exploiting their clients' information?

The CFTC fined J.P. Morgan a record fine of $920 million for using a technique known as "spoofing."[1] Spoofing is a form of market manipulation in which a trader places one or more highly visible orders but has no intention of keeping them (the orders are not considered bona fide). While the trader's spoof order is still active (or soon after it is canceled), a second order is placed of the opposite type.[2]

Increasing liquidity is the main objective of such practices. What is their added value?

Trading Platforms

Most electronic securities trading platforms are considered brokers, not exchanges. They do not offer any certainty of best execution. When the European Union, through the Markets in Financial Instruments Directive (MiFID) regulation, tries to enlarge the market beyond the "monopoly" of the exchanges, it enlarges the scope of the platforms but ignores the risks that this regulation poses to the integrity of the equity market and to the credibility of the stock price. When a "delicate" or "important" order is likely to make prices fluctuate, the investor will not make the mistake of exposing the entire order. He or she will split it or act through several brokers.

In 1999, the NASDAQ, along with 28 of its brokers, was to be sanctioned for collusion and illegal practices. NASDAQ has indicated that it is currently conducting 11 in-depth investigations into suspected price manipulation by independent brokers. These manipulations would be based on the technique

---

[1] https://www.cftc.gov/PressRoom/PressReleases/8260-20
[2] investopedia

known as "phantom orders," which consists of the trader entering false orders into the electronic trading system, intended to create an illusion of liquidity. If he wishes, for example, to buy at a price lower than the market price, it sends false sell orders well below the current trading price, forcing the other brokers to fall in line, which then allows him to buy at the best conditions. Immediately after making his purchase, he then cancels his first fake sell order. This technique is particularly effective when the "buy-sell" spreads of stocks are high. Goldman Sachs and Morgan Stanley have refused to use this technique.

Digitalization has led to an exceptional improvement in market efficiency, but it does not solve all the problems. It has allowed for faster order execution and, more importantly, for the "matching" of buy and sell orders electronically rather than by "specialists" on the floor of an exchange.

Confusion has become such that investors who place an order do not know how it is executed. The fragmentation of conduits and platforms creates a lack of transparency that allows large institutions to cannibalize exchanges. The obligation to provide "best execution" is the only protection, but the transparency is not there.

Pseudo Markets: Crypto Exchanges and Other Platforms

All that glitters is not gold, so says the proverb.

Every crypto exchange is under investigation by the Securities and Exchange Commission (SEC), claims an official from US Senator Cynthia Lummis' office.[3] Lawyer John E. Deaton may have correctly predicted that SEC Chair Gary Gensler is going to "sue an exchange whether it's Coinbase, Binance, or another exchange by the end of the year."[4]

It is worth noting here that none of the crypto exchanges provide the guarantees of a regulated stock exchange. They are market makers who hold cryptos and have no neutrality. This is one of the many deceptions surrounding Bitcoin and its offspring. It is surprising that regulators have not managed to protect the "exchange" denomination and limit it to exchanges that correspond to their regulation, creating confusion for investors who do not know when prices are manipulated.

---

[3] https://www.forbes.com/sites/michaeldelcastillo/2022/08/04/every-us-crypto-exchange-and-binance-is-being-investigated-by-the-sec-says-senator-lummis-staffer/

[4] https://coingape.com/breaking-sec-investigating-all-crypto-exchanges-will-gensler-sue-another-exchange/

There are electronic platforms like Bloomberg and Reuters that have the appearance of exchanges but are not subject to the obligations of transparency and equal treatment of orders.

As far as bonds are concerned, the situation is even more opaque. Although international bonds are often listed on the Luxembourg stock exchange, this is a regulatory formality that the Grand Ducal Palace has made a specialty of, but the bulk of bond transactions are executed "over the counter," which once again favors the large operators who are not subject to any regulatory constraints.

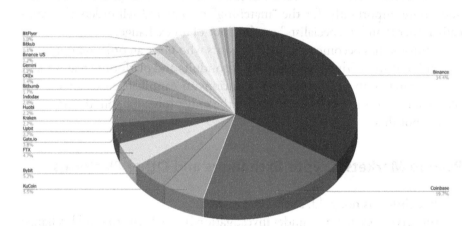

Share of web traffic amongst crypto exchanges
Data for November 2021

https://www.theblock.co/linked/126790/web-traffic-to-crypto-exchanges-in-november-werethe-second-highest-in-2021

There is little information available to enable an investor to know where and how transactions have been executed. This is a concern of the supervisory authorities who are trying to set up audit systems that ensure compliance with regulations.

I recognize that the announcement by BlackRock that it will partner with a crypto platform in August 2022 increasingly raises questions. "Blackrock Partners With Coinbase to Offer Crypto Services to Institutions."[5] BlackRock, the world's biggest asset manager, has formed a partnership with publicly traded crypto exchange Coinbase to make crypto directly available to institutional investors.[6]

---

[5] https://cointelegraph.com/news/coinbase-partners-with-blackrock-to-create-new-access-points-for-institutional-crypto-investing

[6] https://www.coindesk.com/video/the-hash-on-cdtv-clips/blackrock-partners-with-coinbase-to-offer-crypto-services-to-institutions/#:~:text=Services%20to%20Institutions-,Blackrock%20Partners%20With%20Coinbase%20to%20Offer%20Crypto%20Services%20to%20Institutions,about%2040%25%20on%20the%20news

In November 2022, the "crypto exchange" FTX collapsed and filed for bankruptcy leaving one million clients and counterparts at bay, followed by Genesis Trading, which suspended the delivery of tokens to its customers.

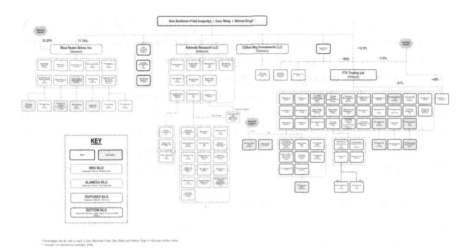

The structure showed an incredible web that carries $ 9 billion of debt for $ 1 billion of cash. The collapse of the cryptos made it unsolvable.

How could exchange regulators have allowed the crypto traders use the word exchange, misleading investors?

It is too early to say what this crypto carnage will mean for the future of this trading space. The lessons will have to be learned.[7]

Liquidity Is the Core of the Market, But It Is Not an End in Itself

For a market to be efficient, buyers and sellers must be able to trade without disrupting the valuation of those assets. This requires traders, investors, and issuers. The liquidity of a company's shares depends on its market capitalization, its ownership structure, the volume of its transactions, and the volatility of the markets themselves.

The liquidity challenges are often ignored by promoters of a stock market for small- and medium-sized companies. There is nothing to prevent them

---

[7] https://clsbluesky.law.columbia.edu/2022/11/30/the-ftx-collapse-why-did-due-diligence-regulation-and-governance-evaporate/

from being listed on the stock exchange, but the trading volume of a stock will be thin, and the prices easily influenced.

Where does the liquidity come from?

- Primary liquidity: Investors, and particularly institutional investors, are the main providers of liquidity. Large investors are more important than brokers. There are the large asset managers, such as BlackRock, the largest in the world, which manages $8 trillion in assets, a significant part of which is in equities. It is also a global firm and operates across all markets.
- Secondary liquidity: The trading of financial assets (bonds, equities, foreign exchange) amounts to trillions of dollars daily. Each of these markets owes its depth to the additional liquidity provided by market makers. They are the ones who adjust supply and demand by injecting their own resources.

The role of regulated exchanges is diminishing in favor of electronic platforms that are not exchanges. The market capitalization of equities, after reaching $120 trillion, retreated below $100 trillion by mid-2022. The trading has reached an annualized $150 trillion for the year.

There is enough liquidity in the financial markets to ensure balanced trading. If $150 trillion changes hands every year, there is no need for central bank intervention to pump liquidity into the financial system nor for speculative innovations that will explode volumes and make managing financial stability increasingly perilous.

The Contribution of the Financial Markets Is Essential

Debt financing in the United States is almost evenly split between bonds and loans. Equity financing is done in exchanges.

Without capital markets, companies and investors would be restricted to bank financing, and their growth would be confined by the limits of bank balance sheets. Direct intermediation is therefore a fundamental element of the economy. It is an essential support to democracy if it respects its principles.

Markets have their raison d'être. Essential functions in our societies are only possible because financial resources can be found, acquired, and sold. The examples below are only a part of this role of markets, but they will make us aware of the necessity of these exchange mechanisms.

The following examples are but a few that show how important the markets are for the functioning of our societies.

Pensions Financed by the Financial Markets

The cicada, having sung
All summer long,
Found herself quite bereft
When the wind chill came (Jean de la Fontaine, The Cicada and the Ant)

The current financing of pensions is not sufficient, and an abyss awaits our children and grandchildren.

Financial markets provide support for this financing:

- Markets provide government pension systems with investments in sovereign bonds but also with more productive investments. However, the regulation of public pension systems limits the use of risk capital. The lowering of interest rates by central banks has made the return on these assets close to zero, further aggravating the shortfall in the pension systems. In many countries, governments' voracious need for capital incites public and even private pension funds to invest in sovereign assets to the detriment of pensions.
- Private pension funds may resort to riskier assets with higher returns, whether stocks or bonds. But above all, they have a propensity to invest in equities, which provide both a higher yield and capital appreciation—in short, a higher return but with greater risks. They have also invested in hedge funds and private equity funds.
- Life insurance companies are committed to paying their policyholders benefits based on the risk insured through the premiums they have paid and the return on their portfolio. Interest rate levels also affect these calculations, which poses a structural problem: Will liabilities have to be reduced if monetary policies continue?

The transfer of corporate pension liabilities to pension funds often clashes with regulations that consider only sovereign assets to be safe. Restrictions on the assets that public pension systems can hold have often deprived them of additional value.

The combination of state debt overhang and policies that artificially reduce asset returns is an unsustainable situation for pensions. States are digging their pension deficits deeper, and central banks are expropriating pensions. Whatever solutions the financial markets offer, they must remain prudent.

This is why the central banks' policy of lowering interest rates is a form of undercutting pension systems. By being overly concerned with market liquidity, central banks are turning their backs on the remuneration of savings instruments and pensions.

If there is one area where financial markets are part of the solution, it is retirement. It is also the area of denial in all its glory. When high school students went on strike in 2010 against the extension of the retirement age in France, they were demonstrating against their own interest: What will be left in the state and pension funds in 25 years, and even more so in 45 years, when they reach retirement?

While governments recognize the risks of underfunding pensions, especially in the public sector, they often ignore the urgency of the problem. As part of its review of countries, the IMF should require governments to disclose the amount of retirement payments they will need to bear. It is often a multiple of sovereign debt.

The Growing Importance of Energy Transition

Finance is certainly part of the solution to the crucial problem of climate change, even if it is not simply a matter of capital. The mere renewal of obsolete infrastructure and machinery is a major challenge for many states. Here again, it would be absurd to put the solutions exclusively in the hands of public authorities. The private energy sector, for example, should bear the replacement cost of its current infrastructure.

But the choice of replacement can no longer be made in the same way as it was after World War II. Coal is no longer acceptable, but whatever the environmentalists think, nuclear energy is indispensable in the current state of energy technology.

The sector has traditionally been financed by issuing bonds and shares on the financial markets since the amounts are so large. The energy transition is such an important challenge that it will be necessary to call upon the public sector and companies but also on public savings through the financial markets.

Sustainable Funds Estimated Annual Flows

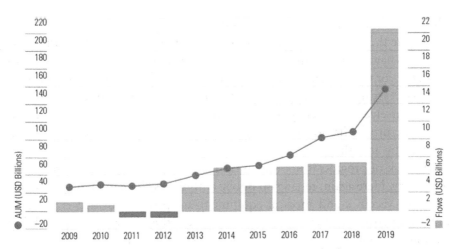

https://www.oecd.org/finance/ESG-investing-and-climate-transition-market-practices-issues-and-policy-considerations.pdf

The combination of European and American programs (under Biden) will reach \$3 trillion. In addition to these interventions, equity and bond financing will have to be provided on the financial markets. In both cases, the United States and the European Union will have to tap the capital markets and increase their debt.

Equity and bond financing will mobilize the financial markets for decades to come, where new "green" instruments are being developed that we must ensure are not just window dressing.

These actions, however, cannot be limited to public sector money. Huge investments will need to be made by companies to reach levels of decarbonization that are acceptable, and they need to be disclosed to ensure that the valuation of those companies integrates the impact of those long-term investments.

The Glasgow Financial Alliance for Net Zero (GFANZ) estimates that corporate spending alone will reach \$150 trillion by 2050. This amount is bearable. "To support the deployment of this capital, the global financial system is being transformed through 24 major initiatives for COP26 that have been delivered for the summit," the group said.[8] "This work has significantly strengthened the information, the tools and the markets needed for the financial system to support the transformation of the global economy for net zero."

Yet the energy crisis following Russia's invasion on Ukraine increases the cost to a point that makes climate plans less urgent.

---

[8] https://www.gfanzero.com/press/amount-of-finance-committed-to-achieving-1-5c-now-at-scale-needed-to-deliver-the-transition/

Healthcare's Thirst for Financing: A Viral Need

The COVID-19 crisis has opened our eyes.

Despite the massive amounts of money invested in health care, most of our countries have found themselves without the minimum resources necessary to avoid the contagion that was sweeping the world. Whether it was the shortage of masks, testing labs, emergency hospital beds, or facilities for the elderly, we found ourselves in a society that had fundamentally disinvested in its health infrastructure. India, for instance, lacked the necessary hydrogen and had to be saved by an airlift.

The lack of progress is not due to insufficient spending. But we are spending poorly. Here again, relying on public authorities alone to manage epidemics while vaccines and medical equipment are privately owned is a deeply unhealthy situation that defies social justice—they bear the responsibility without the means to exercise it. Where would we be today if governments had not massively supported vaccine research?

The table below impressively demonstrates how much the leading countries spend in USD per person in health care.

United States	10,586
Switzerland	7317
Norway	6187
Germany	5986
Sweden	5447
Austria	5395
Denmark	5299
Netherlands	5288
Luxembourg	5070
Australia	5005

Health care is much more important than the pharmaceutical industry, and we have a health policy problem. Nursing homes, hospitals, and maternity clinics are currently accusing our society of decennia of negligence.

The United States has organized a system that puts the population at risk for the benefit of insurers and the pharmaceutical industry. The same drug in the United States costs one-tenth as much in Canada. Health-care expenditures reach 14% of the American GDP, while the Western average is 4%.

Throughout the world, the cohabitation of private and public systems allows for a balance in financing. The debate in the United States on the financing of health care offers a perfect illustration of this attempt by the pharmaceutical sector and private insurance companies to capture the profitable part while leaving the losses to the public sector.

The financial markets are a source of funding for biotech, pharma, hospitals, medical equipment, and many other health-related industries. They are essential to the financing of public health.

The Growing Impact of Financial Markets on Households

One of the most pressing issues is the protection of individual investors.

It is the number one priority of the securities regulators. It should be non-political, but it is fundamentally political. They are government agencies. Yet on a number of occasions, regulators did fail to protect retail investors.

It is important that the assets offered to households do not represent an exaggerated risk for their situation. This may sound paternalistic, but it is a financial regulation known by its acronym KYC (know your customer), which requires financial institutions to take into account the customer's financial situation. Although the influence of the financial markets is far from being limited to investing households as investors, it dominates many debates where the issue is societal. Public opinion must be interested in these financial developments and seek to educate itself. The impact of financial markets on the well-being of our populations is infinitely more insidious or indirect than immediate.

It is in education, communication, and explanation that the long-term solution to the dependence of individuals on financial markets lies. Once again, one of the causes of this evolution is the policy of central banks that have—however unintentionally, but knowingly—deprived individuals of any form of return that they have sought in riskier assets or equities.[1]

---

[1] https://www.sec.gov/rules/final/2020/33-10824.pdf

The proposing release and the amendments we are adopting are part of a broader effort to simplify, harmonize, and improve the exempt offering framework under the Securities Act to promote capital formation and expand investment opportunities while maintaining and enhancing appropriate investor protections.

© The Author(s), under exclusive license to Springer Nature Switzerland AG 2023
G. Ugeux, *Wall Street's Assault on Democracy*, https://doi.org/10.1007/978-3-031-29094-7_16

Sophisticated Investors: The United States vs Europe

The United States has banned access to certain sophisticated or unregulated products for qualified institutional buyers (QIB). This may give an undemocratic impression. The scope of these sophisticated investors was just expanded by the SEC in September 2020. This has not prevented the development of specialized markets: Their products have not been offered to individuals.

Experience shows that this avoids frauds such as the Lehman Brothers bonds or Bernard Madoff's assets—individuals in Europe were able to subscribe to these scams while nonqualified investors in the United States did not have access to these dangerous investments and avoided the worst.

Of course, financial institutions have a limited appetite for regulation that reduces the scope of their distribution, and they are constantly trying to make a dent in it. But that is precisely why Europe should develop legislation that limits access to overly complex or inappropriate financial products. This is an essential reform to avoid frauds by unscrupulous intermediaries.

Europe needs to take steps to differentiate between restricted securities and public securities if it wants to develop a robust Capital Market Union. The 2017 MiFID II recategorization remains ambiguous and has not been effective.[2]

Know Your Customer: The Golden Rule for Brokers and Financial Advisors

Financial intermediaries who offer assets to their clients must conduct a review of their financial situation.

Access to an electronic platform raises the question: What products are on it? By definition, these platforms cannot "know" their clients, and young investors use them more often than they use an advisor.

The term "know your customer" (KYC) first appeared in the United States in the late 1960s to refer to the specific duty of loyalty imposed on the broker, implying that the latter must know his or her client in order to recommend investments adapted to the client's situation and needs. It is only since the beginning of the 1990s that this obligation to know one's client has progressively permeated all banking and financial activities and has been assigned a

---

[2] https://www.fca.org.uk/publication/impact-assessments/mifid-ii-client-categorisation.pdf

new function in the fight against money laundering. Surprisingly enough, this term was mainly used in France from the end of the 1990s to designate the obligations of identification and surveillance of the client in the fight against money laundering.

Investment in Funds: Indirect Influence?

The role of individual investors is most often indirect: They buy funds and the funds, in turn, intervene in the capital markets. In the United States, mutual funds account for more than $20 trillion of the $55 trillion worldwide. Exchange Ttrading Funds (ETFs) add another $4.4 trillion in the United States and $9 trillion worldwide. This indirect force is significant, but it is the fund managers who provide the governance.

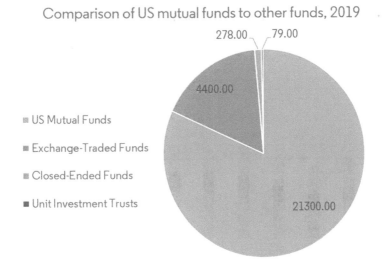

Comparison of US mutual funds to other funds, 2019

278.00   79.00
4400.00
US Mutual Funds
Exchange-Traded Funds
Closed-Ended Funds
Unit Investment Trusts
21300.00

Investor protection exists at several levels in funds:

- Asset diversity: The fund manager invests, depending on the purpose of the fund, in a variety of securities that alone constitute diversification of investor risk.
- Responsibility of the fund issuer: The fund manager is a regulated institution that has a fiduciary duty to put the interests of the fund's investors first.
- Easy entry and exit: Funds can either be sold on the stock market or redeemed at the closing price within three days. This makes it easy for an investor to buy and sell mutual fund units.

For unsophisticated investors, investing in specific stocks can be a tremendous success or loss. What is more, the number of unscrupulous "advisors" that abound on social and other media is distressing. This is the main reason investing in a fund is a protection against sudden losses and a diversification of risks.

Fund managers are subject to changes in public opinion. Thus, societal pressure in favor of the environment is resulting in a proliferation of funds specializing in this type of investment. The most recent figures show that there are $7 trillion in ESG funds.

The meteoric growth of funds that have decided to specialize in "green" investments confirms the influence of individuals on ethical investments.[3]

Barriers to Entry

Assets under management in ESG funds

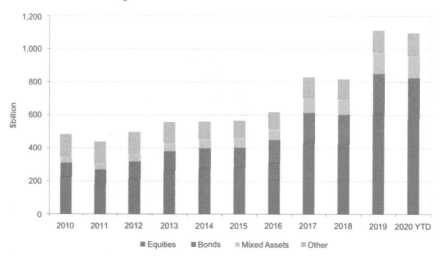

Source: Broadridge as at May 2020 in USD. Includes all domiciles ex North America.
Includes ETFs but excludes fund of funds. Excludes Islamic funds.

If retail investors want direct access to the market, they must understand that only qualified institutions have that privilege. Whether their securities account is with a bank or a broker, it is subject to precautionary rules, and it is therefore through this bank or broker that the order will pass, even if transmitted electronically.

---

[3] https://medium.com/illuminate-financial/2020-will-be-the-decade-esg-climate-and-sustainable-finance-turn-financial-services-on-its-head-a90a88f20a66

On the other hand, through such an intermediary, the investor can choose his investment directly without going through the filter of a fund. He also has access to information available to the intermediary he has chosen.

In the first half of 2020, for reasons ranging from millennials' passion for electronic platforms to simply wanting to pass the time, individual investors have become a growing part of direct stock buyers. These transactions have been done through applications linked to a securities account but without informing the investor.

The barriers to entry are reduced by digital access. For regulators, these e-brokers represent a considerable challenge: how to modify the information and precautions represented by electronic brokers?

After the suicide of one of its clients, who was convinced that he had lost hundreds of thousands of dollars, the online broker Robinhood came under heavy criticism. Popular with millennials, the platform is accused by its critics of trivializing stock trading.

Incomprehensible Language

It has become impossible for an individual faced with an investment decision to have understandable information. Prospectuses are a mishmash of legal terms. Everything is done as if the issuer was protecting itself against lawsuits, without any concern for the understanding of

its client. The financial logomachy is so abstruse that it forces an explanation of the risks and benefits of an asset such as a derivative, a "token," or whatever. But like any language, financial language requires some basic knowledge. The lack of financial education makes it difficult for the individual to understand this language. For example, very few college students (although well educated) understand that when interest rates go up, bond prices go down and vice versa. And of those who do, even fewer know why.

The SEC has issued a rule that requires prospectuses to dispense with legalese and speak plain English. European prospectuses are still quite abstruse for a nonspecialized reader.

Addressing a diverse population of investors is a challenge that technology, without education, cannot meet.

The Onslaught Through Financial Marketing

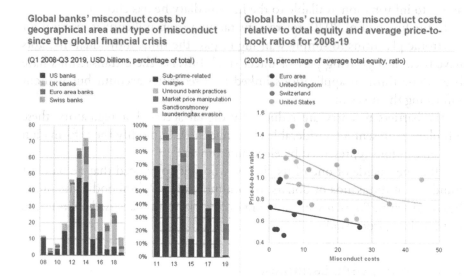

Global banks' misconduct costs by geographical area and type of misconduct since the global financial crisis

(Q1 2008-Q3 2019, USD billions, percentage of total)

Global banks' cumulative misconduct costs relative to total equity and average price-to-book ratios for 2008-19

(2008-19, percentage of average total equity, ratio)

https://www.ecb.europa.eu/pub/financial-stability/fsr/focus/2019/html/ecb.fsrbox201911_03~511ae02cc5.en.html

At the root of the financial crisis of 2008 and its impact on the public were marketing techniques that misled the borrower. Banks had to pay $321 billion in fines for misleading their customers, even though they refuse to be held responsible. This is a small price to pay for the human tragedy that the crisis has caused.

This "regulatory compliant" marketing plays on ambiguity and uses words that the individual cannot understand. This also applies to funds, share issue prospectuses, and annual reports. Lying by omission is a common practice in financial marketing. As for financial advertising, it is most often a red herring.

To do this, we must go beyond appearances, debunking the marketing discourse that seeks to incite the buyer without explaining exactly what he is acquiring.

Addiction to Debt

Debt is like alcohol—abuse can be fatal.

Financial markets are not neutral. They have a direct impact on savings or even on pensions or insurance policies. This is why the 2008 crisis originated among individual borrowers in a sensitive sector: home loans.

Even if households are more cautious than businesses or governments, their indebtedness remains significant.

The interest rates of mortgage loans are intricately linked to the rate of government bonds, to the banks' appetite for risk, and to the duration of these loans. They are therefore subject to the monetary policy of the central banks and the borrowing rate of the banks that grant these loans. They enjoyed the lowest interest rates in recent history.

Europe has seen a flourishing of mortgage lending at excessively low rates thanks to the monetary policy of central banks, which have bought up government bonds and thereby reduced benchmark rates below zero in many countries. Some Swiss mortgages had negative interest rates.

The ratio of household debt to disposable income shows substantial disparities between households around the world. More than half of the countries surveyed have household debt in excess of 100% of income.[4]

The way financial institutions of all stripes have campaigned to convince individuals to take on more debt than is reasonable has destroyed millions of households. Lies about borrowing rates or investment risks are as widespread as they are unacceptable. Only education with common sense will defend you against the sirens that continue to ruin the poorest. The Federal Reserve imposed new regulation for these mortgage originators.[5]

Unequal Access to Financial Markets

The question raised by the evolution of capital markets is, in ultimo, that of the ownership of financial assets. It is difficult to know exactly how much of the population is a shareholder or bondholder, either directly or indirectly. This part of the population, which has been the beneficiary of the quadrupling in10 years of shareholder wealth in the United States, is one of the driving forces behind the inequality that has become indecent. Europe has not experienced a similar growth. At most, the Stoxx 50 index has doubled. But these averages do not tell the whole story. Europe has not been able to generate the spectacular growth of technology company stocks.

---

[4] https://data.oecd.org/hha/household-debt.htm
[5] https://www.federalreserve.gov/supervisionreg/regzcg.htm

An OECD's (Organization for Economic Cooperation and Development) study attempts to approach the distribution of share ownership. It only allows a sketch of the inequality of access to financial markets, but it gives an account of the enormous inequality between the regions of the world[6].

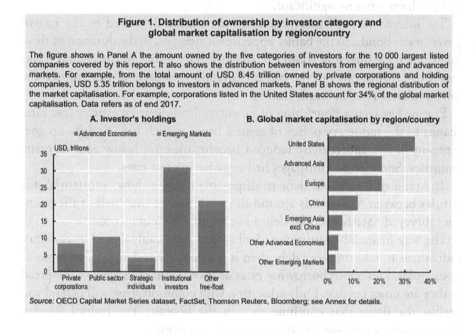

Figure 1. Distribution of ownership by investor category and global market capitalisation by region/country

The figure shows in Panel A the amount owned by the five categories of investors for the 10 000 largest listed companies covered by this report. It also shows the distribution between investors from emerging and advanced markets. For example, from the total amount of USD 8.45 trillion owned by private corporations and holding companies, USD 5.35 trillion belongs to investors in advanced markets. Panel B shows the regional distribution of the market capitalisation. For example, corporations listed in the United States account for 34% of the global market capitalisation. Data refers as of end 2017.

Source: OECD Capital Market Series dataset, FactSet, Thomson Reuters, Bloomberg; see Annex for details.

A Source of Enrichment for the Wealthy?

Many articles are published in the media about the enrichment of billionaires. The existence of mega wealth explains this media attention. Journalists just give figures that are impressive rather than investigate the underlying reasons. What is the role of the financial markets in this enrichment? The role of companies as a benchmark of value is also a measure of shareholder's wealth. Bloomberg has created a billionaire index. One hundred individuals have assets exceeding $20 billion.[7] However, it does not cover their possible indebtedness.

One of the most impressive examples is Bernard Arnault, the chairman and CEO of LVMH, the French luxury company. He is the third largest fortune after Tesla's Elon Musk and Amazon's Jeff Bezos with $200 billion as of 2021.[8]

---

[6] https://data.oecd.org/hha/household-debt.htm

[7] https://www.bloomberg.com/billionaires/

[8] https://www.forbes.com/real-time-billionaires/#218bc7cd3d78

The share price of LVMH has risen from 350 to 650 euros, an increase of over 80% in 18 months. Bernard Arnaud's fortune has therefore increased by $80 billion over this period.

In this function, the financial markets reflect the value attributed by investors to a company. But this does not mean that Bernard Arnaud could, if he wanted to, sell his LVMH shares on the stock market at the market price. Holding almost half of the company's capital, it is impossible for him to dispose of his shares in a significant way through the stock market.[9] Moreover, this shareholding of an exceptional entrepreneur is one of the sources of the company's value. His shareholders trust him. We must therefore be wary of the definition of big fortunes.

To understand this paradox, let us recall that a passive buyer of 1,000 shares of LVMH has earned 300,000 euros in one year. This wealth is not only real but also liquid since the investor can sell shares at any time.

This case is symptomatic of the creation of value by entrepreneurs. It exists all over the world.

We must differentiate between the enrichment of entrepreneurs and passive investors (such as Warren Buffett). Those who follow them and are passive investors have access to purely passive growth of their wealth.

Ninety Percent of the World Population Has No Access to Financial Markets

In a 1964 article, the *New York Times* asked the question: Do the 17 million Americans who own stocks mean that the United States is a people's capitalist? By the end of 2019, that number reached 10 times that of 1964. Is this a sufficient indication? The distribution of this stock ownership is remarkably uneven. Gallup's study released in April 2020 gives the following picture at the end of 2019: Fifty-five percent of the American population is a shareholder. European estimates are close to 25% but also show a huge difference between the north and the south of the continent. Uneven developments deepen inequality.

In a country where the vast majority of people live on weekly payments, it is not surprising that the bottom of the social and economic ladder is not concerned with access to capital markets. Wealth, education, and race continue to influence this distribution. The United States has the largest part of

---

[9] https://www.nytimes.com/1964/02/23/archives/what-17-million-shareholders-share-more-americans-own-stock-in-us.html

its population invested in stocks. Stock holdings among US households increased to 41% of their total funds in 2021.[10]

Stock Ownership Among Major U.S. Subgroups, 2020				
	Yes, own stock	No, do not	No opinion	No. of interviews
	%	%	%	
U.S. adults	55	45	*	2,027
Men	58	42	*	1,052
Women	52	47	1	975
18-29	32	68	*	298
30-49	59	41	*	526
50-64	66	33	*	541
65+	58	41	1	642
Non-Hispanic white	64	36	1	1,458
Non-Hispanic black	42	58	*	200
Hispanic	28	72	*	224
Postgraduate	85	14	*	401
College graduate only	77	23	*	462
Some college	54	45	1	678
No college	33	66	*	459
$100,000+	84	15	*	601
$40,000-$99,999	65	35	*	766
<$40,000	22	77	*	540

https://news.gallup.com/poll/266807/percentage-americans-owns-stock.asp

Driven by debt and zero interest rates, this astronomical growth in the value of stocks and bonds has created a bubble which, in 2020 and 2021, has been fueled by central banks and economic stimulus operations that have found their way into the stock market.

The inequality of the financial markets is therefore increasing indirectly thanks to the state's indebtedness and central banks' money printing. Is it their role to promote this selective enrichment? What will be the impact of a severe equity market correction on households?

---

[10] https://www.conference-board.org/research/economy-strategy-finance-charts/Central-Banks-US-Feb2022

Is Financial Innovation Making Financial?

It is as absurd to be "for" as it is to be "against" technological and financial innovation.

This does not mean that all innovation is neutral. Very often, when I see an innovation coming, I try to understand its purpose and what is "new" about it. This has led me to ask what is the true purpose of certain innovations. Does the innovation add value, or is it simply a way for financial markets to grow beyond any social or economic utility?

Can anyone demonstrate the added value of separating the various elements of a financial product, such as trading the dividend and the non-dividend share? These are false innovations—they are simply splitting casino chips. It is pure speculation that allows traders to get paid twice.

The same is true of cryptos: They do not correspond to any value other than that of a token that is exchanged and to which a genius marketing campaign has falsely tried to give a technological or financial value. But their useless impact represents billions if not trillions of dollars.

To dare to question the usefulness of these innovations and to adopt a simply critical mindset that asks the question of their utility is a crime of lèse-majesté. It is essential, however, to separate the innovations that create value from the others. Innovation is a religion that now has its "evangelists."

The governance of technology companies has regularly been caught in a regulatory or ethical bind. It is only now that some voices are being raised against the "technological terrorism" that dominates the capital markets.

It is the injections of liquidity that have driven up the value of large technology companies, not their often-mediocre performance. Their founders and executives are almost all billionaires. The world's five largest financial

G. Ugeux, *Wall Street's Assault on Democracy*, https://doi.org/10.1007/978-3-031-29094-7_17

capitalizations each exceed $1 trillion. Apple, Microsoft, Amazon, Alphabet (Google), and Tesla are worth a combined $10 trillion, compared to country economies.[1]

The key theoretical finding of a study by Roxana Mihet at New York University published by the European Central Bank (ECB) is that "…even if investors have increased access to the equity premium through cheap funds, improvements in financial technology disproportionately benefit wealthy investors and induce an information-biased technological change that helps the wealthy become wealthier and hurts the poor. Further undirected advances in modern computing, big data, and artificial intelligence, in the absence of any gain's redistribution, could accelerate this process. US macro data from the last 40 years, interpreted through the lens of my theory, suggests that the gains from financial technology stopped accruing to low-wealth investors after the early 2000s, and started to benefit high-wealth investors disproportionately more, amplifying inequality."[2]

This does not disqualify every financial innovation. It calls for an accountability of the promoter's innovation—to justify the purpose of the innovation. However, those who attempt to escape the rule of law (and there are plenty of them) assault democracy.

The Innovative Products

One way capital markets have been innovative is in the creation of new products. They have enriched the asset classes that investors can access, and they have sometimes even developed their own markets and regulations.

They can reach substantial valuations based on a new set of parameters that apply to the specific nature of the asset classes. We will analyze some of them through the lenses of their impact and purposes but also their beneficiaries.

Are they made to make riches richer? Do they create bubbles for their own sake? Are they simply beneficial to the market makers? Could they represent a risk of instability? Those are some of the questions we are asking ourselves. They deserve an answer—innovative products cannot be justified only by themselves.

---

[1] https://www.ey.com/en_ch/news/2022-press-releases/07/the-most-valuable-companies-in-the-world-switzerland-continues-to-be-one-of-they-key-players-while-the-tech-sector-loses-ground
[2] https://www.ecb.europa.eu/pub/conferences/ecbforum/shared/pdf/2020/Mihet_paper.en.pdf

Derivatives: Who Benefits?

So far, we have been content to focus on the 100 trillion or so market capitalizations of stocks listed around the world. One might naively think that this is enough and impressive. But the financial markets did not stop in such good company.

Derivative products, as the word indicates, derive their value for other assets. They make it possible to hedge risks and portfolios, foreign exchange, or interest rate exposures and even default risks. As such, they are important for companies, issuers, asset managers, and investors and provide them a convenient way to manage their financial risks. However, the sheer size of these markets raises a question: Is this asset class entirely used for such purposes, or have derivative markets become a gigantic universe where speculation dominates?

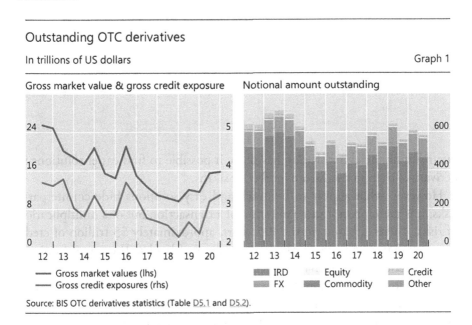

Outstanding OTC derivatives

In trillions of US dollars   Graph 1

Gross market value & gross credit exposure   Notional amount outstanding

— Gross market values (lhs)   ▮ IRD   Equity   Credit
— Gross credit exposures (rhs)   ▮ FX   ▮ Commodity Other

Source: BIS OTC derivatives statistics (Table D5.1 and D5.2).

https://www.bis.org/publ/otc_hy2105.htm

The above Bank of International Settlements (BIS) chart rightly distinguishes between the notional amount, the gross market value, and the gross credit exposure.

When J.P. Morgan announced that, in the midst of the coronavirus crisis, it had made a profit of $2 billion in equity derivatives trading alone, do we not have the right to ask ourselves who benefits from this market and what risks are attached to it?[3] When BNP Paribas recognizes in its balance sheet $247 billion in derivatives (i.e., 12% of its assets) as financial instruments and only $12.5 billion for hedging purposes, one can imagine what proportion of the derivatives market supports risk hedging and the speculative asset class.

From time immemorial, companies and investors have wanted to "hedge" against certain market fluctuations. Whether it be currency, credit, or interest

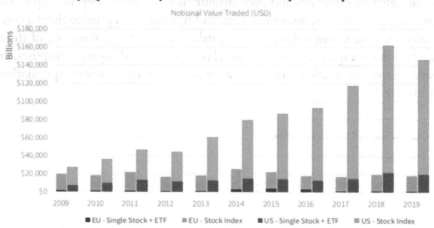

Equity + Index Options Market Landscape – Europe vs U.S.

Notional Value Traded (USD)

rate risks, financial innovation has made it possible to find easier solutions in derivatives than in the future market or swaps.

However, what appear to be quick and easy solutions hide counterparty risks. It is therefore not just a question of a transaction but of a multiplication of risks. There is, based on the BIS chart, approximately $3 trillion of credit exposure. Most of it lies in the balance sheet of banks. The question of the capital needed to cover that risk is unclear.

The following is a simplified example: In the case of a borrower in Swiss francs with a floating interest rate, even if they can obtain a loan or issue bonds at negative rates, there are few companies worldwide that need Swiss francs. But if it is a US company looking to borrow dollars at a fixed rate, derivatives will allow it to "swap" its dollar loan with a Swiss bank, swap its floating-rate interest to a fixed rate with a Japanese company, and swap its Swiss franc fixed interest to dollars with a US bank. In this example, there are three counterparties involved to achieve fixed-rate dollar borrowing. It is

---

[3] https://www.ifre.com/story/2436650/jp-morgan-set-for-equity-derivatives-gains-l8n2e92p6

therefore assumed that this mechanism reduces the cost compared to a bond issue. But in the event of a crisis, the risk of counterparties can be multiplied. These products are cheaper precisely because they do not take credit risk into consideration.

The explosion of the derivatives market into an asset class has been facilitated by complacent regulation that, instead of considering the risks associated with the transactions, weighs only the net amount of risk. Reforms have been put in place to ensure greater transparency of these risks. The European market infrastructure regulation (EMIR) has introduced new obligations for the actors intervening in the derivative markets—financial or nonfinancial counterparties conducting a transaction on these markets, clearing houses, or trade repositories.

A paper by the International Monetary Fund (IMF) summarizes the potentially systemic risk associated with the derivatives market:

> The central counterparties dominating the market for the clearing of over-the-counter interest rate and credit derivatives are globally systemic. Employing methodologies similar to the calculation of banks' capital requirements against trading book exposures, this paper assesses the sensitivity of central counterparties' required risk buffers, or *capital requirements*, to a range of model inputs. We find them to be highly sensitive to whether key model parameters are calibrated on a point-in-time versus stress-period basis, whether the risk tolerance metric adequately captures tail events, and the ability—or lack thereof—to define exposures on the basis of netting sets spanning multiple risk factors. Our results suggest that there are considerable benefits from having prudential authorities adopt a more prescriptive approach to for central counterparties' risk buffers, in line with recent enhancements to the capital regime for banks.[4]

Short Selling: What Is the Credit Risk of Securities Lenders?

Short selling is another mechanism that tends to help hedge the risks associated with a particular type of asset. However, it also increases the size and the liquidity of financial markets for the benefit of financial institutions. We will come back to the role that this technique plays in activism. The purpose here is to account for the lack of consideration of the risks associated with this type of operation.

---

[4] https://www.imf.org/external/pubs/ft/wp/2013/wp1303.pdf

Selling financial assets, one does not own (naked shorting), is done through a parallel operation that consists of borrowing the assets from other owners of the securities concerned. Without them, this market could not exist. In the United States alone, naked shorting represents an additional very short-term liquidity of about 3% of the capitalization of the Standard and Poor (S&P) 500 index, approaching $2 trillion. The securities lender is incurring a credit risk that is not reflected in any financial regulation.[5]

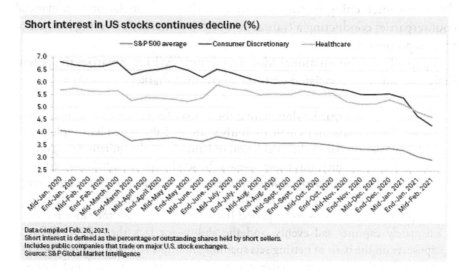

Short interest in US stocks continues decline (%)

Data compiled Feb. 26, 2021.
Short interest is defined as the percentage of outstanding shares held by short sellers.
Includes public companies that trade on major U.S. stock exchanges.
Source: S&P Global Market Intelligence

Is That All?

That narrative is what the securities lenders and short traders would have us believe by touting the benefits of uncovered sales for the liquidity of the financial markets. The reality that puzzles me is the motivation of the securities lenders. By definition, they will receive the securities in return. Why lend to a counterparty (and thus take a credit risk) in a transaction that will aim to lower the price of the security, to their disadvantage as an investor?

Investors are generally unaware that securities they hold with a financial institution might be used to lower the value of their investment in the name of market liquidity. They have in fact given this permission to their custodian in a 200-page document in small print.

---

[5] https://www.spglobal.com/marketintelligence/en/news-insights/latest-news-headlines/s-p-500-short-interest -retreats-further-as-hedge-funds-remain-wary-62934129

Should not regulators prohibit such manipulations with securities held by individuals? Should not the same question apply to pension funds and insurance companies? Should not lenders be required to have a capital ratio to cover borrower risk?

On December 3, 2019, the $1.5 trillion Government Pension Investment Fund of Japan sent shockwaves through the stock lending market by announcing it would no longer lend securities. As described in BNY Mellon's *Aerial View* magazine, "GPIF explained its decision on two grounds. The first was that the transfer of stock ownership rights during the course of a securities loan is 'inconsistent with the fulfillment of the stewardship responsibilities of a long-term investor.' The second reason was just as succinct: 'the current stock lending scheme lacks transparency in terms of who is the ultimate borrower and for what purpose they are borrowing the stock.'"[6]

The question is rarely addressed, and this decision by one of the largest pension funds in the world means that it is aware of the risks associated with short selling. As we will see later, the use of the short selling technique to manipulate the markets or put pressure on companies could profoundly disrupt the orderly functioning of capital markets, to the detriment of both companies and investors.

Increasing the Size of Financial Markets for Liquidity Reasons?

The crisis of 2008 saw short selling flourish, which precipitated declines in value. Sometimes they even had to be banned. From March 18 to May 18, 2020, in the midst of the stock market crisis, the French regulator Autorité des Marchés Financiers (AMF) banned short sales and all other transactions that create or increase a net short position. This prohibition was applicable to any person established or residing in France or abroad investing in shares traded on French markets under the authority of the AMF.

Europe has been at the forefront of regulatory restrictions on short selling. The EU Short Selling Regulation (SSR) and certain aspects of credit default swaps aim to increase the transparency of short positions held by investors in certain EU securities, to reduce settlement risks and other risks linked with naked short selling, and to ensure that member states have clear powers to

---

[6] https://www.bnymellon.com/us/en/insights/aerial-view-magazine/stock-lending-dispelling-the-myths.html

intervene in exceptional situations to reduce systemic risks and risks to financial stability and market confidence.[7]

Short selling impacts the company that is targeted. During the financial crisis, several financial institutions desperately sought Securities and Exchange Commission (SEC) support to ban short selling. At a time when a crisis is causing profound distress, is it ethical and justifiable to allow speculative operations that increase this level of distress? Where is the equity? Is not it fundamentally antisocial? Should not those operators be made accountable for the impact of their actions? In September 2008, the US Securities and Exchange Commission temporarily banned most short sales in nearly 1,000 financial stocks.[8]

Companies whose shares are subject to significant short positions must effectively manage not only their market capitalization but the value of these "short" positions.

Does the increase of the size of the equity markets have a beneficial effect on the economy? Absolutely not. Effect for the market size? Maximum. We will not be able to reduce the pressure of the markets without imposing an assumption of the credit risk associated with these operations.

This does not condemn short positions: It all depends on the motivation of the players, the risks they take, and the purpose of those operations.

The GameStop affair was a real-life example of this type of risk. The hedge fund Melvin Capital started the year 2021 with $12.5 billion in assets, which fell to $8 billion at the end of January due to the rise of the stock market. It had taken a bet that GameStop, a video game distribution company whose stock had just risen, would fall back. When the attack on this position was launched by activists opposed to this type of operation, this fund lost 53% of its value in a few days in February against a rise of 1.625% in the company's stock price. How did they manage to borrow these shares? Who took the credit risk on Melvin Capital?[9]

---

[7] https://www.esma.europa.eu/regulation/trading/short-selling
[8] https://corpgov.law.harvard.edu/2013/05/23/shackling-short-sellers-the-2008-shorting-ban/
[9] https://www.thestreet.com/memestocks/gme/gamestop-stock-short-sellers-under-scrutiny

The Crypto (In)experiment or the Creation of Assets Without Substance

The creation of new financial products is often born from the meeting in the capital markets of the desires of borrowers and lenders. Others, more artificial, have found an environment in the markets that allows them to flourish without responding to an economic or financial need.

Among them, Bitcoin remains the most important attempt at a new type of asset that was called—wrongly—an alternative currency by the Federal Reserve. It is also the most controversial. An ecosystem has been created around Bitcoin using known terms but still causing confusion: currency, stock market, and casino chip?

Even today, the main difficulty to regulate what once was a $2 trillion market remains the identity of digital assets. Contortions have been made to find the basis of regulation. However, there is still no consensus that exists on what "it" is.

Cryptos Are a Gigantic Ponzi Scheme

Do cryptos have a social purpose or are they a manifestation of investor distrust? Have they been the source of gigantic criminal money laundering frauds? Was it a gigantic fraud to avoid regulation?

I remain convinced, as I wrote in 2014, that this is a Ponzi scheme built on sand.

> Since November 2013, Bitcoin has been the victim of a manipulation that is similar to a Ponzi scheme. Let us remember that Bernard Madoff had set up a business from scratch that allowed him to collect $50 billion that collapsed like a house of cards. There were no assets behind these funds. The mechanism is simple: exceptional performance based on nothing. Investors have to keep filling the abyss, until the music stops. But in this case, there is no chair missing, they all fall together. There is no economic or financial reality behind Bitcoin, only a value of convenience between parties.[10]

It took eight years and the collapse of the value of cryptos for pundits to recognize the reality. These eight years of irrational valuation were mostly attempts to avoid any form of accountability to regulators or investors. [11]

---

[10] https://www.lemonde.fr/blog/finance/2014/02/09/le-bitcoin-est-devenu-un-ponzi-scheme/
[11] https://markets.businessinsider.com/currencies/btc-usd

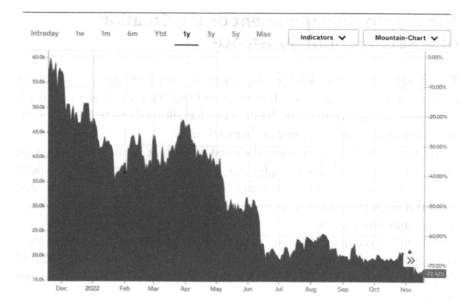

With a $1.5 trillion value and a vibrant ecosystem, it is possible that Bitcoin is here to stay. It is defined by supply and demand, with an opaque investor base and no transparency on manipulation or possible fraudulent participants.

That is what makes cryptos suspect.

A Net Loss to the Economy

Unlike a stock or a bond, cryptos have a negative impact on the economy. They are a flight away from money, and the savings that flow into these instruments go to sellers and out of the economy. They have no inherent social value. It is a huge game between rich people who have invited the less rich to speculate on an asset of an indefinite nature, traded on exchanges that are not, and are unfit to be, a means of payment or a unit of account. It must be recognized, however, that the problem lies elsewhere: a more or less educated fringe of the population has acquired such a distrust of banks or monetary authorities that they are ready to invest in anything as long as the traditional authorities and institutions reject them.

This problem is a question of democracy: if we do not recognize the added value of a currency or a central bank, then the system has lost some of its credibility. This is the challenge facing governments and central banks: the mistrust of money.

Facebook and Its Libra, or an Arrogant Company's Dreams of Grandeur

It is not because Facebook was innovative that it was right.

In 2019, Facebook embarked on a venture whose ambition alone should have provoked suspicion: a universal digital currency, the Libra. For any number of reasons, it crashed. Taking the sovereign privilege of "minting money" by storm with its arrogance, and deaf to the regalian questions that this attempt raised, Facebook had to retreat and abandon Libra.[12]

When Facebook decided to launch its own version of a "universal digital currency," I wondered for a moment if Mark Zuckerberg and his French deputy, David Marcus, former French CEO of the PayPal payment system, were utopians or mystifications or maybe simply ignorant.

What shocked me the most was Facebook's exorbitant claim that Libra would solve the problem of those who do not have access to a bank account and therefore to money other than in paper form. Presenting itself as the savior of these populations, it sounded paternalistic and false. Even the United Nations fell under the spell of Libra's sirens.

After months of suspicion about how the company was "monetizing" the data of its monopoly, harvesting it by selling it, sometimes to lackluster governments, Mark Zuckerberg had to face the US Congress and the European Parliament in May 2018.[13] Guy Verhofstadt asked him if he wanted to be a monster who built a machine to destroy democracy. The debate in the French newspaper *Le Figaro* was entitled: Is Facebook laughing at us?

Ignoring the political dimension of the problem, Facebook announced the Libra in competition with fiat currencies and took the full force of the opposition by governments and central banks. The project was blissfully received by the worshippers of technological innovation, as it was an amazing engineering concept, but it completely ignored that money is a core sovereign privilege and that their hubris would not pass the minimum test of legitimacy. In short, they played with fire and failed.

Libra, as predicted, was immediately under attack from all sides by central banks and world political leaders, who cited the many risks: the development of money laundering, the increase in economic instability, and new possibilities of abusing user data. However, the major risk political leaders wish to avoid is the privatization of their monetary supply by a consortium of private companies, which would imply that states would be dispossessed of their economic and monetary sovereignty.[14]

---

[12] https://techcrunch.com/2022/07/04/meta-novi-pilot-ends/
[13] https://www.youtube.com/watch?v=7uRFY1AtocE
[14] https://clsbluesky.law.columbia.edu/2019/07/11/libra-the-regulatory-challenges-facebook-ignored/

Libra has brought to light one of the great challenges of financial innovation, which seeks to substitute itself for the authorities of various countries. In a Columbia Law School blog, I analyzed the dimensions that Facebook had chosen to ignore. It is in the arrogance that characterizes this company, whose governance is increasingly imperialist, that we find the answer to this remarkable failure of Facebook "who can do no wrong."

This is the most obvious case of a challenge to democracy from the digital universe. Do I need to add to this Mark Zuckerberg's support for Donald Trump, which led to a Facebook staff strike, and his refusal to block foreign sites attempting to influence the 2020 US presidential election?

For another example, look no further than the latest adventures of Elon Musk, a great influencer, announcing the payment of Tesla cars in Bitcoin, swallowed in a week. He accompanied his statement by purchases of Bitcoin and other contradictory statements, earned him a remission of order from the SEC.

Central Bank Digital Currencies, or the Defensiveness of Currency Issuers

The end does not justify the means, even in technology.

Democratic rules apply to social media, whatever country they come from. But the challenge for central banks has only just begun: how to digitalize traditional currencies? The launch of digital currencies operated by central banks raises issues that go beyond technology.[15]

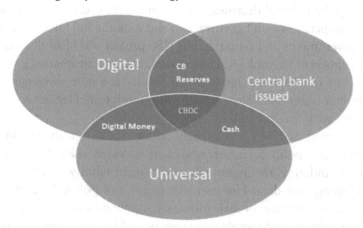

A more interesting question is what will happen when governments finally get serious about regulating Bitcoin and its brethren. Most policymakers have

---

[15] https://www.mdpi.com/2199-8531/7/1/72

instead tried to change the topic by talking about central bank-issued digital currencies (CBDCs).[16]

At a recent forum on financial regulation organized by the Journal of Financial Regulation of Oxford University, Columbia Law School, and Cornell Law School, a senior Federal Reserve participant confirmed my worst apprehensions: "Nobody has been able to explain to me what kind of problem CBDC is aiming to resolve."

The *Economist* was even more direct: "What is the fuss over central bank digital currencies?"[17] It is not obvious what the point is. Many people already use digital currency, whether in mobile apps for payments or on bank websites for transfers. What are these new digital currencies and why are central banks creating them?

The defensiveness of governments, central banks, and regulators toward financial innovation is alarming. It is not a coincidence that the push for CBDC coincided exactly with Facebook's announcement of Libra. Was it a proactive push or a reactive one? Was it a distraction from their core responsibility to control inflation?

Exchange Traded Funds (ETFs): A Useful Innovation[18]

ETF Ecosystem

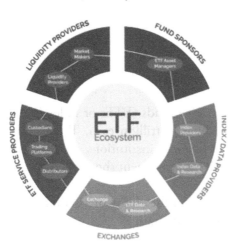

---

[16] https://www.project-syndicate.org/commentary/will-advanced-economies-ban-cryptocurrencies-by-kenneth-rogoff-2022-06?utm_source=project-syndicate.org&utm_medium=email&utm_campaign=authnote&barrier=accesspaylog

[17] https://www.economist.com/the-economist-explains/2021/02/16/what-is-the-fuss-over-central-bank-digital-currencies?utm_medium=cpc.adword.pd&utm_source=google&utm_campaign=a.22brand_pmax&utm_content=conversion.direct-response.anonymous&gclid=Cj0KCQjw_7KXBhCoARIsAPdPTfi2WdpIMAKtH_wyrCESfYfh5g5flIjYAuJF9BDkangxW9m3AXXeGnYaAkVrEALw_wcB&gclsrc=aw.ds

[18] https://www.etftrends.com/etf-strategist-channel/celebrating-14-years-of-etf-growth/

Born out of an opportunity to avoid capital gains tax in the United States, ETFs have become an essential component of the financial markets. They met a need that explains their success: they provided a listed instrument whose value reflected stock market indices. This is a challenge to the active management model. Their great advantage? They trade like a stock and can be bought and sold at any time, which is not the case with mutual funds.

They now reach $15 trillion worldwide, nearly half of which are in the United States. Recently, ETFs have moved into variations that do not provide this transparency or liquidity, to the point that the SEC in the United States has regulated these instruments, excluding dozens that were using the name for illiquid assets. The growth was impressive as it does have a purpose: to allow investors to acquire an asset that is backed by underlying securities that replicate a country or a sector's index.

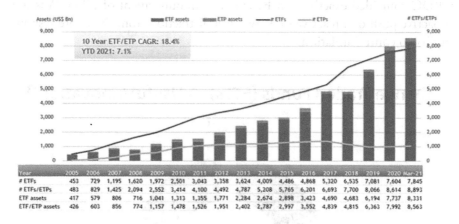

Year	2005	2006	2007	2008	2009	2010	2011	2012	2013	2014	2015	2016	2017	2018	2019	2020	Mar-21
# ETFs	453	729	1,195	1,620	1,972	2,501	3,043	3,358	3,624	4,009	4,486	4,868	5,320	6,535	7,081	7,604	7,845
# ETFs/ETPs	483	829	1,425	2,094	2,552	3,414	4,100	4,492	4,787	5,208	5,765	6,201	6,693	7,700	8,066	8,614	8,893
ETF assets	417	579	806	716	1,041	1,313	1,355	1,771	2,284	2,674	2,898	3,423	4,690	4,683	6,194	7,737	8,331
ETF/ETP assets	426	603	856	774	1,157	1,478	1,526	1,951	2,402	2,787	2,997	3,552	4,839	4,815	6,363	7,992	8,563

Active funds and passive funds (ETFs or index funds) have grown to the same size, now exceeding $4 trillion each. This threatens one of the most lucrative businesses of financial institutions: wealth management and private banking. And yet, active management should be able to dissociate itself from stock market indices.

This raises the question of the ability of asset managers to produce returns that exceed indices and benchmarks.[19]

---

[19] https://www.gam.com/en/our-thinking/investment-opinions/beyond-peak-passive

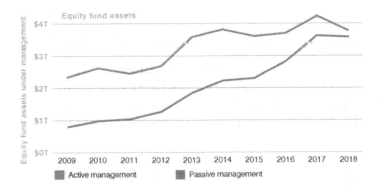

High-Frequency Trading, or the Race to the Nanosecond for the Strongest

In his book *Flash Boys*, the most outstanding author and commentator on American finance, Michael Lewis, tells the story of how a 1,331-kilometer high-frequency cable was built to reduce trading times between Chicago and New Jersey for the modest sum of $300 million. The goal, to create a competitive advantage in speed of execution and especially in capturing orders before others, could even identify them.

The cable was to connect the Chicago Mercantile Exchange to the operations of the Nasdaq Stock Market in Carteret, and the goal was to reduce as many milliseconds as possible for the orders that traders send between the two markets. This is how the role of the Garden State in the new Wall Street is formed—where, inside the anonymous warehouses of Secaucus, Weehawken, and Mahwah, swirl the computerized backbones of the major exchanges.[20]

Technology has allowed a frantic race to reduce the speed of transactions—this has been the case for stock market transactions, where trading platforms have been equipped with microsecond capabilities.

This costly technology has created a form of inequality among operators, defeating the need for regulation in terms of access to the market itself. Those who have access to these extraordinarily expensive technologies can beat those who cannot afford them.

In June 2020, the US futures regulator, the Commodity Futures Trading Commission (CFTC), buried "Reg Automatic Trading (AT)." It dropped the requirement that automated trading firms register with it and reveal their code—the algorithm that underlies their strategy. This last proposal "was probably unconstitutional," acknowledges Brian Quintenz, one of the four

---

[20] https://www.amazon.com/Flash-Boys-Wall-Street-Revolt/dp/0393351599

CFTC commissioners. Where is the added value of speed of execution if not the power to go faster than a competitor? In any case, once again, there is no societal added value to this race.

The root of the problem is the unequal nature of this access to markets: Only the most powerful computer systems have the means to capture the flow of orders before the others. And only traders benefit from this innovation. Once again, this is where the question of democracy and inequality arises.

The Regulation of Innovation Is Essential

The Problem of Regulators

These innovations pose a singular problem for regulators.

What they have in common is that they substantially increase the size of financial assets that will be traded on financial markets, whether regulated or not. They represent a race for size and speed, the social utility of which is uncertain, but this type of question is not part of their mandate.

While it is not their role to intervene at the level of innovation laboratories, it was not until Bitcoin reached $500 billion that the Federal Reserve became concerned. It has tripled since then. Even today, the legal debate on the nature of these innovations is not over. In such a context, the lack of limitation on public access to these innovations has been the source of large-scale extortion.

I did co-author a paper with Takeshi Nagai on the regulation of digital assets. The conclusion was as follows:

> The current regulation of digital assets in the US and in other countries has been a brave attempt to put new assets in old structures. They are unsatisfactory, even though they are understandable. It covers different regulators and regulations. It has not been seriously tested in court. The urgency of a legal framework to cover those assets is obvious from our review. Are relevant agencies willing to get together to do so?[21]

The innovation of financial markets cannot develop to the detriment of democracy and transparency rules, let alone serve to organize fraud or tax evasion. How can this be done without having a dissuasive effect on innovation?

The Fintech sector, which targets financial services technology and its various components, cannot be a means of unfair competition with banks or

---

[21] https://georgesugeux.com/wp-content/uploads/2021/06/Nagai_Ugeux_2021_JIBLR_Issue_5_Press_Proof.pdf

insurance companies, which, unlike the Fintech sector, are regulated. It is up to the Fintech sector to demonstrate that it does not fall into abuse, and it is up to the supervisory authorities to verify the veracity of this information.

Before the rise of this innovation, the concept of the "sandbox" had been developed to allow for experimentation between innovators and regulators. This kind of mentality would allow for a more harmonious evolution.

A Culture Above the Law?

As we have seen, the proliferation of innovations creates an ecosystem that is difficult to regulate.

The root of the problem, however, is the culture of the technology world, which considers any form of limitation on its development as an aggression of the "old economy." Turning this into a generational conflict makes the discussion difficult.

Navigating between the interests of markets and investors will only be possible if regulation itself evolves. The large technology players are increasingly acting as if they are above the law. This is antidemocratic.

The guiding principle for this evolution has to be accountability. This must be exhibited not by the regulators but by those who promote such innovations—when they submit their project, demonstrate its usefulness, and identify the risks of their initiatives.

A recent paper of the OECD published by Stephen Lumpkin frames the debate, exploring "various regulatory issues related to financial innovation. It starts from a premise that financial innovations are neither always helpful (or benign) nor always threatening. Innovations have the potential to provide for a more efficient allocation of resources and thereby a higher level of capital productivity and economic growth. Many financial innovations have had this effect. But others have not. Examples of the latter include products that may have been misrepresented to end-users and resulted in delinquencies, bankruptcies or other problems among them, or products that have been inadequately managed with respect to the various credit or market risks they entail."[22]

---

[22] https://www.oecd.org/finance/financial-markets/44362117.pdf

When the Ideology of the Markets Defies Democracy

Do Financial Markets Have an Ideology?

The road we have travelled comes from an observation of unbearable inequality. In order to dismantle its source, we must focus our attention on both the behavior of the actors and the detour of the capital markets from their primary mission toward the interests of the markets and their actors, becoming an end in itself.

We cannot leave it at that: The exacerbation of inequalities in this last decade forces us to question the ideology that underlies this evolution, which increasingly enriches the holders of securities and leaves the largest part of our populations on the pavement. To do this, we are going to try to flush out this ideology.

As Engels puts it in his letter to F. Mehring from July 14, 1893: "Ideology is a process accomplished by the so-called thinker consciously, indeed, but with a false consciousness. The real motives impelling him remain unknown to him, otherwise it would not be an ideological process at all. Hence, he imagines false or apparent motives. Because it is a process of thought he derives both its form and its content from pure thought, either his own or that of his predecessors. He works with mere thought material which he accepts without examination as the product of thought, he does not investigate further for a more remote process independent of thought; indeed, its origin seems obvious to him, because as all action is produced through the medium of thought it also appears to him to be ultimately based upon thought.... True, external facts belonging to its own or other spheres may have exercised a co-determining influence on this development, but the tacit pre-supposition

G. Ugeux, *Wall Street's Assault on Democracy*, https://doi.org/10.1007/978-3-031-29094-7_18

is that these facts themselves are also only the fruits of a process of thought, and so we still remain within that realm of pure thought which has successfully digested the hardest facts."[1]

The first paragraph of Thomas Piketty's latest book *Capital and Ideology* offers us one of the fundamental answers to the question of whether financial markets have an ideology. "Inequality is neither economic nor technological; it is ideological and political. This is no doubt the most striking conclusion to emerge from the historical approach I take. In other words, the market and competition, profits and wages, capital and debt, skilled and unskilled workers, natives and aliens, tax havens and competitiveness—none of these things exist as such. All are social and historical constructs, which depend entirely on the legal, fiscal, educational, and political systems that people choose to adopt and the conceptual definitions they choose to work with."[2] After those quotes, I could be taken for a Marxist or a socialist, which I am not. But a philosophical and humanist angle to inequality is necessary if we want to go beyond the core of the beliefs of those who are implementing this ideology.

It is the acceptance of the inequality of the allocation of resources that lies at the heart of this ideology. At the core of this inequality, the structure of the financial markets favors the rich minority and disadvantages the poor majority. This raises the very question of democracy. How, in societies where the majority of the population suffers from inequality, do these inequalities not only fail to diminish but have further increased during the pandemic crisis?

A democracy where the majority of voters suffers from inequality is a failure. Even the principle of "one share, one vote" is flouted by multiple voting shares, from Facebook in the United States to Alibaba in China to the Florange Law in France.

Still today, American capitalism dominates the financial markets throughout the world, particularly in Europe. Unlike European values, American capitalism is fundamentally a "financial" capitalism and is measured by wealth, ignoring the social dimension. This explains the exorbitant presence of financial markets in American political discourse.

---

[1] https://www.marxists.org/archive/marx/works/1893/letters/93_07_14.htm

[2] Thomas Piketty, Capital, and Ideology. The Belknap Press of Harvard University Press. 2020 https://www.hup.harvard.edu/catalog.php?isbn=9780674980822

The Invasion of American Financial Capitalism

I will be laser-focused on working families, the middle-class families I came from here in Scranton. Not the wealthy investor class. They do not need me.
  Joe Biden[3]

The Marshall Plan

At the end of the war, Europe was financially drained. Its dependence on the United States, which had just liberated Western Europe, was total. My generation continues to feel immense gratitude, not only for our liberation but also for the help the United States provided in the form of the Marshall Plan.

Contrary to a widespread perception in Europe, General Marshall, Secretary of State of the United States, did not intend to impose American solutions on Europe, as his Harvard speech of June 1947 shows:

"It is already evident that, before the United States Government can proceed much further in its efforts to alleviate the situation and help start the European world on its way to recovery, there must be some agreement among the countries of Europe as to the requirements of the situation and the part those countries themselves will take in order to give proper effect to whatever action might be undertaken by this Government. It would be neither fitting nor efficacious for this Government to undertake to draw up unilaterally a program designed to place Europe on its feet economically. This is the business of the Europeans. The initiative, I think, must come from Europe. The role of this country should consist of friendly aid in the drafting of a European program and of later support of such a program so far as it may be practical for us to do so. The program should be a joint one, agreed to by a number, if not all European nations."[4]

A Series of Big Bangs

The fundamental ideology of American capitalism is incompatible with the social democratic principles of the European continent. Financial capitalism is one of its most extreme deviations.

In the prevailing Cold War climate, Russian banks, and especially the Moscow Handlowy Bank, the only one authorized to conduct international

---

[3] https://www.cnbc.com/2020/07/09/biden-says-investors-dont-need-me-calls-for-end-of-era-of-shareholder-capitalism.html
[4] https://www.marshallfoundation.org/marshall/the-marshall-plan/marshall-plan-speech/

operations, sought ways to deposit dollars outside the United States. On February 28, 1957, a transfer of $800,000 made by this bank in London, without the intervention of the United States, set in motion a market that today dominates the world: the Eurodollar market, which became the Eurocurrency market.[5]

As far as bonds were concerned, there was a market in dollars in New York commonly called "Yankee Bonds," issued on the American market by foreign issuers in dollars. The Interest Equalization Tax that taxed these bonds was established in July 1963. While dollar bonds outside the United States were executed in New York, this tax made these transactions too expensive for non-American issuers through a withholding tax that had just been created.[6]

A Eurobond market quickly developed outside the United States, and the major American players, either directly or through acquisitions, quickly came to dominate the City of London. It was the place where, at 11 a.m., the London Interbank Offered Rate (Libor) was setting the daily interest rate between banks.

At the same time, for political and sometimes financial reasons, several countries "opened up" their capital markets through reforms known as "big bangs." This is how London saw, one after the other, its merchant banks being bought out, absorbed, and transformed into large institutions, mainly American. Margaret Thatcher's 1986 reform put an end to the uniquely British character of the London Stock Exchange. Now, Wall Street dominates the City.

What will happen after Brexit? The City would like to be able to propose regulatory arbitrage, but it cannot do so by defying the regulations of the European Union unless it loses the privilege of equivalence with the European Union.

This transformation of the structure of international equity markets has put their control in the hands of large American companies, which have imported the cult of the shareholder and the "stock market" remuneration of managers.

---

[5] https://www.sfu.ca/~poitras/EEH_Eurodollar_98.pdf
[6] https://www.jstor.org/stable/40909967

The Arrival En Masse of American Players on the London Market

When the US market ceased to be internationally competitive, the large American banks developed their capital markets activities around the world. They began by exporting to London but are now omnipresent:

> During a six-month internship at Midland Bank in 1972, I discovered the city of London in all its uniqueness. Merchant banks were everywhere, and one sign was more artistic than the next. Ten years later, we moved to London for Morgan Stanley. We were pioneers, but the professionalism and power of the American firms would soon transform the City into an international marketplace. The methods of issuing bonds were soon to be modelled on those of the U.S. market. It was an irresistible takeover that only the exceptionally large European banks such as Deutsche Bank, BNP, or UBS could compete with.

It is difficult to imagine a "natural" evolution of market ideology without understanding the extent to which the Anglo-Saxon world dominates international finance. The market capitalization of companies listed in the United States (adding NYSE and NASDAQ) reaches $36.76 trillion. Japan comes next with $5.1 trillion. And the European stock exchanges together reach almost $15 trillion.

The Cult of Shareholder Value

> Corporate managers must conduct the business in accordance with [shareholders'] desires, which generally will be to make as much money as possible while conforming to the basic rules of the society, both those embodied in law and those embodied in ethical custom.[7] *(Milton Friedman, 1970)*

This was the quote that launched what is called the financial or Anglo-Saxon capitalism. Interestingly, the "ethical custom" that he refers to was never taken into consideration, and only the "law" was applied.

There is another version of capitalism: Rhine capitalism and social capitalism are a socioeconomic model combining a regulated free market capitalist economic system alongside social policies that establish both fair competition

---

[7] https://www.chicagobooth.edu/review/its-time-rethink-milton-friedmans-shareholder-value-argument#:~:text=In%201970%2C%20the%20late%20Milton,those%20embodied%20in%20law%20and

within the market and generally a welfare state. It emerged in Germany and was promoted by German Chancellor Konrad Adenauer. It remains the conceptual gap between Europe and the United States. Yet in an article in the *New York Times* in 1970, Milton Friedman explained that the doctrine of "social responsibility" involves the acceptance of the socialist view that political mechanisms, not market mechanisms, are the appropriate way to determine the allocation of scarce resources for alternative uses.[8]

Without Shareholders, There Would Be No Companies

At one stage or another of a company's development, its shareholders have enabled it to develop and grow. They are entitled to their share of the company's assets, with dividends distributed if the company is profitable, and one vote per share at the general meetings. This is a basic principle of property rights.

But while they do get a share, a company's performance is not the result of their capital contribution alone. In order to succeed in growing and beautifying, it must benefit from the work of the managers, employees, and workers who work there, from the environment in which the company operates, from the community in which it develops, and from a whole range of goods and services made available to it.

In one word, if the company exists only for the exclusive good of its shareholders, as Milton Friedman said, and not for the good of a larger whole, it betrays its citizenship. There are other dimensions to its success besides capital. Corporate executives are more than "servants" of the owners, as Friedman described them.

The Dogma of the Primacy of Shareholder Value Conflicts with Social Purpose

Stakeholders are not limited to shareholders alone, and while the latter deserve their share of the results, the dogma of "shareholder value" has invaded the financial markets, even though it does not correspond to their societal project or their values.

The company "belongs" to its shareholders in the sense of civil property law and commercial law. But the right of ownership is not absolute. Beyond this,

---

[8] https://www.nytimes.com/1970/09/13/archives/a-friedman-doctrine-the-social-responsibility-of-business-is-to.html

the company is a social body that can only function if the different elements that comprise it and that it influences live in harmony. Without the contribution and motivation of its workers, its subcontractors, and the society in which it operates, in a business that itself has its own regulations and ethics, the company cannot limit its raison d'être to creating value for shareholders.

In August 2019, for the first time, the Business Roundtable, which brings together business leaders, opened the door with a statement that caused a stir. It redefined the purpose of business and expanded it:

> The Business Roundtable announced the release of a new Statement on the Purpose of a Corporation signed by 181 CEOs who commit to lead their companies for the benefit of all stakeholders – customers, employees, suppliers, communities, and shareholders...It affirms the essential role corporations can play in improving our society when CEOs are deeply committed to meeting the needs of all stakeholders.[9]

The magnitude of the economic, social, and financial power of business has finally caused corporations to rethink their operating principles and broaden the definition of their value. Will it be followed with action?

As the World Economic Forum has assessed: "We believe that shareholders and stakeholders are equally important, and that their requirements are irreversibly entwined over time. If a company does not deliver value to its stakeholders, it won't deliver value to its shareholders in future – and vice versa."[10]

Is Shareholder Enrichment Going Beyond What They Deserve?

The Question of Inequality Cannot Be Avoided

Does shareholder enrichment correspond to improved corporate performance? Are there other factors that explain why the Standard & Poor's 500 index has quadrupled while corporate profit growth has stagnated since the 2008 financial crisis? This chart is a demonstration of this disconnection.

---

[9] https://www.businessroundtable.org/business-roundtable-redefines-the-purpose-of-a-corporation-to-promote-an-economy-that-serves-all-americans

[10] https://www.kearney.com/web/world-economic-forum/shareholder-vs-stakeholder-value

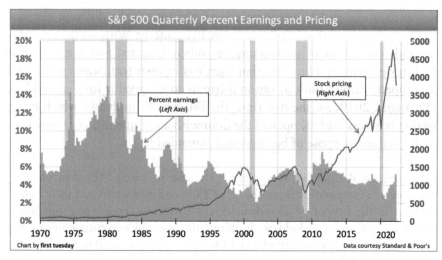

This poses a fundamental question about the mechanisms that allowed this quadrupling. Lower interest rates made bonds less attractive while companies continued to raise their dividends. Debt was cheaper. Market liquidity led investors to move into equities. The exponential growth in the price of technology companies did the rest.

But the democratic question beckons. These piles of liquidity and the fall in interest rates have a formidable actor: the central banks. With new missions imposed by governments, they have injected so much liquidity that asset inflation has rendered the very notion of value meaningless.

Thanks to these mechanisms, companies have favored shareholders to the extreme, diverting public money in favor of the richest.

Could it be that public money has been used in a way that was increasing shareholder returns while fixed income yield was reduced by quantitative easing and low interest rates? Have we reached a point where monetary policy has started to influence the spreads rather than focusing on a balance between borrowers and lenders and using their balance sheet to do so?

These questions are not theoretical. These factors make the public sector an agent of inequality rather than being neutral.

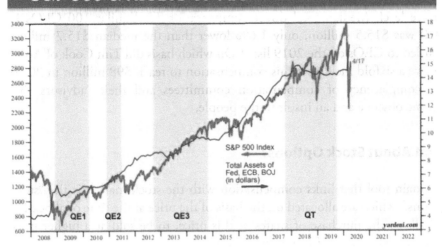

This chart is, to put it mildly, profoundly disturbing. Such a correlation cannot be purely accidental when it spreads over a long period. Does it explain part of the quantitative easing (QE) objectives?

Executive Compensation Tied to Market Prices

To complete the circle, it was necessary to correlate the enrichment of executives with the evolution of the stock market price. This American system created fortunes, but it also provoked massive crises like those of 1929 and 2008. Nobody dares to question this system, yet it is not justified either in law or in morality.

There is something paradoxical in the all-out use of key performance indicators (KPIs) that link bonuses to performance, while enrichment is achieved through mechanisms that multiply wealth on the stock market. A classic case of having your cake and eating it too?

Making an executive's remuneration dependent on the performance of his company's shares means that he benefits, beyond the performance of his company, from factors specific to stock market supply and demand. As we have seen, earnings growth was not a factor in the quadrupling of the stock market index. What we have seen is the development of enrichment exogenous to the performance of companies and, in the event of a market downturn, forms of compensation that limit their risks.

The COVID-19 pandemic caused upheaval throughout the US economy in 2020, and executive pay does not appear to have felt intense effects at a surface level. Median total direct compensation for Equilar 100 CEOs in 2020 was $15.5 million, only 1.6% lower than the median $15.7 million awarded to CEOs on the 2019 list.[11] On which basis did Tim Cook of Apple deserve a sixfold increase of his compensation to reach $98 million in 2021? The complacency of compensation committees and their "advisors" has become obscene and an insult to the people.

What About Stock Options?

The main tool that links compensation with the stock market is the "stock options," which are allocated on the basis of the price at the time of allocation and allows the purchase of shares at this price, to be sold at a higher price without having to pay for the current value.

This mechanism adds to the focus on the stock price from executives and often staff. It is a way to "align" their interest to those of shareholders. The problem is that it amplifies the search for shareholder value. I vividly remember when Morgan Stanley went public: It did profoundly influence the way the firm was managed and the focus of the most senior partners on the value of their stocks. It is a cultural change, as if a new "external" partner, the market, had become a key drive of corporate activities.

The relations between CEO stock options and analysts' earnings forecast bias has driven attention from researchers. "We argue that a higher level of stock options may induce managers to undertake riskier projects, to change and/or reallocate their effort, and to possibly engage in gaming (such as opportunistic earnings and disclosure management) and hypothesize that these managerial behaviors will result in an increase in the complexity of forecasting and, hence, in less accurate analysts' forecasts. We also posit that analysts' optimistic forecast bias will increase as the level of stock options pay increases," explains a German publication.[12]

What is more, when stock prices did not evolve in the direction of the managers' enrichment, corrective measures were taken. Heads I win, tails you lose!

The example of the billionaire Steve Jobs who defrauded his own company is worth looking at. Apple Computer disclosed in a regulatory filing that

---

[11] https://www.equilar.com/reports/80-highest-paid-ceos-2021-equilar-100.html

[12] https://www.springerprofessional.de/ceo-stock-options-and-analysts-forecast-accuracy-and-bias/11230780

Chief Executive Officer Steve Jobs was aware that some stock options granted to him and other executives at Apple between 1997 and 2002 were backdated and that the company was restating financial results for the past few years as a result of the backdating. But the maker of the popular iPod also said that Jobs did not financially benefit from the options and added that a special committee that investigated the options granting practices at Apple found no wrongdoing by Jobs or other current managers.[13] Apple is just one of many companies accused of fraudulent backdating of stock options. Steve Job's personal fortune was estimated at $10 billion at the time.

The Race for Shareholder Return

The shareholder is remunerated for his investment according to a calculation of his return, which is a combination of the dividend and the appreciation of the share value.

As we have seen, this appreciation is not only due to an increase in the profitability of companies but also to factors external to the company. Dividends have been growing steadily in the face of declining profitability, and boards of directors have favored steadily increasing dividends. As interest rates have fallen, the search for yield has led to a wave of dividend-fueled equity investments. Over the past five years, the investor in the US market index (Standard & Poor's 500) has earned a return of 189%.

What About the Dividend?

It is normal that dividends paid to shareholders are higher than interest rates on bonds. Shareholders take the risk of the company's performance and bondholders the risk of its failure. However, when central banks lower interest rates, companies are able to increase dividends thanks to the profits from their lower financing costs, which increases the valuation of stocks.

As central banks have been responsible for a massive drop in bond yields, sometimes through negative interest rates, the search for yield has led investors to stocks because of the dividend and the absence of "animus societatis." It was in equities that most of the 2020 injections were invested. That trend changed as central banks reduced their purchases and started to increase interest rates in the first half of 2022.

---

[13] https://money.cnn.com/2006/12/29/technology/apple_jobs/

But behind a company's dividend policy is an ideology that constantly favors the shareholder: the dividend must grow. The yield on shares varies from country to country and from sector to sector. It is expressed as a percentage, not of equity but of the share price. The higher the share price, the higher the dividend and vice versa.

S&P 500 dividends on track for minor 2020 decline

Dividends paid by S&P 500 companies are likely to dip just 1% in 2020 after several companies resumed payouts suspended earlier due to coronavirus uncertainty, according to S&P Dow Jones Indices

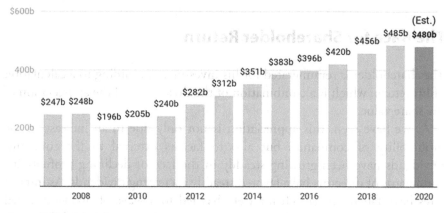

Source: S&P Dow Jones Indices

The chart above shows that dividends in the United States have grown at a compounded rate of 6% over 20 years. They have also been almost constant despite all the financial crises of the last 15 years. In the middle of the inflationary crisis, Eurozone companies increased their dividends by 28.7%![14]

The company tends to increase or maintain the amount of its dividend every year even if the results are down. One might doubt that this policy reflects fluctuations in the company's performance.

Not paying a dividend is considered a bad signal. It is a perfect example of the iron law of the markets that deviates from what the dividend is: one of the remunerations and a positive signal for good companies that have enough cash to finance investment opportunities and to remunerate their shareholders' loyalty. A company will boast that it has always paid its dividend over the

---

[14] https://www.euractiv.com/section/economy-jobs/news/european-dividends-grow-by-28-7-in-q2-2022/

last 100 years—war, natural disasters, or viruses have not been able to undermine what has become an obligation. "Dividend Diplomats" are clear: Dividends are the foundation of our goal to reach financial freedom. We continuously invest in dividend growth stocks to grow our passive income. If you have not figured it out by now, we eat, sleep, and breathe dividends! FedEx will increase its dividend by 53%.[15]

All these considerations raise the question of the hierarchy of corporate payments. During the coronavirus crisis, I suggested that dividends should be paid in shares, which protects the company's financial position, relieving its cash flow.

But a more radical movement has called for dividends to be dropped during 2020. The 2019 dividends of large, listed companies could go out the window or be quarantined. The idea is for companies to preserve their cash flow. Too bad, because they were expected to reach almost 55 billion euros, their highest amount in history.

Among the contradictions of the financial markets, a policy of steadily increasing dividends is a contradiction "in terminis," and this principle must be questioned. This steady upward trend in companies, including banks, which continue to increase their shareholders' remuneration, is one of the forms that financial capitalism takes to the detriment of employment.

The comparison with Europe is astonishing: The average dividend has been 3.52% since the financial crisis, about twice as high as in the United States. But what is more serious is the disconnection between the United States and Europe. The graph below goes back to 2016, but it shows the trend: While the percentage of profits distributed to American shareholders is around 40%, Europe reaches 55%. Contrary to various claims, Europe is more generous than the United States in remunerating its shareholders through dividends. US companies prefer share buybacks.

To put it plainly, European companies invest a smaller share of their profits in investments than American companies. In a world of negative interest, this European policy must absolutely be questioned. It excessively favors shareholders. It also explains why the stock price will grow less rapidly. However, how could dividends increase by 28.7% in Q2 of 2022.[16]

---

[15] https://seekingalpha.com/article/4520653-8-expected-dividend-increases-in-july-2022

[16] https://www.euractiv.com/section/economy-jobs/news/european-dividends-grow-by-28-7-in-q2-2022/

Share Buybacks to Boost Returns… and Threaten Financial Stability

Share buybacks are not neutral but rather an admission that the earnings and equity of a company cannot be put into action to create shareholder value. Nevertheless, it is hard to identify the motivation of companies and boards.

Trillions of dollars have been used by listed companies to buy back their own shares. In June 2021, the banks started this buyback again. We must understand the consequences of these actions:

- The first impact is the increase of the stock price. It is understandable why investors and executives join in this bonanza that will enrich them beyond their regular compensation.
- A number of companies financed their share buybacks by increasing their debt, creating a double leverage.
- The result of these operations is a decrease in the company's equity, sometimes coupled with an increase in debt. This scissor effect weakens the company. The pandemic grounded airlines worldwide but "when the breeze came" (COVID-19), they had to be saved by billions of dollars spent by Donald Trump's government to avoid bankruptcy.
- It is not because we live in a utopia of stock market valuations that share buybacks can be analyzed according to short-term situations.

Buybacks & Dividends

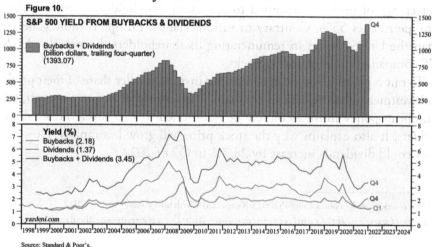

Figure 10.

Source: Standard & Poor's.

The Short and Long Term: Shareholder Activism

It is difficult to measure the proportion of investors who seek to increase the value of their financial assets over the long term. It is true that pension funds and insurance companies have a long-term investment horizon. However, they are not the most active traders.

Hedge funds have a time horizon that consists of maximizing short-term returns (alpha). Their transparency and regulation are light, and in the United States, they are reserved for qualified investors. One of the ways to generate short-term profits is through activism.

Shareholder Activism Can Be Useful Depending on Its Purpose

There is nothing inherently wrong with using various means to influence corporate policy. But these means must be legitimate, which is not always the case. When activists use shares in a company to put pressure on its strategy and management, they have the means to address the management of the companies to express their grievances. This does not give them a preferential right to information. If they are honestly interested in making their opinions and objections known, this is the right place to do it.

It is disturbing to see that the first obstacle to this dialogue is the companies themselves. Yet for companies to manage this is to learn about the activists, their background, and their attitude. There should be room for an initial good faith conversation. Refusing to do so is often an admission of weakness by management. At best, activists are the only recourse against collusion between management and the board of directors to the detriment of shareholders.

Because of a lack of dialogue or because the conversation has turned sour, activists have several arrows in their bow. Some specialize in extortion: They will try to obtain a profit that they have sometimes carefully prepared by accumulating short positions.

Shareholder activism is definitely no longer a purely Anglo-Saxon phenomenon. In search of new investments, activist funds have crossed the Atlantic to establish themselves in Europe, taking their practices with them. The degree of disclosure of the conversation remains variable.

The active involvement of shareholders in the life of listed companies is a condition for the companies' proper functioning and sound governance. In this respect, it should be encouraged. However, the recent abuses on the part of certain activist shareholders can have harmful effects, both for the company, which must know how to respond to them, and for the proper functioning of the market. The lack of transparency on the positions of the shareholders concerned, on their intentions, or their conflicts of interest, and the destabilization of companies at important moments in the life of the company have to be corrected.

Boards of directors often do not play their role and refuse any interaction with activists when, in many cases, their fiduciary duty should require them to investigate the case and see whether or not the activists' claims have merit.

Activism is sometimes a wake-up call worth listening to. In some cases, however, it is fundamentally self-serving.

Activism and Abuse of Rights

Big battles between activists and corporations do not paint a positive picture of corporate governance and activist morality.

In most cases, it is through aggressive statements in the media that a company's management is challenged. These are cases where the activist knows that they will not be able to make their point of view known through the channels of corporate democracy, particularly in general meetings. Moreover, the market authorities are caught between the support obtained by the companies at the highest level of the state and their role of guardian of shareholder equality.

The ingredients of a classic activist attack are gathered: One wants to raise the share price to favor the shareholder, one uses the media before having even started a dialogue with the company. Using normal corporate channels is below their status. Often, they do not have sufficient voting rights to influence the general assembly.

There are jackals among them who take advantage of a weak situation and go directly to court. They are known and spotted and will not hesitate to put obstacles in the way of the restructuring of Greek or Argentinean debt, for instance, at the risk of provoking a crisis in these countries.

It is essential to be able to separate the wheat from the chaff.[17]

---

[17] https://www.sullcrom.com/files/upload/sc-publication-review-analysis-2021-US-shareholder-activism.pdf

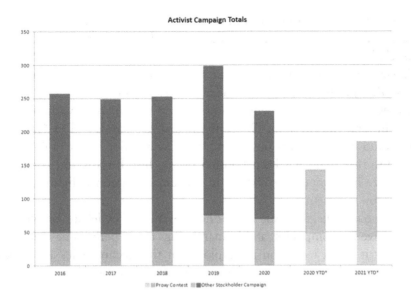

While the number of shareholder activist campaigns in the United States remained flat in 2021 compared to 2019 and 2020, going into 2022 companies should anticipate that activism will continue to be a powerful lever for certain opportunistic shareholders seeking to extract value and produce "alpha" returns. Specifically, companies should look out for an uptick in activist campaigns focused on ESG (environmental, social, and governance) issues. Activist campaigns may be launched against "de-SPACed" companies that are underperforming and companies with depressed stock prices.[18]

This analysis shows the complexity of regulating activism between those who aim at improving the future of the company and those who look for immediate profits. It does not give activists a supremacy that they often attribute to themselves.

Is Shareholder Value a Threat to Employment?

When a company announces a reduction in its workforce, its share price rises. It is the shareholder who benefits first from the layoffs.

Many people are shocked by this. The explanation, however obvious it may be, is simple. If the company reduces its staff, its costs will fall, and its profits will rise. Faced with the prospect of higher profits, the stock price rises. This

---

[18] https://www.skadden.com/insights/publications/2022/01/2022-insights/corporate/activism-landscape-continues-to-evolve

is both logical and automatic. But the implicit choice in favor of the shareholder and against employment opens a Pandora's box where capital and labor clash.

Amazon is accelerating its growth with a view to developing cashierless stores. The number one online retailer has just announced an "express cart" that uses a combination of sensors and cameras to scan items without having to go through the checkout. With its Amazon Go stores and its "Just Walk Out" solution, Amazon is positioning itself as a major player in contactless payment. This trend has been boosted by the health crisis and could soon materialize in Europe. Meanwhile, in Alabama, Amazon is fighting against trade union representation.[19]

Make no mistake, this issue is at the heart of this book's debate: Employment is expensive for companies, and human beings could perhaps be replaced by robots. Is it not a reduction in employment that technologies are working toward?[20] And this is at the expense of the taxpayer, who will have to pay taxes to cover unemployment benefits.

Dividends vs. Jobs

One question keeps nagging at me: Why are corporate executives more reluctant to cut dividends than to reduce employment? Do they apply double standards between capital and employment? It is understandable that the public is shocked by this new form of inequality. The conflict between the financial returns and the social dimension of the company is a question of balance.

Contrary to what the financial ideology would have us believe, the debate is not only between technology and employment but also between capital and labor—in short, between shareholders and workers. This is the most dramatic conundrum of American capitalism, made possible by the fact that the labor market is fluid and the labor force mobile.

This is not as often the case in Europe. This is why the profit growth of European companies cannot compete with that of American companies: Europe is not as easily prepared to sacrifice jobs for the sake of shareholder value. Even in their own countries, however, they compete with global companies who prioritize shareholder value over stakeholder value.

---

[19] https://www.cnbc.com/2021/09/08/amazon-brings-its-cashierless-tech-to-two-whole-foods-stores.html

[20] https://news.crunchbase.com/startups/tech-layoffs-2022/

Has employment effectively become the enemy of shareholders even though the latter can only benefit from profits thanks to the contribution of employees? Unemployment is in fact paid for by the taxpayer. States are forced to go into debt to finance unemployment benefits. We always come back to the taxpayer.

Companies have the means, as we have seen during the lockdown of the coronavirus, to separate themselves more or less temporarily from their employees and their workers, all at the expense of the state and therefore of society. Needless to say, they were surprised to see the shrinking of the workforce that ensued from their lack of support for their staff.

They can "lobby" politicians to avoid societal measures that are not favorable to them. This is how the markets and the race for profits combine to ignore the societal responsibilities of large corporations.

No subsidies should be given to companies whose survival is not threatened. Subsidizing oil companies to make the necessary investments in new technologies is outright theft from the taxpayer for the benefit of the shareholder. To make things worse, fossil fuels received \$5.9 trillion in subsidies in 2020, according to a Yale University study.[21]

The paradox is that it is the dog who wags the tail. Increased unemployment reduces consumption, which reduces growth. We need capital and work and an equitable distribution of wealth in relation to their respective contributions. This search for the reduction of employment through technology is suicidal.

---

[21] https://e360.yale.edu/digest/fossil-fuels-received-5-9-trillion-in-subsidies-in-2020-report-finds#

Capital Markets, Politics, and Policies

Yes, financial markets need political support to promote their ideology and politicians coalesce around capital.

Political influence is all the more difficult to quantify because it is part of a set of decisions that, either directly or indirectly, affect the redistribution of wealth. Inevitably, the most powerful have the means to influence these decisions in their favor. Why is democratic control of major financial and budgetary decisions so favorable to large publicly traded corporations?

The answer lies, namely, in political contributions: The table below is an illustration of the ways Donald Trump contributions exceeded those of the Republican Party in the 2020 elections.

Finance Is Not Included in the Political Debate

Is it because of a lack of knowledge or experience? Is it the result of a short-term electoral vision? How can citizens not understand that the legislative system and governments make decisions that ultimately weigh on their shoulders? Why is it that neither the parties nor the unions seem to attach any systemic importance to these decisions, which are often considered "technical" when they are eminently political?

Explosive corporate and government debt, interest rate policy, and the fiscal outlook are, in all countries, carefully removed from the electoral debate. You cannot blame the candidates. Most would not be able to articulate a program on this subject. How could we improve the training of our congress people and senators to help them understand the implications of government

© The Author(s), under exclusive license to Springer Nature Switzerland AG 2023
G. Ugeux, *Wall Street's Assault on Democracy*, https://doi.org/10.1007/978-3-031-29094-7_19

or corporate decisions? In 1968, during student demonstrations, one of the slogans was "If you don't take care of politics, politics will take care of you."

Even in Joe Biden's campaign, the fiscal impact of extraordinary spending was not discussed in terms of how it would be funded. It must be said that his advisers defended the theory that denies the risks of debt. The connection between Bernie Sanders and Professor Stephanie Kelton, the primary advocate of the Modern Monetary Theory, led to her becoming co-chair of the Biden Campaign's economic think tank. The recent opposition to the White House plan and its reduction from $3.5 to $1 trillion are due to concerns about the US fiscal policy and debt.

How much leeway do governments have in a world where corporations do not contribute to the budget and the wealthy have sophisticated ways of avoiding taxes?

It is critical to find ways to force this discussion, which has as much impact as unemployment, pensions, immigration, and health care. Each of these central topics of political debate is heavily influenced by fiscal considerations. They directly affect the issues of the state and regional budgets, the way they are financed, and the impact on jobs.

The Financing of Elections

For several years, we have been witnessing a worrying trend in many countries: the questioning of elections. Three months after the French presidential election, the yellow vests took the right to demand "Macron out!" in defiance of democracy. Behind this development, one issue continues to feed all populisms, whether of the left or the right.

Total cost of US elections

$US, adjusted for inflation

■ Congressional Races   ■ Presidential Race

Year	Congressional Races	Presidential Race
2020 (projected)	5,674,950,826	5,163,276,829
2016	4,450,842,959	2,575,855,503
2012	4,133,954,529	2,957,531,496
2008	2,949,270,438	3,321,525,519
2004	3,068,367,148	2,620,070,625
2000	2,510,772,607	2,125,546,201

https://theconversation.com/the-scale-of-us-election-spending-explained-in-five-graphs-130651

In the United States, the Republican Party, convinced that it could not have a majority if all votes were counted, has launched actions to restrict voting rights. It even contested the result of the Joe Biden election, against all evidence. Financing elections is a way to make sure democracy is corrupt and public trust vanishes.

This is where the Citizens United decision enters: Twice, in 2010 and 2014, the Supreme Court lined up with those who did not want any limit on political contributions. Chief Justice Roberts wrote that "The government has a strong interest, no less critical to our democratic system, in combating corruption and its appearance. We have, however, held that this interest must be limited to a specific kind of corruption — quid pro quo corruption — in order to ensure that the government's efforts do not have the effect of restricting the First Amendment right of citizens to choose who shall govern them."[1]

Is there a more striking example of finance as an instrument of inequality and anti-democracy?

The astronomical cost of elections is a barrier to entry that does not allow a candidate to run unless he or she is wealthy, able to raise considerable funds, or funded by a political party. This creates a financial advantage for incumbents.

Democratic Institutions Funded by Interest Groups

Once in office, elected officials are indebted to the interest groups that finance them. Democratic institutions are seen to be dominated by money. When the US primaries began in 2019, the question asked was not who the best future president would be but who among the 24 candidates could raise enough money.

The funding of political parties and candidates favors those with a pro-business and pro-wealthy agenda. This is true everywhere: The accumulation of wealth makes it possible to bribe or even buy votes.

The situation in the United States is obviously much more serious, both in terms of the amount of money and the way it is funded. The National Rifle Association is just one example of a lobby that refuses to regulate the carrying of weapons whose main beneficiaries have received more than $3 million. Some may be surprised that the champion of all beneficiaries of gun money was John McCain.[2]

---

[1] Official Report of the Supreme Court volume 573.
[2] https://www.nytimes.com/interactive/2017/10/04/opinion/thoughts-prayers-nra%2D%2Dfunding-senators.html?mtrref=www.google.com&assetType=REGIWALL&auth=login-email

What About the World?

The cost of elections in Europe appears to be much lower. The reason is that they are mostly national. The ceiling on contributions is often and easily circumvented. Several elections in France have turned to spectacle when prominent people have circumvented the law. What will be the penalty?

Unfortunately, there is no transparency of corporate contributions to the campaigns of the various candidates in Europe. If the costs of the many elections in Europe were aggregated, the figures would be close to those of the United States.

There are no estimates for the Japanese elections.

As to China, the cost of their communist party "elections" is unknown, while popular elections are nonexistent.[3]

The mammoth cost of US elections in context

Total expenses of all parties and candidates*

USA	2016 presidential**	£2.3bn
UK	2015 general	£71m
France	2012 presidential	£55m
Germany	2013 general	£54m
Italy	2013 general	£34m
Japan	2013 general	£9m

* Converted from EUR to GBP on 27 July 2016
** Projection. 2012 = £2bn
Source: Handelsblatt

THE WEEK @StatistaCharts   statista

Financial Markets and International Politics

The globalization of international capital markets is a relatively recent phenomenon. It can be traced back mainly to the privatizations of large international groups that had to or wanted to call on international savings.

---

[3] https://www.statista.com/chart/5371/the-mammoth-cost-of-us-elections-in-context/

Today, the shares of global companies are listed on several stock exchanges. International competition is intense. In recent years, we have seen an intensification of the use of financial markets in the conflict between the United States and China.

The Fight Against International Corruption

The United States has managed to dominate this space because of the large amount of American capital that can be invested in these companies around the world. In 2010, the US government mandated that the Securities and Exchange Commission (SEC) play a role in implementing the Foreign Corruption Practices Act.[4]

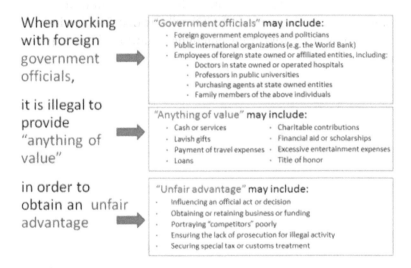

When working with foreign government officials,

"Government officials" may include:
- Foreign government employees and politicians
- Public international organizations (e.g. the World Bank)
- Employees of foreign state owned or affiliated entities, including:
  - Doctors in state owned or operated hospitals
  - Professors in public universities
  - Purchasing agents at state owned entities
  - Family members of the above individuals

it is illegal to provide "anything of value"

"Anything of value" may include:
- Cash or services
- Lavish gifts
- Payment of travel expenses
- Loans
- Charitable contributions
- Financial aid or scholarships
- Excessive entertainment expenses
- Title of honor

in order to obtain an unfair advantage

"Unfair advantage" may include:
- Influencing an official act or decision
- Obtaining or retaining business or funding
- Portraying "competitors" poorly
- Ensuring the lack of prosecution for illegal activity
- Securing special tax or customs treatment

Enforcement of the Foreign Corrupt Practices Act (FCPA) continues to be a high-priority area for the SEC. In 2010, the SEC's Enforcement Division created a specialized unit to further enhance its enforcement of the FCPA, which prohibits companies issuing stock in the United States from bribing foreign officials for government contracts and other businesses.[5]

This is just one example of the imposition of the Lex Americana on the international financial markets, and it is a measure of the distortion of the responsibilities of the capital market regulator, which must now police international contracts that may have involved active or passive bribery. On what

[4] https://export.duke.edu/working-foreign-nationals/foreign-corrupt-practices-act
[5] https://www.sec.gov/enforce/sec-enforcement-actions-fcpa-cases

grounds should an agency regulating securities and exchanges have a mandate to chase corruption?

Far be it from me to say that efforts to reduce the business corruption taking place everyday around the world should not be praised. Using the presence of non-US companies on a US stock exchange to give the regulator authority is an abuse of the law.

Why is there no equivalent regulation in Europe? Because member states want to maintain the ability to bribe at the national level?

The Challenge of Emerging Countries

Is it necessary to remind ourselves that 85% of the world population (6 billion people) live in an emerging country? The Organization for Economic Cooperation and Development (OECD) tells us that 25% of international shares are held by investors from emerging countries. Fifteen percent are Chinese.

Fig 7: **The expansion of EM financial markets**

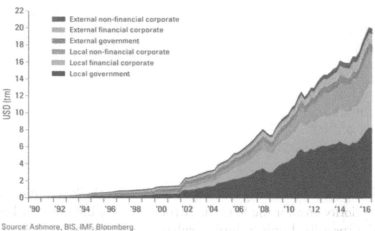

Source: Ashmore, BIS, IMF, Bloomberg.

This does not mean that emerging countries do not have their own capital markets. The financial markets of these countries have reached levels that have supported growth far in excess of that of industrialized countries. However, they are underdeveloped because of the lack of a strong domestic investor base. They are also dependent on capital flows from investors in other countries, some of whom are long-term but who sometimes act in a speculative manner, creating tremors that amplify local difficulties.

It is difficult to see how regulators in these countries could impose transparency of their activities and financial accounts on state-owned enterprises listed on the stock exchange.

The immaturity of emerging financial markets is the result of an underdeveloped institutional and individual investor base. Their elites usually invest abroad. Forced to finance themselves, they will seek aid from multilateral agencies (World Bank, IMF, etc.). Even this aid is politicized. At the heart of this challenge is obviously Africa, which has practically no access to private financial markets.

One of the key risks of 2023 will be the default of foreign currency debt issued by emerging market sovereign, banking, and corporate borrowers whose yield has increased because of a strong dollar, higher interest rates, and a higher spread.[6]

The Chinese Case or the Misled Listing War

After 20 years of regular interaction with Chinese authorities, investors, and financial markets, I think I can outline some aspects of China's approach to capital markets.

The first phase was the privatization of SOEs, which make up the largest portion of Chinese companies listed outside of China. This phase emerged at a time when the US and Chinese markets were trying to find a way to cooperate. China needs the US capital market to raise funds and keep these state-owned enterprises going. It is also the sector where state control is the most severe, not to mention the "red princes" or "princelings" who run the vast majority of these enterprises. Needless to say, foreign investors in these state-owned companies have had to accept China's state governance.

The second phase was the arrival of private companies whose shareholders were desperate to raise money in the United States. It was a flourishing period, but the US stock exchanges at that time accepted companies that did not meet the minimum listing standards. It took only a few years to discover that the accounts of some of these companies were fraudulent. Unscrupulous Chinese intermediaries were promising these companies good times and taking outrageous commissions.

In the third phase, things had to be put right. American regulations had changed and imposed a form of quality control on the local accounting

---

[6] https://gugeux.medium.com/an-emerging-market-financial-crisis-is-unavoidable-and-probably-massive-9bfceb1a3a23

system. The Chinese objected. It was to Hong Kong and Shanghai that Chinese companies were now turning.

I am in Beijing at the headquarters of the national market authority, the China Securities Regulatory Commission. The person I am talking to is in charge of the international department. The President of the Shenzhen Stock Exchange introduced me to him. I tell him about the concern of the American authorities regarding these listings that use a vehicle in tax havens. It is important that the Chinese authorities, who refuse the interference of the SEC, ensure a control of these companies. The Chinese government has decided not to concern itself with these companies on the pretext that they are foreign companies, whereas their assets represented 100% of the shares of a Chinese company. [7] The conversation will allow an opening. At the exit, I hear the footsteps of a man who runs to join me: He asks me not to publish anything about our talks...Everything is said.

In the fourth phase, Donald Trump threatened Chinese companies with being delisted from the American stock market as part of an executive order listing companies with connections to the People's Liberation Army (PLA). The exchanges followed course, and the victims of this action were mostly US investors, who saw the value of their shares sometimes halved.[8]

In the fifth phase, in 2021, it was the Chinese authorities putting on the brakes on the listing of Chinese technology companies, such as ANT and Didi, for fear of seeing their data used by the United States.

The New York Stock Exchange (NYSE), however, had managed a coup by obtaining the listing of Alibaba stock in June 2014. In November 2019, the stock would be listed on the Hong Kong Stock Exchange, which had changed its listing criteria in the meantime. Like all White House actions under Donald Trump, the move backfired on the US market and diminished US influence over foreign corporate governance. Once again, nationalism reduced a lucrative US capital market business and its influence on Chinese companies.

The bill, already passed unanimously in May by the Republican-majority Senate and unanimously by the Democrat-controlled House of Representatives, was signed into law by Donald Trump, giving him one more tool in his conflict with China before he left the White House. The Holding Foreign Companies Accountable Act promoted by Sen. John Kennedy Jr. prohibits foreign companies from being listed on US stock exchanges if they have not

---

[7] http://www.ashmoregroup.com/sites/default/files/article-docs/MC_10%20May18_2.pdf

[8] https://clsbluesky.law.columbia.edu/2021/01/25/the-backlash-against-chinese-company-listings-on-u-s-exchanges-has-a-long-history

complied with the auditing rules of the US Public Accounting Oversight Board (PCAOB) for three consecutive years.

International Cooperation of Regulators

The International Organization of Securities Commissions (IOSCO), better known by its acronym, is an international organization created in 1983 with its general secretariat in Madrid. It gathers the regulators of the main stock exchanges in the world and meets once a year. Its main objective is to establish international standards to enhance the efficiency and transparency of securities markets, to improve investor protection, and to promote cooperation among regulators to combat financial crime.[9]

However, its means are limited: The United States, of all parties, refuses any form of sanction or control of its domestic activities. While the World Trade Organization has the means to act; this is not the case for the capital markets.

At the global level, there is only cooperation on technical problems. For the rest, regulatory competition between financial markets knows no limits.

---

[9] www.iosco.com

complied with the auditing rules of the US Public Accounting Oversight
Board (PCAOB) in this transaction.

International Cooperation of Regulators

The International Organization of Securities Commissions (IOSCO), better
known by its acronym, is an international organization created in 1983 with
its central secretariat in Madrid. It gathers the regulators of the main stock
exchanges in the world and meets once a year. Its main mission is to establish
standards and methods to enhance the markets and transparency of securities
markets, to improve investor protection, and to promote cooperation
among regulators around a financial crisis.

However, in some countries, the IOSCO standards are still particular to some
forms and are interpreted in accordance with the World Trade
Organization. Also, the regulators are connected to a global protection system.

The Role of Taxation in Capital Inequalities

Tax fairness is an essential element of democracy and trust in corporate leaders and governments. Corporations have succeeded in shifting taxes to consumption through taxation that penalizes the poorest. They have used globalization to force the political world to reduce the direct tax burden on them. https://blogs.imf.org/wp-content/uploads/2019/07/tax.png

Corporate Income Tax Stumbles Around the World: The Cost of Globalization

The most resounding victory of the haves over the have-nots, of the knowers over the unknowers, and of globalization over communities, is taxation. The mechanisms that allow this inequity are complex and subtle. They do not have the simplicity of slogans against the rich. We need to know how taxes are distributed to understand why large corporations do not pay taxes, why the rich can deduct the cost of acquiring assets that are swelling at a rapid rate, how tax evasion is organized, and how the proceeds of crime escape taxation.

How long will this imbalance last? How long will democratic countries survive the abuse of power that is becoming widespread in the industrialized world? What will become of the millions of people on the brink of financial collapse, particularly in the emerging countries? Will it take a popular revolution to set the record straight?

© The Author(s), under exclusive license to Springer Nature Switzerland AG 2023
G. Ugeux, *Wall Street's Assault on Democracy*, https://doi.org/10.1007/978-3-031-29094-7_20

Race to the bottom
Corporate income tax rates have fallen
significantly over the past three decades.
(combined corporate income tax rates by country group, in percent)

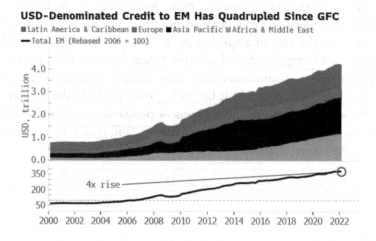

High-Income   Middle Income   Low-Income   OECD Europe

OECD Non-Europe

Source: IMF Fiscal Affairs Department Tax Policy Rates Database.

INTERNATIONAL MONETARY FUND

In recent years, the European Commission has embarked on a program
that specifically targets the taxation of finance and investment. On July 15,
2020, it adopted a new tax package to support Europe's economic recovery
and long-term growth. This initiative is based on three important components: fighting tax abuse, helping tax administrations keep pace with a changing economy, and reducing administrative burdens for citizens and businesses.
It also ensures better cooperation with third countries.

USD-Denominated Credit to EM Has Quadrupled Since GFC
■Latin America & Caribbean ■Europe ■Asia Pacific ■Africa & Middle East
━Total EM (Rebased 2006 = 100)

Tax Inequality: Households Are the Cash Cow of the State

The transformation of taxation has probably escaped the vast majority of our fellow citizens. Designed after the war as a means of redistributing income between the most and least fortunate, it has lost this function, which is essential to a solidarity-based economy, with a drastic increase in the unequal tax on consumption and a decrease in corporate taxes.

The most important source of state tax revenue comes from so-called indirect taxes or taxes on consumption. Value-added tax (VAT) is the main tool of this taxation. A 1% increase in VAT on cigarettes affects a household or a millionaire equally. This is also the case for the tax on petroleum products, which affects motorists at the pump. Half of the resources therefore come from individuals.

Let us add to this the collection at source of income tax on salaried workers—unavoidable, but at least with a gradation that ensures a certain redistribution between the highest and lowest incomes.

Let us make no mistake: Not all individuals are subject to the same treatment. The tax on consumption is asocial. One dollar of tax on cigarettes or gas reflects identically on the billionaire and the single parent.

Large Companies Do Not Pay Income Taxes

In the OECD countries, only 9.8% of the tax revenues come from corporate taxes. In the United States, it is 7.8%. The indecency of this abysmal contribution should revolt citizens. Everything was done to prevent their awareness of this. This is one of the main sources of tax of inequalities.

The tax minimization makes what is cynically called "the search for the least taxed path" extremely easy. One of the fruits of globalization has been the possibility for companies to "park" their profits in low-tax countries. The recent European Court of Justice ruling in favor of Apple and Ireland is a reminder of how difficult it is to achieve tax fairness even within the European Union. The story is not over yet.

If small- and medium-sized companies cannot generally escape taxation; it is the multinationals that are having a field day. As they also manage to get subsidies from the state for more or less justified reasons, the contribution of large companies to the state budget is negative.

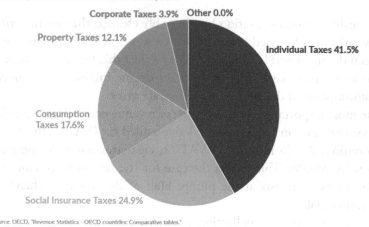

Individual Taxes Are the Most Important Tax Revenue Source for the United States

Sources of Tax Revenue in the United States, 2019

Corporate Taxes 3.9%   Other 0.0%

Property Taxes 12.1%

Individual Taxes 41.5%

Consumption Taxes 17.6%

Social Insurance Taxes 24.9%

Source: OECD, "Revenue Statistics - OECD countries: Comparative tables."

Contrary to what popular vindictiveness claims, what is most lacking in the balance of public finances does not come from the big fortunes but from the companies themselves.

"In absolute terms, the United States experiences the highest annual corporate tax losses of any country by far with an estimated $189 billion unaccounted for every year. That's 1.13 percent of GDP. China comes second with $66.8 billion while Japan also records substantial losses of about $47 billion" writes Forbes, who publishes this table.[1]

A Major Shift in Corporate Taxation?

The Biden administration's announcement of a global corporate tax reform that has been accepted by most OECD countries is encouraging news. For the first time, an attempt to harmonize the taxation of large corporations including the allocation of this tax where the income was generated is a revolution.

The G20's approval of this project, on the weekend of July 11, 2021, in Venice, is the first step in a process that will be complex but indispensable if we want to restore some form of tax fairness. There is no alternative if we want to put an end to the massive tax evasion of large multinational corporations.

---

[1] https://www.statista.com/chart/8668/the-global-cost-of-tax-avoidance/

The Global Cost Of Tax Avoidance
Estimated annual corporate tax losses in selected countries (billion U.S. dollars)

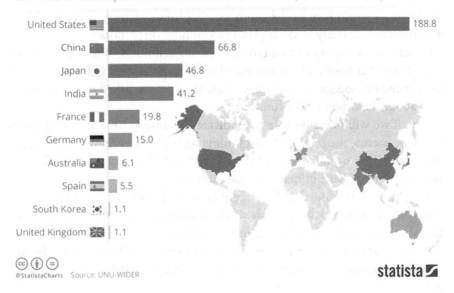

United States	188.8
China	66.8
Japan	46.8
India	41.2
France	19.8
Germany	15.0
Australia	6.1
Spain	5.5
South Korea	1.1
United Kingdom	1.1

@StatistaCharts   Source: UNU-WIDER

statista

This one piece of good news could change the corporate taxation landscape. The agreement would impose a minimum 15% corporate tax rate in nearly every country in the world and punish the few holdouts who refuse to go along. The OECD estimates the accord will raise $150 billion per year globally from tax-fleeing companies.[2]

It aims particularly at companies who managed to avoid paying taxes. The US champions are impressive. At least 55 of the largest corporations in America paid no federal corporate income taxes in their most recent fiscal year despite enjoying substantial pretax profits in the United States. This continues a decades-long trend of corporate tax avoidance by the biggest US corporations, and it appears to be the product of long-standing tax breaks preserved or expanded by the 2017 Tax Cuts and Jobs Act (TCJA) as well as the Coronavirus Aid, Relief, and Economic Security (CARES) Act tax breaks enacted in the spring of 2020.

The tax-avoiding companies represent various industries and collectively enjoyed almost $40.5 billion in US pretax income in 2020, according to their annual financial reports. The statutory federal tax rate for corporate profits is 21%. The 55 corporations would have paid a collective total of $8.5 billion for the year had they paid that rate on their 2020 income. Instead, they received $3.5 billion in tax rebates.[3]

---

[2] https://www.nytimes.com/2021/10/30/world/europe/g20-biden-corporate-tax-agreement.html?
[3] https://itep.org/55-profitable-corporations-zero-corporate-tax/

Wealthy Tax Evasion

The financial world is not solely composed of honest actors. There is a fringe of actors who are ready to do anything to launder dirty money.

It includes a category of participants who are criminals. With the increased precautions that banks take when transferring large amounts of money, organized crime has sought to find areas where they are not asked too many questions about the origin of the funds.

Even if we will never be able to eradicate organized crime and its more or less rogue agents, the public, through films such as Oliver Stone's Wall Street, is becoming increasingly aware of these practices.[4] The catch phrase "Greed is good" remains present in many people's minds.

The markets themselves, their regulators, and police forces continue to refine their tools for identifying shady deals and their operators. But there are still escape routes like Bitcoin and other cryptos.

What crypto assets offer is a rare service: anonymity. Over the past decade, however, governments have developed increasingly sophisticated investigative tools. Unfortunately, international cooperation remains flawed and allows organized crime to continue to profit from criminal money.

The information is in the hands of financial intermediaries and particularly banks and brokers; not without reluctance, they have increased their means of surveillance. It is true that fines are expensive and hurt.

It is in this context that the market of cryptos, and particularly Bitcoin, has developed, which has been used to provide the money for crime known as "ransomware" or ransom that is paid to the perpetrators of all forms of digital piracy. This was the case for the payments, fortunately recovered, that were necessary to unlock the attack on the US East Coast oil pipeline.

---

[4] https://www.imdb.com/title/tt0094291/

An Undemocratic Coalition of Hostile Interests

The various aspects of this section demonstrate the urgency of a reform that will avoid the fact that large companies who fund political parties and candidates, and other contributors albeit to a lesser extent, constitute an objective coalition of interests. Taxes in developed economies have now become a critical part of inequalities.

The reduction of tax rates, the subsidies, and the absence of companies' contributions to the budget create an "ecosystem" that threatens democracy by exacerbating inequalities.

As inflation looms, interest rates are increasing and wars are being fought, and what was barely acceptable comportment by public authorities has now become indecent. The rebalancing is urgent to say the least, to avoid a series of social unrests and explosions.[1]

The IMF (International Monetary Fund) commented on this chart by launching a stern warning in May 2022: "Any rise in social unrest could pose a risk to the global economy's recovery, as it could have a lasting impact on economic performance." In a paper last year, IMF staff showed that unrest can have a negative economic impact as consumers become spooked by uncertainty and output is lost in manufacturing and services. As a result, 18 months after the most serious unrest events, gross domestic product is typically about one percentage point lower than it would have been otherwise.

Capital markets are at the heart of an ideology that feeds inequality through the cult of the shareholder, its most important supporter. The corporation leads to wealth disparities and does not assume its social responsibility when

---

[1] https://blogs.imf.org/wp-content/uploads/2022/05/Social-Unrest-Blog-Chart-for-post.jpg

© The Author(s), under exclusive license to Springer Nature Switzerland AG 2023
G. Ugeux, *Wall Street's Assault on Democracy*, https://doi.org/10.1007/978-3-031-29094-7_21

Taking to the streets

Social unrest events are rising but remain below pre-pandemic peaks.
(percent of countries with Reported Social Unrest Index-identified events)

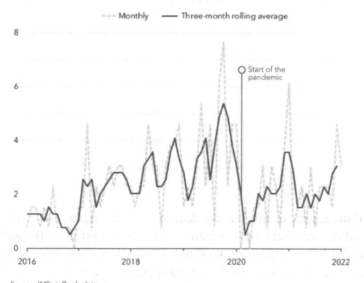

Source: IMF staff calculations.
Note: Due to differences in media coverage and perception across countries, social unrest events
(defined as large peaks in country-specific series) are a more robust measure of
international trends in unrest.

IMF

it conflicts with the return of the shareholder. Executive compensation makes this system opaque and incentivizes executives to favor capital over labor.

The support given to this ideology by governments around the world, and especially in the United States, has been the source of unbalanced pieces of legislation that have allowed various ways to grow the importance of capital markets to the detriment of ordinary people.

This system can only work with the implicit or explicit support of political leaders, governments, or parliaments that are susceptible to corruption. Faced with this situation, it is urgent to take drastic measures that will turn good intentions into realities whose environmental, social, and governance impact will redefine our democracies.

The problem of corruption when it comes to taxation is a long-haul fight against financial crime, which is often made easier by new technologies or products, like the crypto assets.

Public trust depends on the ability to rebalance the benefits of shareholders and workers. As Katharina Pistor puts it, "The battle between the two codes, the digital and the legal, is on."[2]

---

[2] https://hiddenforces.io/podcasts/katharina-pistor-code-of-capital/

For a Democratic Reform of Financial Markets

A Complete Change of Perspective

The rebalancing of financial markets requires a profound revision of the objectives of the institutions and individuals who participate in them. Few of them will even accept a diagnosis that has become obvious: the prevailing ideology is the search for individual interest in this great Circus Maximus.

Few of these participants question the legitimacy or the impact of their actions as long as they are legal. The first class I took at law school made it noticeably clear: law and ethics are different, and it would be incorrect to expect the law to propose an ethical path to justice.

The enrichment of shareholders and financial institutions has reached levels whose obscenity escapes them. That the leaders of the technological sphere find it normal that their salary is around $100 million is an insult to their employees and workers and to society at large.

The change of perspective requires these decision-makers to ask themselves a rather simple question: what impact will their actions have on society? This change of perspective will take a long time to translate into actions that reduce these inequalities. It will therefore be necessary in the meantime for public authorities to make decisions that mitigate them. To do this, they must transform themselves and recognize the importance of taking care of communities.

The future of our democracy is at stake.

 G. Ugeux, *Wall Street's Assault on Democracy*, https://doi.org/10.1007/978-3-031-29094-7_22

A Change of Mentality Is Always a Challenge

It would be naive to underestimate the many obstacles that stand in the way of transforming the ideology that underpins financial markets. Whether it is the rejection of financial capitalism, the reduction of exorbitant shareholder benefits, executive compensation, central bank policies and government debt voracity, or the mechanisms that increase inequality even in moments of crisis such as COVID-19, these are fundamental reforms whose magnitude would discourage many.

It is not an impossible task; it is both multifaceted and diverse. Even if I am ready to be considered a utopian, I am not intending to fight like Don Quixote against windmills.

What is needed is for the parties involved to see their fundamental and long-term interest and be convinced that capital markets cannot exacerbate inequalities and threaten an already weakening democratic world. On each of the necessary reforms, there is abundant academic and legal literature that explains why these reforms are not necessary, or at least not useful, and in any event impossible. The great insincerity is that the actors in this enormous commedia dell'arte refuse to recognize their responsibilities in the growth of inequalities, the weaknesses in the system, and the necessary transformations.

My confidence in this necessary evolution comes from a democratic conviction: the magnitude of inequalities has become intolerable, and the risks are translating into social and political tensions. Our leaders are able to anticipate them but seem powerless to defuse such tensions before the worst happens. Between 75 million and 95 million, additional people could be living in extreme poverty in 2022 compared to pre-COVID-19 projections, due to the lingering effects of the pandemic, the war in Ukraine, and rising inflation.[1]

We simply do not have the right to increase the number of people thrown below the poverty line every year. Seventy-five million of them have already dropped below the line as a result of the pandemic measures. We do not have the right to privatize wealth in the hands of the few. I would like to believe that the calls of social leaders and the need for solidarity will create a powerful movement, driven by a recognition of the imbalance of capital markets. My experience, however, is that self-interest speaks louder than justice.

It is not a question of rejecting financial markets but of redefining a social and political organization to prevent the systematic abuse of power. Beyond their economic purpose, these markets have become an instrument that

---

[1] https://www.worldbank.org/en/topic/poverty/overview

increases inequality and controls public powers. Democracy is increasingly threatened by the selfish hunt for individual interests.

The imbalance of financial power that threatens democracy and promotes unfairness leads us to an exacerbation of inequality. This change of perspective is intellectually easy, while the implementation of this new vision of the role of financial markets and their operators will have to be embodied in specific and concrete measures. It is the enforcement of these measures that the imbalance is most resistant and difficult to put in place because it will do the reverse of what markets believe in: There will be short-term sacrifices and losses of value to create long-term equity.

The model that has developed since World War II has privatized financial resources and imposed expenditures on a public sector that has become largely drained. This model of financial abuse is condemned by popular opinion for good reason. It must be replaced by a model in which finance is under democratic control.

The financial markets are at the origin of a rapid increase of income inequalities. There are solutions that can allow for the rebalancing of finance's contribution to society. But this rebalancing that advanced countries must undergo is fundamental. Which democratic forces will be able to initiate and maintain this process of consultation and decision?

A Social and Solidarity-Based Capitalism Is Possible

In 2020, the OECD (Organization for Economic Cooperation and Development) launched the Global Action "Promoting Social and Solidarity Economy Ecosystems," funded by the European Union's Foreign Partnership Instrument, to support the development and internationalization of the social and solidarity economy. The Action focuses on two critical policy levers that can help unlock the potential of the SSE, namely, legal frameworks and social impact measurement, while considering the entire policy ecosystem as a framework. The SSE designates a group of companies organized in the form of cooperatives, mutual societies, associations, or foundations, whose internal functioning and activities are based on a principle of solidarity and social utility. It gives good conscience.[2]

A social form of capitalism must emerge and be embraced by the various participants. Yet as soon as this idea is proposed, the vast majority of Americans

---

[2] https://www.oecd.org/cfe/leed/social-economy/OECD-global-action/

cry "socialism." They would be surprised by the widespread philosophy that considers solidarity to be a core value. Without public opinion pressure, the system of the coalition of interests that dominates the world of finance will not change. As the saying reminds us, you cannot ask a turkey to vote for Thanksgiving. And yet, it is in the interest of companies, governments, and civil society to do so, since it is not a question of following the destructive discourse of populism or nationalism but of rebalancing the forces at work.

This requires an awareness on the part of citizens that our votes and our financial means count and that they are capable of halting a trend that leads to societal rupture, most likely a violent one. The path we have taken highlights the structural inequality imposed by a model that American investors have exported and that we, as citizens have, sometimes unconsciously, accepted.

This also demands a transformation of the investment horizon: It is essential that the technical means of increasing the size of markets be limited to those that are socially and economically useful. The domination of short-term actors imposes a short-term vision on which no economy, no society, can be built.

Moreover, financial capitalism does not respond to European and Asian values of solidarity. If Europe is capable of conceiving this new model, will it succeed in transforming it into a political force that transcends parties and cleavages and unites Europe around a societal consensus? Such a European reform in turn would affect global financial markets.

In order to achieve this, the financial leadership needs to stop denying this imbalance. Do they want to change it? They have the democratic and financial means—do they have the will? Do they see what the current model condemns us to?

The Public Sector Must Reduce Its Dependency on Wall Street

The power of financial markets, their regulation, and the support of central banks have diverted the public sector from its social and economic responsibilities. At the heart of this observation is the question of the purpose of the state.

The subheading of Governor Raghuram Rajan's book *The Third Pillar* says it all: "How Markets and the State Leave the Community Behind." Markets endanger themselves when they stop working for the broader citizenry because they may then rise up to shut the markets down.[1] In the name of what democratic principle would the authorities intervene other than as a control and regulatory authority in the daily life of these markets?

The multifaceted involvement of the public sector in the financial markets can serve economic policies and make the state a neutral user of its means of financing. We are well beyond this stage in a world that makes public authorities' active partners in capital markets. There can be no question of the citizen and the taxpayer using the state's money, directly or indirectly, to favor the financial markets and the companies that populate them.

It is democracy that is at stake.

---

[1] https://www.penguinrandomhouse.com/books/566369/the-third-pillar-by-raghuram-rajan/

© The Author(s), under exclusive license to Springer Nature Switzerland AG 2023
G. Ugeux, *Wall Street's Assault on Democracy*, https://doi.org/10.1007/978-3-031-29094-7_23

The State and Financial Contributions Corrupt the Decision-Making Process

Corruption takes many impenetrable forms, whether it is the "revolving door" in the United States or "pantouflage" in France, subsidies, or financing of elections. The big banks have made a specialty of hiring former political leaders for well-paid positions in exchange for their political influence.

What is true for business is regularly translated into the financial markets. One can be chairman of the Federal Reserve and continue one's career in a hedge fund. One can be a regulator and end up in a stock exchange or a trading house. José Manuel Barroso, for instance, was the president of the European Commission and then joined Goldman Sachs, which a number of central bank governors had worked for, including the ECB Chairman Mario Draghi and the Bank of England Governor Mark Carney. J.P. Morgan was sued for hiring Chinese scions of political leaders, unbelievable as it may seem, "and paid $264 million in fines."[2]

It is important that there is a system for gaining experience in the public and private sectors. We do not need to isolate ourselves. But in what spirit? Careerism or enrichment? This could create a generation of business leaders with a sense of res publica, of the common good. There are remarkable examples of the benefits of these mixed paths. But they remain the minority.

The Holy Alliance of Special Interests

Let us take a closer look at how we can reconcile the two enemies: finance and democracy:

- **Governments** are the first willing victims of the weakening of democratic institutions. They are in a position to make decisions that balances the well-being of the population or the profitability of companies. They are regularly audited by some form of Court of Auditors, which denounces abuses but does not have the means to correct them.
- **Regulatory authorities** cannot be partisan. Their actions should be controlled by parliament, especially since they emanate from the executive branch. This ambiguity remains the source of significant weaknesses in the enforcement of financial contributions. The state is judge and party. How is it possible to impose sanctions on a state agency? Government agencies are controlled by parliaments, but indirectly.

---

[2] https://www.reuters.com/article/us-jpmorgan-settlement-idUSKBN13C1Z8

- **Lawmakers** are themselves likely to follow the money and have always opposed ethical control of their own members. Parliaments are in a position to stop decisions and, sometimes, to prevent the worst. Their most powerful weapon is the budget: resource allocation and taxation. But each representative or senator will have to finance his or her election or reelection, and some private interests will be happy to help them. How would the US House of Representatives achieve these goals, when its members are replaced in their entirety every two years and are therefore constantly looking for funding for their election campaigns? How could we expect the media to be independent when they are the prime beneficiary of these funds?
- **The judiciary** in most democratic countries has more integrity than the executive and legislative branches. In the United States, prosecutors are elected and therefore subject to the same pressures as members of parliament. But the appointment of judges is a political matter—Donald Trump boasts of having appointed hundreds of federal judges for life. We remember the accusations of rape against US Supreme Court nominee Brett Kavanaugh, which were ignored by Senate Republicans. Everything is there to confirm that even criminals manage to be appointed to the highest levels of the judiciary. We just saw such a result in the Supreme Court's repealing of the Roe v. Wade's decision on abortion.[3]
- **Political parties** would not survive on state or constituent contributions alone. They are tied hand and foot to the fortunes and corporations that fund them. Even if they seek to fund themselves directly from their constituents, the amounts obtained are insufficient, and the lion's share of their budget is financed by corporations.

How does one cut the Gordian knot of this alliance of interests? Nothing escapes it, and the financial markets are part of this gearing. When will politicians treat citizens as human beings rather than commodities they can use and abuse?

Eliminate Tax Deductibility of Political Contributions and Lobbying

Most countries allow tax deductions for political contributions to varying degrees. This means that indirectly, in the form of reduced revenues, the state and local budgets are reduced by the amount of these contributions. What it

---

[3] https://www.supremecourt.gov/opinions/21pdf/19-1392_6j37.pdf

effectively means is that taxpayers are paying for the tax deduction of those contributions.

Preventing these amounts from being deducted for tax purposes will reduce the amount of money going to political activities from the wealthiest and largest corporations. These deductions reduce government revenues and are a democratic practice in name only since they favor the large "donors," which include the rich and large corporations.

The same treatment should be applied to tax-deductible payments that are used to "finance" authorities in foreign countries. Despite US efforts under the Foreign Corrupt Practices Act, such payments remain widespread. I must admit that when I worked for the General Electric, which did not allow such payments, I was ashamed to see large European companies winning contracts by bribing governments. Deductible, they are part of the purchase or sale price of the product or service. Nondeductible, and they become much more expensive. I have not lost my capacity for indignation in the face of obvious and unsanctioned fraud.

Among the main contributors to the political parties are the big players in the financial sector: large companies and ultrarich individuals. They are seeking to obtain advantages that will allow them to continue to favor large, listed companies, in particular by avoiding the taxation of dividends, share buybacks, and capital gains. They are also seeking to weaken the regulatory power of financial markets.

Wall Street corporations made a record $2.9 billion in total political contributions over the course of the 2019–2020 election cycle.

The Opacity of Political Contributions

"Scandals, which have been widely reported in the media and which have led to judicial investigations, have opened the eyes of public opinion to the problem of illicit financing of political parties and to the link between this phenomenon and that of corruption. While these scandals have not undermined the importance of political parties as pillars of representative democracy, they have highlighted those clear rules and transparent accounts are key to restoring or preserving citizens' trust in politics" writes Walter Schwimmer, the Secretary General of the Council of Europe.[4]

Several initiatives have been launched to ensure the transparency of funds paid indirectly to public authorities by economic and financial interests. But

---

[4] https://eos.cartercenter.org/uploads/document_file/path/310/Financing_Political_Parties_fr.pdf

they do not go far enough because parliamentarians are themselves the beneficiaries of the bribes that finance their campaigns.

When it comes to money in politics, transparency is about strengthening democracy and preventing the manipulation of the government for private ends.[5]

It is not enough to limit the amount or to publish global figures. One effective way to reduce the power of these interests is to force the publication of the identity of the beneficiaries and the amount of these contributions, as is the case in the United States.

Many efforts are underway to do this. But it is essential that the accounts of political parties, candidates, and campaign contributors be published in a transparent manner. It will also be necessary to detail the amounts paid by companies. Which government will propose such a measure? Which parliament will vote for it?

Under the presidency of George W. Bush in January 2010, the Supreme Court of the United States removed the limits put on these contributions under the hypocritical name of "Citizens United Act," which proves that, on the contrary, financial interests do not want to be capped. Not to do so is to give unlimited influence on the powers of money, inflated by hallucinating stock market returns.

We are no longer in the business of financing campaigns but in the business of shaking down democratic institutions. It spreads widely outside of the United States. Through complex mechanisms, Russian and Chinese influences are undermining confidence in the electoral system, the key to democracy. Saving democracy implies a transparency that makes democratic control of foreign or ideological influences possible.

---

[5] https://www.brennancenter.org/our-work/analysis-opinion/transparency-democracys-sake

Refocusing Central Banks on Monetary Policy

What do central banks have to do with funding governments? When did they decide to reach out to the liquidity of the stock markets? How did their interest rate policies spread from short-term to long-term interest rates, managing and massaging the yield curve? Why are they expected to follow policies for growth and employment? How could they have grossly ignored the inflation risk of their massive injections of funds during the pandemic?

These are not and should not be their roles. The excuses put forward, such as growth, employment, or the defense of the euro, are far from convincing. The effect has been to favor borrowers at the expense of savers and favor corporates at the expense of retirees.

Without accusing them of bad intentions, I can only note the consequences of their actions. The weakening of democratic control and independence of central banks threaten financial stability. They are already trapped with the quintupling of their balance sheet, and they do not know how to get out of the hole they dug themselves and from which they knew they could not escape.

In late October 2020, Bill Dudley, the former president of the Federal Reserve Bank of New York, argued that the effectiveness of additional Federal Reserve actions is now extremely limited and that further economic stimulus must come from fiscal policy. No central bank wants to admit that it has no firepower. Unfortunately, the US Federal Reserve almost certainly does. This means that America's future prosperity depends more than ever on government spending plans—something the President and Congress must recognize. Much of today's easy money comes at the expense of future growth. So,

G. Ugeux, *Wall Street's Assault on Democracy*, https://doi.org/10.1007/978-3-031-29094-7_24

while the Fed should certainly continue to support the US economy, opinion is likely to waver over the future economic burden this will create.[1]

They sincerely hoped that the sprawling measures they have taken over the last ten years could revive growth and employment. Prisoners of an economic theory that they refuse to question, they have acted in good faith. They have simply turned their backs on their essential mission of monetary policy to favor borrowers (mostly sovereigns) over savers. This is an ethical problem.

The Failure of the Custodians of Inflation

It is difficult to accept what happened over the past years. As custodians of inflation, central banks have tried to increase it in vain to 2%. By fueling demand and ignoring the consequences of pandemic lockdowns, they were instigating a double inflation: the asset inflation in real estate, energy, and financial assets, as well as the price inflation that would inevitably come from too much money chasing too few opportunities. As Mohamed El-Erian writes, "…for the well-being of the U.S. and global economy, the answer to these questions is less important than whether the Fed shows seriousness about fixing four failures that continue to fuel one of the worse policy mistakes in decades: Failures of analysis, forecasts, response and communication."

As noted in the *Economist*, "It is the Fed, however, that had the tools to stop inflation and failed to use them in time. The result is the worst overheating in a big and rich economy in the 30-year era of inflation-targeting central banks. The good news is that inflation may have peaked at last. But the Fed's 2% target will remain a long way off—forcing agonising choices on the central bank."[2]

A Politically Impossible Mission?

Central banks (willingly or unwillingly) have given up much of their independence and have assumed risks for which they are not competent to manage. Moreover, they have accumulated assets that they will not be able to dispose of. They are trapped in the fiscal policy of governments.

---

[1] https://www.bloomberg.com/opinion/articles/2020-10-28/the-federal-reserve-is-really-running-out-of-firepower?srnd=opinion
[2] https://www.economist.com/weeklyedition/2022-04-23

Says Paul Tucker, the former deputy governor of the Bank of England, "We need some principles: political principles. Anyone committed to the separation of powers that lies at the heart of constitutional government should want central bank independence to be preserved. Otherwise, presidents and prime ministers could use the printing press to fund their pet projects and enrich supporters without having to go to the representative assembly for legislated approval. Aspirant authoritarians, on the left or right, will be alert to the attractions of seizing or suborning the monetary power; the IMF should catalogue past examples."[3]

Considering that central banks should promote sustainability and climate change, the fact that employment and growth elements have been added to their missions in recent years compromises the integrity of their monetary policy role. In the case of the ECB (European Central Bank), its role as "guardian angel of the euro" adds to its functions and explains why it has resorted to negative interest rates.[4]

It is extraordinarily difficult for central banks not to be influenced by the executive branch, of which they are the financial weapon, and become the financial arm of the state, relinquishing their primary function of conducting monetary policy. As absurd as it is to pursue such a monetary policy in opposition to economic policy, the dilemma for them is heartbreaking: by becoming the water carrier of public debt, they weaken their independence.

Stop Printing Money

Central banks have killed the risk premium of all financial assets and deny the impact this had on retirees, savings, and insurance companies or pension funds. If their actions had been useful and effective, they would have at least renounced their principles for a noble cause. But it was a failure on all counts.

If unconventional monetary policies have failed over the last ten years, it is also because the torrents of liquidity brought into the system by central banks via the purchase of financial assets through QE operations were not relayed by the action of governments and banks in the real economy. The money thus remained in the financial system and only increased the stock market indices. You do not put artificial rain on inundated soil.

---

[3] https://www.imf.org/external/pubs/ft/fandd/2020/05/paul-tucker-unelected-power-on-central-bank-independence.htm
[4] https://files.stlouisfed.org/files/htdocs/publications/review/12/03/117-134Thornton.pdf

The central banks failed in their task during the quantitative easing operations and used all their artillery too hard and too fast in 2020. They did it in a reactive way to events, without moral compass or structural backbone. They argue that the foreseeable adverse consequences of their actions were not intentional. This moral argument does not absolve them of responsibility for the consequences of their actions.

Central banks are no strangers to the sovereign debt market. They perform several functions in this area, but their most important role is that of so-called open market policy. This is a regularization function, not an investment function. The redefinition of monetary policy has led central banks to accumulate sovereign bonds for reasons that are monetary in name only. In so doing, they have become the partner of the issuing state, and their balance sheets are full of these assets.

The Bank of Japan is the last major central bank that continues to purchase Japanese Government Bonds. The Bank of Japan will maintain its ultra-loose monetary policy as the economy has not been affected much by the global inflationary trend, Governor Haruhiko Kuroda said, stressing the country's 15-year experience with deflation is keeping wage growth subdued.[5] What it did, however, is devalue the Yen. The untimely assassination of former Prime Minister Shinzo Abe on July 8, 2022, further increased the uncertainties of a country that fights to ignore how the rest of the world is evolving.[6]

Conflicts of Interest Require a Change in Governance: Central Banks as Supermarkets

The risk of unrecognized conflicts of interest are inherent to the multiplicity of their responsibilities. The book of Paul Tucker, the former deputy governor of the Bank of England, is called *Unelected Power: The Quest for Legitimacy in Central Banking and the Regulatory State.*[7]

They have favored borrowers to the detriment of savings, weakening the balance of the markets. Having become a central player in the financial markets, they now have an influence on the stock and bond markets well beyond their financial stability policies.

---

[5] https://www.reuters.com/markets/currencies/bojs-kuroda-vows-keep-easy-policy-japan-less-affected-by-global-inflation-2022-06-29/

[6] https://capital.com/usd-to-jpy-forecast

[7] https://press.princeton.edu/our-authors/tucker-paul

Conflicts of interest are not new. But at that time, there was not much to avoid them, to control them, and to prevent them, because there was less movement from a public to a private function and vice versa. Today, these comings and goings are legion and even encouraged. At the same time, and with the help of scandals, public institutions are adopting codes of good conduct and conflict of interest prevention. Even the European Central Bank has had to do so since January 2019, under pressure from the European Parliament, NGOs (nongovernmental organizations), and the Ombudsman of the European Union.

Unless there is a profound reform that refocuses central banks on their core business as guardians of monetary policy, they will no longer regain the trust they enjoyed before the 2008 crisis. To do so, they must unambiguously specify their monetary policy goals: not just interest rate policy but the motivations behind massive purchases of long-term assets and the lowering of rates to zero or negative.

Transparency Is Not Optional

Central banks have made great strides in their communication, but they refuse to be accountable.

These questions relate to the criticality of some of their actions and the opacity of their policies:

- What is the impact of their policies on savings and why do they agree to this expropriation?
- What are the reasons for the sudden drop-in interest rates if there is no growth?
- How do they manage the consequences of not remunerating duration or credit risk in a world where governments no longer pay for their loans but instead have a field day?
- What systemic risk is likely to appear if the creditworthiness of sovereign risks deteriorates to the point of causing a sharp rise in long-term rates?
- What risk is attached to the lack of an exit strategy for their long-term assets, which have just increased by $10 trillion?
- What role did central banks play in the evolution of stock prices, forcing investors to rush into the stock market despite the mediocre performance of companies?
- What is the motivation of central banks in holding corporate risks instead of focusing on the liquidity needs of banks?

- Is it possible to regulate banks that deposit with and borrow from central banks on a regular basis?
- How could central banks have ignored the inflationary risks of their quantitative easing and zero interest rates?

Could it be that central banks are tired of worrying about the level of interest rates on short-term loans to banks and the support of the government bond market and instead have become a gigantic mutual fund for sovereign bonds, intervening in the credit market and even in the junk bond market?

The monetary policy that must be called "classic" is the one that ensures price stability through short-term interest rates and open market operations. The central bank is also the lender of last resort for the banking system.

The Supervision of Banks Needs to Be Transferred to an Independent Agency

When it comes to banks, central banks are judge and jury.

The concentration of powers in the hands of central banks—the power of supervision, of financing their balance sheet by banks, and loaning to banks to ensure the liquidity of their interventions—has never been seriously analyzed. Yet banks fear central banks more than they should.

The Volcker Alliance, a think tank created by the former Federal Reserve Chairman, outlines its "vision to reshape the financial regulatory system for the 21st century. The system for regulating financial institutions in the United States is highly fragmented, outdated, and ineffective." There are 23 institutions that impact the financial world—a veritable theme park for financial institutions. A multitude of federal agencies, self-regulatory organizations, and state authorities share oversight of the financial system in a framework riddled with regulatory gaps, loopholes, and inefficiencies. Virtually every autopsy of the financial crisis cites the convoluted regulatory system as a contributing factor to the financial crisis. The Alliance's goal is a simpler, clearer, adaptive, and resilient regime, equivalent to modern regulatory frameworks in other developed countries, which is mandated to deal with the financial system as it currently exists and is capable of keeping pace with the changing financial landscape. The alliance argues that a properly reconfigured regulatory system is a necessary step toward effective regulation and long-term stability of the financial system.[8]

---

[8] https://www.volckeralliance.org/publications/reshaping-financial-regulatory-system

Need we say it, is this reform still on the Congressional table? Too many institutional, political, and personal interests stood in the way of this improvement in US regulation. But the challenge is to ask ourselves what kind of regulation corresponds to our values.

Europe has developed leadership in such sensitive areas as competition law and privacy, which are essential to financial markets. It has even succeeded in imposing it on non-European financial institutions. This role is essential.

Redefining the Independence of Central Banks

Central Banks Pretend to be Independent: Are They?

Central banks' independence is relative and needs to be qualified.

The multiplication of central banks' functions has sounded the death knell of their independence. By becoming the financier of the executive branch, they compromised the very essence of their mission. This has allowed the executive branch to intervene in reserved areas of monetary policy.

Creating regimes of autonomy in which central banks have real decision-making power is the only way to avoid the entirety of central bank functions coming under the control of the executive branch. Donald Trump's constant attacks on the Federal Reserve are the very example of this political drive to interfere abusively in the decisions of central banks. Central bankers are the first victim of all dictatorships—Egyptian, Greek, and Turkish; the list goes on.

This does not make them dependent on their governments, and it is important to respect those who run these central banks. But their communication is ambiguous and sometimes misleading. They will only be truly independent if they provide consistency between their public discourse and the consequences of their actions. In no case can they depend on the Ministry of Finance, which has an interest in using central banks to reduce their financing costs to the detriment of the risks of the central bank balance sheet and stability.

Redeploying the Corporate World on Its Mission

Large corporations have a fundamental trust problem, and it is growing.

Like every large institution the corporate world is between admiration and hate. But it needs trust.

From the merger between Monsanto and Bayer to the authorization of the pesticides—including glyphosate—that they produce, we know that hundreds of millions have been spent by lobbies to force the European Commission to approve a massive entry of the most polluting chemical company on the planet into the European Union on the basis of reports by experts recruited by the companies themselves. During the financial crisis, the banks spent billions on fees to large law firms to limit the consequences of lawsuits against them.

What is the corporate purpose of financial markets? To make the financing of companies possible and to provide investors with the necessary framework to enable them to make informed choices. Over the past 20 years, the financial markets have evolved in such a way as to make their own interests an end in themselves. They are at the service of shareholders, not of the company or society.

They have succeeded in enlisting public authorities, and particularly central banks, to manufacture returns that are disconnected from the real economy and from the performance of companies, which are forced to manage themselves in the short term instead of taking the risks of building a solid industry. Corporate share buybacks and dividend policies have weakened companies and rely on the state to bail them out, as we saw in 2020.

The time has come to change course and define objectives that consider broader and more complex goals and to hold the private sector accountable

G. Ugeux, *Wall Street's Assault on Democracy*, https://doi.org/10.1007/978-3-031-29094-7_25

for its impact on the environment and society and for the governance it will put in place to achieve it.

This is not an illusion. The changes of the last few years, under pressure from public opinion, are a step in the right direction. We must ensure that these actions continue.

Making Corporate Officers and Directors Personally Accountable

It is people who commit fraud, not institutions.

The transparency and integrity of corporate information are nonnegotiable. Numerous frauds have punctuated the life of the financial markets over the past ten years. They have often resulted in fines being imposed on companies rather than the executives themselves being indicted. Europe is quicker to incarcerate executives suspected of fraud. The United States did not put anyone in jail during the 2008 crisis.

The US practice of companies paying fines for all forms of fraud and other illegal practices without acknowledging responsibility is blatantly insufficient. Why would corporate executives be untouchable when they commit fraud, while politicians can be replaced for their actions?

Individualizing Responsibility

Without strong personal accountability, no respect for leaders is possible.

It is the individuals within companies or governments who are responsible and accountable and who must be penalized, either financially or through deprivation of liberty. It is too easy to have power and not take responsibility for one's actions, while demanding remuneration commensurate with the risk. Ignorance and lack of intent are moral excuses. The company's managers or directors cannot absolve themselves of their responsibility, and ignorance is a failure. There is a discordance between the sometimes-obscene remunerations of executives of large companies and the way they plead ignorance when the situation deteriorates.

It must be said that acquisition bonuses, bonus shares, and golden parachutes fall into this category. US market regulations have mandated that, in extreme cases, executives must return the bonuses of those who have abused the system.

Gary Cohn, the former chairman of Goldman Sachs, who is also a billionaire, refused to return part of his bonuses when a scandal in Malaysia that took place under his authority earned several billion dollars in fines and as much in compensation to the Malaysian government for fraud. This provision was recently challenged in court, and it took the intervention of the SEC (Securities and Exchange Commission) to restore this "minimal" sanction. They were only very partially successful.[1]

This raises a profound ethical question. Individuals or groups of individuals who might be otherwise kind, sincere, and honest in their personal lives seem to change their uniforms when they enter the upper echelons of companies. The disconnection between law and morality is real. After the crisis of 2008, regulators had to remind us of this duty by introducing a new "conduct and culture" rule.

Without individual responsibility, we will never be able to reform a system that enriches the wrongdoers without making them responsible for their actions.

Disconnecting Executive Compensation from the Stock Market

When he rose to the top of Apple, Tim Cook received free shares as the new CEO. They did not compensate any performance since he had not yet proven himself. They were worth $700 million, and he had not taken any risk. Now, these shares are worth more than double. A "loss" of $700 million had to be recorded when these shares were granted. Where is the fairness? Where is the logic?

There are many factors that affect a stock price. The main one is certainly the company's performance, but for several years, particularly in 2020, experience has shown that the stock price can be influenced by various actions, the most obvious of which is the buyback by a company of its own shares. As we have seen in the United States, profits have stagnated while stock price has tripled and with it the remuneration of executives.

The imbalance of the stock option system is that the beneficiary does not have to invest in order to benefit from the capital gain. What is more, it is a

---

[1] https://www.ft.com/content/ef6e63bd-92df-42f3-be7a-aeef31ed8ff8

one-way street. If the share price falls, it is a loss of earnings but not a loss. If the price has risen, the exercise of the option allows for an immediate profit.

The bonus system is also influenced by market developments. Without being strictly correlated to the stock market price, the bonus pool will evolve according to the famous shareholder value. In addition, stock prices are also influenced by government subsidies and stimuli and by injections by central banks.

It is on the results of the company that the remuneration of the manager's performance should be based.

Making Directors Accountable for Avoiding Difficult Questions and Not Sanctioning Management

The board of directors is the weakest link in corporate governance.

The board of directors is a privileged place where members are expected to support the company as a whole, not only the shareholders. Asking the tough questions or challenging the actions of a company or institution's management is a perilous exercise, and I have personally experienced situations where this attitude means the certainty of exclusion or an obligation to resign. It is too easy to hide behind collective responsibility, unless one considers that in the case of a typical management fraud, the entire board of directors must resign.

This is not theoretical: I was on the board of a NASDAQ-listed U.S. company owned by an Indian pharmaceutical group. When we were informed that the various reprimands from the Federal Drug Administration had not been heeded and that the plant had been shut down by the marshals, my blood ran cold. The local outside counsel was willing to do anything to challenge the board's investigative authority. I was removed from the Board Audit Committees by the Chairman of the Board. I resigned and informed the SEC of the reasons for my resignation; the SEC was quick to...do nothing.

Efforts have been made to ensure that audit committees have a certain financial literacy. Before this evolution, the audit committee at J.P. Morgan was headed by the director of a New York theater. The professionalization of boards and the diversification of board members have progressed.[2]

Yet, the presence of lawyers around the board table strips boards of one of their essential roles: taking responsibility. Often, the debate drowns in the waters of compliance. The selection process goes through recruiting firms that are the clients of the executives, and they do not hesitate to propose personalities that fit the mold of "friends of the CEO."

During a seminar organized by the French association of women directors, I was asked the question: What is the most important quality of a woman director? I answered: the courage to ask the difficult questions.

In addition, the risks of legal action against the board are covered by special insurance for directors and officers, and so a form of impunity has taken hold on boards. It is interesting to note that when measures to increase director responsibilities were announced, the main objection was that if too much responsibility was placed on directors, there would be no good candidates.

In some cases, boards and executives have an incestuous relationship. It is time to decouple these two bodies and prohibit the CEO from chairing the board. Directors do not have to manage companies nor are they irresponsible spectators.[3]

There is no way to sanction the actions of directors within the board except the resignation of a director or the entire board. One example comes to mind: the case of Eurostar, the channel tunnel linking England to France and Belgium, whose board was replaced in its entirety during a general meeting. They remain the exception.

However, it would be wrong to generalize. Even if the safeguards are not robust in the event of difficulties, most boards of directors are composed of personalities who have both the necessary skills and the outspokenness. I have known cases where directors have taken personal risks by standing up to management despite threats from lawyers. Rarely they have prevailed, but they have sometimes exposed operational weaknesses that could no longer be ignored.

Courage around the boardroom table is a rare commodity. Asking the right questions can be perilous.

---

[2] https://www.ncsl.org/research/financial-services-and-commerce/financial-literacy-2022-legislation.aspx
[3] https://www.nacdonline.org/insights/publications.cfm?ItemNumber=35784#:~:text=In%20 brief%3A%20As%20the%20corporation's,involvement%20in%20everyday%20company%20 operations

Separating the Functions of Chairman and CEO

Every CEO wants long-standing employees, but their ineffective leadership causes organizational stress that cripples the workplace culture. Quite often, we read articles or hear of CEOs abusing their power and tarnishing their company's reputation. This is due to their neglecting feedback from their team and making decisions based solely on their own judgment. Not only does this erode trust, but it sets a standard that employee and leadership voices are not welcomed.[4]

The last years have demonstrated the immense difficulty (assuming they so desire) for directors to confront toxic CEOs. The vicissitudes of the behaviors of Mark Zuckerberg and Elon Musk of the corporate world are troubling. Their institutional investors will not confront them. A company that is run by such autocrats cannot be labelled ESG, since their governance fails.

The composition of boards and their organization reflects different cultures. Most countries distinguish between the two functions. Recently, however, the number of large companies that have opted for a distinction has increased.

What is important in this separation is a distinction of roles. While the chief executive officer manages the company on a day-to-day basis, the chairman of the board is responsible for the proper functioning of the governance. This is a different responsibility, and the distinction makes sense. It is also the place where strategy, environment, social, and other policies should be discussed—they rarely are.

The limit of the distinction is the relationship between the two leaders. As long as it is positive, everything is fine. However, it would be an illusion to believe there will be no conflicts, and these sometimes give way to real hostility. The appointment of a new CEO or president can also threaten this relationship.

One of the rules that has been imposed in the UK is to prohibit the former CEO from becoming the chairman of the board of the same company. It prevents the new CEO from being kept under the thumb of his or her predecessor or even chosen for his or her sympathetic submission to the latter.

---

[4] https://www.forbes.com/sites/heidilynnekurter/2021/06/27/high-turnover-here-are-3-things-ceos-do-that-sabotage-their-workplace-culture/?sh=1c9c72d3288f

Shares Buybacks Are Strategic Decisions That Must Be Justified

It is essential to impose additional disclosures that justify that, despite these buybacks, the company will not need equity in the next five years. A prospectus that reveals the real reasons for these buybacks, as is done with capital increases, would be welcomed. It is a statement that the future will not provide opportunities. If debt is used, companies are weakened and risk bankruptcy. They have to play their cards right. Equity capital is not a toy in the casino of the stock market.[5]

As of 2022, US companies are currently on pace to spend $1.2 trillion on buybacks—this includes Apple's recent $82.6 billion and Alphabet's $70 billion in share repurchases. Apple alone has spent almost $500 billion in the past decade on buybacks.

Where Are the Banking Regulators?

This trend makes the banking system less robust, and the next crisis will, once again, force central banks to come to the rescue of the banks to protect public savings. But their share buyback programs are there to favor shareholders. Even the pandemic rescue plans supported an indirect form of bailout of the banks, who made enormous profits thanks to the monetary policy.

We understand why these actions, which will prove lethal for many companies, are conducted with the greatest discretion, even if they are not confidential. They must be capped as a matter of urgency. But it is investors, and particularly large wealth managers, who push dividend and share buyback decisions, who ensure a return that is not connected to the performance of the companies.

It is interesting that the Federal Reserve announced that Bank of America Corp., Citigroup Inc., and JPMorgan Chase & Co. face higher-than-anticipated increases in their stress capital buffers under the Federal Reserve's stress tests, likely constraining stock buybacks.[6]

---

[5] https://clsbluesky.law.columbia.edu/2019/04/29/do-share-buybacks-deserve-more-regulatory-scrutiny/
[6] https://www.spglobal.com/marketintelligence/en/news-insights/latest-news-headlines/fed-stress-tests-worse-than-expected-at-bofa-citi-and-jpmorgan-chase-70934399

Making Investors Accountable

What happened after the release of the Larry Fink and the Business Roundtable statement that companies should include values other than profits?[1]

That would be the recent announcement that "Support at BlackRock for U.S. shareholder proposals on environmental and social issues fell by nearly half in this year's annual meeting season, as the world's largest money manager voted for just 24% of them."[2]

Investors like discretion. Some take it to extremes: I remember a meeting with one of the partners of the Eton Park Capital whose website was limited to their name and address. All other access was reserved for investors. A few years later, this hedge fund, which had lost half its value, returned $7 billion to its shareholders. In 2009, several hedge funds rebelled against the SEC (Securities and Exchange Commission) to prevent any form of control of their activities and took it to court in Washington, where they won their case.[3]

But investors are accountable for their influence, through votes or otherwise, on the management and regulators. Large institutional investors themselves are subject to the quarterly earnings constraint and push companies toward actions that have a short-term gain without justifying their position in the long run.

I am increasingly concerned to see major investors make their views known while voting for resolutions that contradict those views. As my colleague Isabel Verkes writes, "Virtually every large asset manager relies on proxy

[1] https://www.businessroundtable.org/about-us/members/laurence-d-fink-chairman-and-chief-executive-officer-blackrock-inc

[2] https://www.ft.com/content/48084b34-888a-48ff-8ff3-226f4e87af30

[3] https://webstorage.paulhastings.com/Documents/PDFs/1188.pdf

© The Author(s), under exclusive license to Springer Nature Switzerland AG 2023
G. Ugeux, *Wall Street's Assault on Democracy*, https://doi.org/10.1007/978-3-031-29094-7_26

advisers in deciding how to cast a ballot at shareholder meetings. That is especially true for managers of mutual funds and ETFs. While their business models are based on scale and low management costs, they still get to vote on many thousands of ballot items for the portfolio companies in their funds. The duopoly of proxy advisory services implies that just two firms—ISS and Glass Lewis—dominate how U.S. shareholders vote their stocks."[4]

Clarifying the Relationship with Issuers

In the system of financial capitalism, the advice of institutional investors is subject to a value system and principles that are all the more important given that these investors who create or run the fund management business are often former investment bankers. Institutional investors are also subject to the iron law of short-term results.

What is more, company executives and portfolio managers are compensated on the same basis: the performance of the stock market price or an equivalent valuation of a private company. Do not count on them to try to influence the company in a different direction than the board or management.

One of the most interesting aspects of this relationship is the voting of institutional investors at shareholders' meetings. We are only beginning to question the influence that institutional investors exert. They have themselves created governance structures that verify decisions on the basis of their own principles.

It sometimes happens that the management principles displayed by the manager are contradicted by the votes.

Promoting Investments Based on Sustainability Principles

The growth of funds that adhere to environmental, social, and governance (ESG) principles is spectacular. This is one of those cases where the power of the people has driven an evolution. It is the younger generation that has challenged us all to not make the planet uninhabitable for humanity. This is a step of considerable importance in terms of democracy. It confirms that the power

---

[4] https://clsbluesky.law.columbia.edu/2020/08/13/the-politics-of-institutional-shareholder-voting-transparency-before-reform/

of the people can bend the powers of capital in a direction they did not want to follow.

Even if the cause of climate change is not taken up by all wealth managers, this disparate population is being transformed before our eyes. Governments should follow—they should ensure that all the institutions that depend on them, be they pension funds, government agencies, or multilateral institutions, are forced to adopt a policy that pursues sustainability principles.

There is a long way to go on the social side. Since employer and employee representatives are not putting this issue on the agenda, it is up to citizens to pressure unions to establish principles of civil society, to ensure that companies, like Apple, that have used child labor in inhumane conditions are shunned by investors. It is not clear that EU countries can agree on common principles.

Applying the governance dimension of ESG would eliminate more than one large technology company, like Facebook, with a poor respect for democracy. The efforts that have been made in this direction are commendable. That Mark Zuckerberg had to testify before several parliaments, where he was criticized for ignoring his role in protecting questionable sources or for the sale of his data without his subscribers' permission, should lead large "ethical" investors to blacklist this company.

The road will be long, and resistance will be strong, but private and institutional investors have the capacity to give their decisions a citizen dimension. It is essentially through the mutual funds in which they invest that, collectively, they can influence the financial markets. But they still need to be informed about how the fund managers vote with their shares.

Promoting Fair Markets

It is vital to understand the various aspects that contribute, both in the public and private sectors, to transforming financial markets into a gigantic machine that crushes equity. A democracy that allows a system that neither imposes nor exercises societal responsibilities is not trustworthy. The events of 2020 were a life-size demonstration of the disconnection of markets in a major economic and employment crisis.

Over the past half-century, financial markets have grown in size and sophistication, which has made their democratic control complex and perilous for those who exercise it. They have grown from 50% to 110% of the GDP at the global level and 150% for the United States, while France, at 85%, has the highest ratio in Europe. This striking force has made it possible to excessively promote inequality in the face of capital:

- The 50 richest Americans now hold almost as much wealth as half of the United States.
- The health crisis has continued to accentuate these inequalities if we are to believe the Federal Reserve's new data from October 15, 2020.
- A quarter of the population has no access to these markets and no means to participate in the collective enrichment of the capital markets. They feel the impact only very indirectly through their bank accounts, insurance policies, mortgage financing, or savings.

The obscene indebtedness of governments is a burden on taxpayers for future generations and threatens financial stability.

© The Author(s), under exclusive license to Springer Nature Switzerland AG 2023
G. Ugeux, *Wall Street's Assault on Democracy*, https://doi.org/10.1007/978-3-031-29094-7_27

As Patrick Artus writes, American households and companies show by their behavior that they are not very risk averse. This explains the reactions of US companies to recessions, the functioning of the labor market, the structure of assets, the levels of debt, and the absence of state socialization of individual risks. Continental Europeans are much more risk averse, which explains the rejection of Anglo-Saxon capitalism's behaviors and types of organization.[1]

The Redistribution of Wealth

At the heart of this system, capital markets have played a crucial role in the redistribution of wealth. In a financial power where states, listed companies, and financial markets take the lion's share, citizen-taxpayers no longer recognize themselves. They have lost confidence in any form of equity. Financial capitalism has transformed economies by financializing them. Financial considerations weigh more heavily than economic and social considerations.

The citizen has come to renounce the only voice that is their own: the vote. Across the world, the abstentionist party outnumbers all others. As impoverishment increases while wealth explodes, they have lost hope that the system can be reformed in their favor. And it is this very despair that poses the most pressing threat to democracy.

The way authorities have responded since the 2008 financial crisis has not improved financial stability. More recently, the handling of the coronavirus crisis has exposed the role of governments in bailing out financial markets for astronomical amounts that will burden taxpayers for decades to come. Moreover, the many other ways in which populations and countries have been affected by the virus has been a further demonstration of inequality, especially in some emerging markets.

Attempting to outline essential reforms to remedy this situation is a difficult and complex task. Reforming the system from within will make it more egalitarian and democratic. Rejecting it all together will not change anything.

Containing the Size of Capital Markets

Financial markets have become too large to be left in the hands of financiers alone.

---

[1] https://www.cairn.info/revue-d-economie-politique-2002-4-page-545.htm

Asset inflation threatens us, as do price increases of services and goods. The essential role of the equity market in financing companies is not in question. But more than ever, the explosion of debt and share buybacks have demonstrated the volatility posed by systemic risks of debt. Growth cannot be achieved without recourse to the capital market.

However, those practices that only serve the interests of shareholders, financial institutions, and their cronies must be stopped. They have represented a multiplier of the "natural" size of the market capitalization without any purpose other than bloating them, which is already overabundant and multiplied by the central banks:

- The coronavirus crisis has caused companies to explode in debt to finance their losses, and almost none of them have issued shares to strengthen their financial structure.
- Investors must have a place where their assets are traded; to take the risk of investing large amounts, they must be able to count on a reasonable possibility of disposing of these investments without upsetting their value.

It is therefore not this primary function of financial markets that is at issue but the various actions that have affected the size of markets outside of this financing function.

Limit the Use of Derivatives Through Capital Adequacy

The usefulness of having means to hedge the risks of companies or investors is real. It is therefore not a question of excluding a technique that has improved and enabled better management of companies. The question is squarely focused on the use of "naked derivatives."

Naked derivatives encourage the development of a speculative market that is completely disconnected from risk hedging needs. The question of its usefulness arises.

Over the last ten years, the outstanding amount of these products has fluctuated between $500 and $700 trillion, according to the Bank for International Settlements. How much of this amount has actually been used to cover risks or to facilitate complex financing?

The only way to limit this market risk is to ensure that financial institutions are forced to allocate a portion of their capital to this activity, not based on their quantification of risk but on the distinction between products used to hedge risks and as a separate activity from those risks. This will reduce the volatility and systemic risk associated with this activity.

Treating Short Selling as Lending

Short selling artificially increases the size of equity markets. They are understandably useful for large portfolio managers who cannot hedge their risks exclusively by selling and buying stocks.

To ensure that this market is contained within reasonable limits and to limit the risks that these positions have posed in financial crises, steps can be taken. The first step is to ensure that the credit risks taken by securities lenders are accounted for in the same way as any equivalent credit transaction.

Prohibiting the use of securities owned directly or indirectly by individuals and pension funds or insurance companies will reduce the availability of securities for such transactions.

Does the existence of "short" and "ultra-short" funds, whether in the form of investment funds or ETFs, really have a reason to exist? Is not it a time bomb that threatens financial stability and leads to massive interventions by central banks? What is their social value?

South Korea's Yoon Suk-yeol administration has declared war on the nation's "deep-rooted" practice of illegal short selling, but retail investors and onlookers are expressing skepticism on whether the practice could really be uprooted.[2]

The financial media Benzinga notes that "Naked Shorts is the biggest risk and greatest scam ever known to man in the stock and associated markets. Now in most financial markets around the world, they have been regulated out of the market or highly restricted. They now own, control, and dominate the SEC regulating body in the USA. This means they are free to attack any company large or small without any worry of consequences."[3]

---

[2] https://www.koreaherald.com/view.php?ud=20220729000527
[3] https://www.benzinga.com/government/22/07/27991938/jr-why-naked-short-selling-is-the-gretest-risk-to-all-stock-investors

Rebalancing Labor and Capital Through Taxation

It is inconceivable to establish an equitable relationship between the social body and finance without raising the question of the contribution of the various players in the financial markets to the state budget. Public finances cannot be based solely on the taxation of work and consumption.

This implies putting in place more effective and robust systems to deal with the use of financial markets for tax evasion or fraud or for laundering criminal money.

Effectively Tax Large Companies

One of the main sources of inequalities is the fact that the bulk of budget revenues comes from salaries and consumption—in one word, households. The decrease of the corporate income tax over the past ten years has reached unacceptable proportions.

One welcomes the Biden initiative that is now adopted by the OECD (Organization for Economic Cooperation and Development) countries. The roughly 200 companies that report profits of more than $1 billion per year, on average and in a three-year period, would pay the new corporate profits minimum tax (CPMT), set at 15% or the amount a company owes under the regular corporate tax—whichever is greater.[1]

---

[1] https://www.americanprogress.org/article/a-corporate-minimum-tax-would-ensure-large-corporations-begin-to-pay-their-fair-share/#:~:text=The%20roughly%20200%20companies%20that,corporate%20tax%E2%80%94whichever%20is%20greater

© The Author(s), under exclusive license to Springer Nature Switzerland AG 2023
G. Ugeux, *Wall Street's Assault on Democracy*, https://doi.org/10.1007/978-3-031-29094-7_28

In the Bristol Hotel in Paris, during the negotiation of a major U.S. acquisition by a French group, I spoke with the group tax executive of the U.S. Group. He was proud not to pay taxes to the Federal Government. However, his tax department worldwide was using 600 tax lawyers to achieve that result.

The obsession of large companies to avoid paying taxes has never been treated as it should be: incivism. It is one of the largest sources of inequality. Are there no other economic challenges that more immediately impact the whole population of a country?

Taxation of Capital Gains

There is no theoretical reason capital gains should not be taxed as ordinary income.

Capital markets are an important part of this inequality, but they are far from being responsible for it. It is therefore necessary to analyze their role in the broader context of the taxation of labor and capital.

There are still tax regimes that do not tax capital gains on the sale of stocks or bonds. The most famous case is that of Bernard Arnault, the CEO of the luxury goods company LVMH, who, after trying to become a Belgian taxpayer (Belgium does not tax capital gains), finally gave up. The situation of Carlos Ghosn, the CEO of Renault, has also been in the news—he is a Dutch tax resident, which allows him to avoid the wealth tax.

The popularity of share buybacks is often due to the fact that they are taxed on a capital gain basis while dividends are taxed as ordinary income. That difference needs to be erased. The same applies to the taxation of the income of hedge funds. While dividends go to all shareholders and are taxable on their full amount, share repurchases distribute earnings only to investors who sell their shares, who then pay capital gains tax on any profits from the sale.[2]

If shares are subject to double taxation, that of dividends and that of company profits, bonds are generally issued on the international markets without any tax being deducted at source.

There is no moral or societal reason to tax capital gains on securities less than other income. It is the greatest source of inequality.

---

[2] https://www.taxpolicycenter.org/taxvox/1-buyback-tax-could-lead-higher-dividend-payouts#:~:text=While%20dividends%20go%20to%20all,any%20profits%20from%20the%20sale

Financial transactions themselves are not taxed. This does not mean that markets are not taxed. Stock exchanges are taxed companies like any other. Stock market players are companies taxed with a corporate tax that, as we know, contributes almost nothing to the state budget.

The idea of taxing financial transactions is not new. Trading activities are taxed through corporate taxation. Investors are subject to taxation in many ways. The most fanciful figures of the tax revenues that would be obtained this way have circulated to the point that the European Union has included such a tax, levied at the European Union level to finance the 750-billion-euro budgetary facility, which helps countries that have suffered the most from the coronavirus.

Promote a Tax on Financial Transactions?

Implemented in France since 2012, the Tax on Financial Transactions is a stock market tax applied to the shares of French companies whose market capitalization exceeds 1 billion euros. Originally 0.1%, the tax rate is currently 0.3% of the acquisition value. With the decrease in brokerage fees and the appearance of low-cost brokers, this tax is becoming increasingly visible and is therefore not negligible in the profitability of a stock market investment.

In the United Kingdom, a stamp duty is required on share transactions. Stamp duty, which dates from 1986 in its current form but existed in other forms long before, is equivalent to 0.5% of the amount of a transaction in the UK.

These 750 billion euros of debt that the European budget will have to carry as part of its stimulus package can be significantly repaid by a tax on stock market transactions, but it is difficult to imagine that this will be the case. Post-Brexit, this would be the best support the City of London could receive from the European Union.

While the measure is obvious, liberals often ignore that financial transactions happen in cyberspace and can avoid national regulations. This is exactly the case with social media companies, which do not get taxed where they earn their revenues.

Agreeing on the principle is fair. Expecting a major source of budget income is not practical.

Fighting Fraud Facilitated by Financial Markets

It is the entire ecosystem of the financial markets that must be mobilized. Whether it is the brokers who give orders, the control of fiscal identity by financial institutions, or the monitoring by stock exchanges and financial markets of suspicious transactions, a mobilization is necessary.

The problem is the anonymity of transactions. It is not the stock exchanges that have the capacity to detect the identity of operators. It is the representatives of the principals, essentially brokers, who are supposed to know their clients.

But this only exists on regulated markets. Cryptocurrency exchanges have made a specialty of money laundering and tax evasion. According to the Directorate General of Public Finance (DGFIP), holding a cryptocurrency is not taxable; it is the fact of converting this cryptocurrency into national currency, which is to say, in a way, reselling it, that "taxes it." Bitcoins have therefore never been included in the wealth tax.[3]

North Korean state-sponsored hackers were likely the perpetrators of a hack that led to the theft of around $100 million in cryptocurrency, according to analysis from blockchain researchers. Russia is rumored to be using cryptos while its foreign currency accounts are frozen.

---

[3] https://www.cairn.info/revue-d-economie-politique-2002-4-page-545.htm

Reconciling Shareholders and Society

There is no reason for the shareholder to be demonized if the remuneration is legitimate and reasonable.

Financial capitalism is in conflict with society, absolving itself of any responsibility toward it. Every member, individual, or institution has a societal responsibility and cannot escape it. Without giving up its raison d'être, the company and its shareholders must identify and assume the role they play in the society in which they operate, in their country and abroad.

Its functioning avoids any form of rebalancing by democracy, which watches helplessly as inequalities explode. If there is a central theme in this book, it is the demonstration of the mechanisms that support the stock market price: dividends, share buybacks, stock options, taxation, debt, interest rates, growth, or recession.

The ideology consists in privileging the value of the shareholder's investment to the detriment of other factors that make the company what it is: society, personnel, and ethics.

The demands of corporate performance rarely allow for a policy that favors the environment, social issues, and governance. Nor does it favor a job-creating investment policy, even if it does affect the immediate results somewhat. The reaction increases as ESG (environmental, social, and governance) investments increase around the world.

© The Author(s), under exclusive license to Springer Nature Switzerland AG 2023
G. Ugeux, *Wall Street's Assault on Democracy*, https://doi.org/10.1007/978-3-031-29094-7_29

A Social and Solidarity-Based Approach to Financial Markets

It is a question of balance and measure.

Efforts have been made to ensure financial regulation combats the excesses of the financial markets, yet it has never been considered that the markets could have a social role, let alone a societal obligation.

Having masses of capital in their hands that can favor the rich and powerful of this world, the financial markets also have the capacity to transform themselves to become, on the contrary, a balancing factor that is in their long-term interest.

Promoting a Long-Term Vision: Publishing a Three-Year Plan Every Year?

It has become almost impossible to discuss the economic and social horizon. The fact that the stock market is riding high while this growth is financed by public and private debt leaves no illusions about what lies ahead.

The publication of quarterly results for companies that rely on the financial markets (whether in the form of bonds or stocks) is useful for some industries, but they are few in number. The decisions that business leaders make are made in the context of their company's purpose. That purpose is ethical, not legal.

My recommendation is not to eliminate the quarterly indications demanded by investors, who are themselves required to publish their performance on a quarterly basis. It is a matter of publishing an annual three-year outlook that will make it possible to measure whether or not the quarterly results are consistent with the three-year plan. If quarterly results challenge this trajectory, an explanation would be provided.

From my conversations with responsible business leaders (they are the majority), I understood their frustration at being corseted in the straitjacket of financial analysts, relayed by the media, who will launch into interpretations comparing Q2 to Q1 and Q2 of last year.

There is no social and solidarity economy with companies whose management horizon is short term. It is time to impose on companies and investors, as well as on analysts, the media, and other acolytes of financial capitalism, disclosures of information that explains how and with what financial, social, and economic objectives the financial strategy is being implemented.

Executive compensation should be based on several years of performance. A single good year does not deserve huge bonuses.

...information that explains how and why a firm's financial... ...identifies the firm's emerging opportunities and... ...executive compensation should be based on several years of performance. A single good year does not deserve huge bonuses.

Strengthening Financial Regulation

Strengthen the Independence of Financial Regulation

Reinforce regulatory independence and resources.

Although it is a sovereign function, regulation must be removed from the clutches of business and government. Too often, we have seen immunities granted to the powerful and harsh penalties imposed for minor misdeeds.

Capital markets are like engines that help power the global economy: they perform best with regular tune-ups. In this spirit, the major regulatory overhaul following the global financial crisis was aimed at shoring up key segments, from over-the-counter derivatives to investment funds and market infrastructure, closing fault lines revealed by the crisis. But now, even after historic enhancements in recent years, countries still need to keep pushing to lower risks and strengthen the tools to manage future crises and ultimately to reduce fluctuations tied to economic cycles.[1]

Market regulators are government agencies and therefore subject to state control. They have limited independence. While the SEC (Securities and Exchange Commission) exercises leadership over global regulation, the European market authority is often limited in its actions by member states.

Most financial scandals have their roots in actions that should have been sanctioned beforehand. Trust in democracy requires this strengthening.

---

[1] https://blogs.imf.org/2022/06/29/capital-markets-regulation-is-stronger-but-some-gaps-still-must-be-closed/?utm_medium=email&utm_source=govdelivery

© The Author(s), under exclusive license to Springer Nature Switzerland AG 2023
G. Ugeux, *Wall Street's Assault on Democracy*, https://doi.org/10.1007/978-3-031-29094-7_30

Party-driven appointments or powerful interests cannot exclusively drive supervisory authorities.

Why would governments appoint heads of supervisory authorities with individuals who might seek to undermine them in their own financial manipulations? Whether it is Veolia-Suez, LVMH-Tiffany, Wirecard, Enron, Airbus, Boeing, and many others, the vulnerability of supervisory authorities is well known. It is not limited to finance—recall how the supervisory authorities were bribed by Boeing for the 737 Max. The list is long and seems to be growing.

This requires a level of remuneration of the regulatory executives and staff that limits the temptation of bribery and allows for the acquisition of talent able to stand up to the bastions of lawyers and large corporations, who are extremely happy to take them on.

Financial Regulation Needs to Be Robust

In recent years, regulators have been embroiled in scandals that have exposed some deficiencies. They are as systemic as they are human.

One cannot help but see this as a meeting of the pot of clay and the pot of iron.

At the structural level, the combination of political leaders at the top of the pyramid with a professional staff creates an imbalance in decision-making and prosecution. The difference in remuneration between the head of a regulatory body and the attorneys and corporate executives he or she regulates does not allow for the recruitment of the necessary talent. One has to be a saint to take these jobs at the price society is willing to pay. And, let us face it, there are many who provide this selfless service to our democracy.

In France, we remember how Société Générale was not sanctioned for its negligent supervision of Jérôme Kerviel, who is in prison. One also remembers the insider trading in Airbus shares, where the facts were proven but where the sanction commission of the Autorité des Marchés Financiers made any serious sanction impossible.

Eric Swanson, the former assistant director of the SEC's Division of Prosecution, is married to Bernie Madoff's niece, who is the general counsel of the Madoff firm. The SEC has been slow to act for two years. It is easy to understand why it did not go all the way in its investigations.

If, in the United States, the methods are sometimes more muscular, the judicial system makes the burden of proof difficult in the face of a lawyer and their expensive services, who will have more than one arrow in their quiver to avoid their client's imprisonment. And yet, cases of insider trading are legion.

Supervising Financial Innovation: The Deceiving Mask of Financial Engineering

The essential economic and social functions of financial engineering are not compatible with some financial innovations that are devoid of any added value for society and that instead have increased the risks attached to these markets, through mechanisms that transform the stock market into a casino.

This field is still in its infancy. The mistakes of central banks and market regulators during the first 15 years of Bitcoin are a reminder of how timid regulators sometimes are and how they react too late and often superficially.

In October 2019, US regulators created a "Global Financial Innovation Network" comprising the four main regulators. Olivier Fliche, the director of the Fintech and Innovation division of the Autorité de contrôle prudentiel et de résolution (ACPR), made the following statement following the Wirecard scandal in Germany:

"We have had exchanges at the European level to coordinate, understand what was happening, and assess the consequences it could have in France for the customers of the regulated subsidiaries of this company. We are of course dealing with these aspects on the spot, but there will also be lessons to be learned in the longer term at the European level, when we have more time to reflect."[2]

Regulating Cryptos

The recent initiatives taken around the world to address the problems raised by crypto assets (it is now admitted that they are not currencies) cannot hide the fact that they came at least ten years late.

The recent collapse of Bitcoin from $68,790 to $17,708 in 52 weeks is not strange given these initiatives. This collapse together with the bankruptcies of crypto exchanges and other operators demonstrates cryptos' absence of substance. There is no way that the world of digital innovation can be regulated using the existing rules and supervisors. They deserve a much more agile type

---

[2] https://www.latribune.fr/entreprises-finance/banques-finance/scandale-wirecard-des-lecons-a-tirer-au-niveau-europeen-experts-acpr-851892.html

of regulation with the ability to force promoters of those assets to explain and present their purpose (if any) to a new type of regulator.

We cannot ignore that regulators have not reacted in a timely fashion with the objective to protect investors. They could have reserved cryptos to QIBs (qualified institutional buyers), imposed the same transparency requirements on "crypto exchanges" as with other trading platforms, and vetted innovative crypto products that proved fatal to investors.

In essence, it is not because it is innovative that it is good. The promoters have to demonstrate the legitimacy of their initiative and its purpose.

The Special Purpose Acquisition Companies (SPACs)

The two-year absence of regulation of SPACs is even more surprising.

SPACs intrinsically arbitrage the IPO (initial public offering) and the M&A (mergers and acquisition) regulation to avoid disclosure. It was pure regulatory arbitrage—how could regulators have missed it? I reached out to the SEC and published a blog on this subject. This is what I wrote in March 2021, following the lack of responsiveness of the SEC:

> Although it has been used in the past, the resurgence of the Special Purpose Acquisition Company (SPAC) has been spectacular in the last two years. According to its promoters, a SPAC offers relatively easy access to a listing on a regulated exchange for a private company looking to go public. The sudden proliferation of SPACs has prompted the SEC to investigate how underwriters are managing the risks involved, according to Reuters. The investigation has so far involved letters from the SEC's enforcement division asking the underwriters to provide the information voluntarily and, as such, has not yet risen to the level of a formal investigative demand.[3]

The recent initiatives have effectively made this regulatory arbitrage useless by making sure that the same requirements apply to SPACs and IPOs. They defeated yet another heavily marketed "innovation" of Wall Street that aimed to enrich the promoters while leaving investors defenseless.[4]

The SPAC was a pure regulatory arbitrage.

---

[3] https://clsbluesky.law.columbia.edu/2021/03/31/regulating-spacs-before-its-too-late
[4] https://www.sec.gov/news/press-release/2022-56

Promote Education, Information, and Honest Communication

The only way to reduce inequalities is through education.

The solution lies between the American model, which puts its students in debt for decades, and the system that provides free or low-cost education. It should come as no surprise that Joe Biden and the Democrats are making this an issue, attempting to provide free access to bachelor's degrees for students with limited family income. Beyond that, a system of scholarships should provide such an education to students who deserve it by virtue of their circumstances and performance.

Without a share of state and local funding, there is no way to balance the budgets of schools and universities. But tuitions, state funding, and research budgets are not enough to provide access to a quality education.

Ideology pollutes this debate between purists who do not want to hear about privately funded schools and those who refuse to recognize the quality of public education.

Here again, the balance tilts toward the wealthy.

Financial Education Must Be Part of Adolescent Education

I know. It is not just about finance.

But high school, technical, and general education curricula do not teach our middle school students about the functioning of the society in which they are starting out and which will soon be theirs.

© The Author(s), under exclusive license to Springer Nature Switzerland AG 2023
G. Ugeux, *Wall Street's Assault on Democracy*, https://doi.org/10.1007/978-3-031-29094-7_31

It should be taught in a clear and objective way (yes, it is possible) in adolescence. It is essential that in the last years of secondary school, a rigorous training in the societal field, including finance, be introduced. At university—for those who have the privilege—specialization dominates. The undergraduate years, however, should teach students how finance works before they become its easy prey.

Finance dominates nothing less than society and democracy. It cannot be ignored by our leaders, whoever they may be. Our students deserve to learn about it.

Whether it is school or university education, it is unspeakable that young students enter life without having received a financial education. At the very least, this education must begin in high school as an important part of the training of those who will enter the world and need to know how it works, especially when they access online trading.

As I prepare to launch a series of podcasts for teenagers to help them understand the basics of finance, I realize that an entire generation has entered into trading without any basis for measuring the risks and rewards that assets bring.

Establishing a True Financial Education of the General Public

This lack of education has led to prominent academics admitting that "they do not understand much about finance" and that they "trust their banker." This resignation in the face of the jargon and manipulations of finance leads to dramatic errors. Ill-informed, how would the notables dare oppose the "financial specialists" or the "bank economists"?

Faced with the information disseminated by companies, managers, politicians, and the media, it has become impossible for any form of citizen control to be exercised, leaving all democratic voices outside the debate. Without sanctions for fake news, our democracy is crumbling.

The debate that has arisen since Donald Trump came to power consists of the value of truth in communication, the use of social media for manipulation, and the value of science.

Money corrupts. We all know that. How do we ensure that this corruption is outlawed in democracy?

Financial Communication in the Age of Fake News

What is well understood is clearly stated,
  And the words to say it come easily. (Nicolas Boileau, L'Art Poétique, 1674)

It must be said that the language of finance has become so technical and abstruse that it is increasingly difficult to understand. Should not graduate schools organize specific training for professionals? Attempts to force share issue prospectuses to be expressed in "plain English" have resulted in the multiplication of pages, making the information amplified and unreadable.

Lawyers know how to secure a monopoly on this language, and we have seen how this monopoly is a source of inequality, since the choice of a defense is measured in hard-earned ducats.

It will never be possible to completely popularize finance, but the summit of its intelligence is not artificial—it lies in the ability to explain a complex reality in simple words.

Even presentations by executives, and especially CFOs (chief financial officers), to their shareholders and a fortiori to the community at large require at least a degree in finance. Vulgarization is the height of intelligence.

Presentations to shareholders at annual general meetings have become incomprehensible to 90% of the participants. Is it too much to ask to present an educational version of these results?

Making the Media Responsible for Financial Information

Where is investigation journalism?

It is not only about the press but about the influence of social media on financial information. Market authorities have tried to regulate the information coming from governments, companies, and investors. We have seen their impact in the GameStop case.

The daily movements of stock prices and their interpretations by journalists often take the place of information. This favors micro-movements and avoids the need to talk about the underlying problems.

Journalists reflect the comments of traders and the messages of companies. Few of them ask questions about the whys and wherefores and are content with day-to-day explanations. The best example was in the first half of 2020. Even while the economy was in decline, a severe recession was underway, central banks were dousing the markets with liquidity, and unemployment was exploding, stock market commentary still focused exclusively on the coronavirus.

As for the comments of the big asset managers, they have only one objective: to lead individuals to buy rather than sell shares.

Rein in Financial Advertisement

The advertising industry has turned to a manipulation of the public.

Each of us is overwhelmed by political, economic, or financial advertising. Elections finance the media. In the cat and mouse game between regulators and advertisers, the latter have the high hand. It is an incredible amount of money that they spend to attract investors into products with a minimum of information and often without any form of veracity.

In the United States, $300 billion are spent on advertising. In the UK, spending on advertising increased by 25%, despite inflation, to $100 billion.

Measures must be taken to avoid some of the plagues provoked by financial advertising. The worst part of it is clearly the promotion of indebtedness to the public. It was one of the causes of the global financial crisis of 2008: the disastrous marketing on mortgages created a crater of debt and pushed families to bankruptcy. It was not prevented by regulators, and after the crisis, it was ultimately sanctioned through fines.

The misleading media who constantly advertise "stocks without risks," "the next Apple stock," or "double your capital" would have been prohibited if Donald Trump had not emasculated the Consumer Finance Bureau, which was supposed to be independent and protect the population from the sharks of fallacious marketing.

A persistent theme in all of CFPB (Consumer Financial Protection Bureau) Director Rohit Chopra's interviews is his concern about the entry of big tech companies into financial services, particularly in connection with payments and the companies' ability to collect and monetize data about consumers.[1]

In the world of fake news, fallacy looks almost benign. Financial advertising will need to become the focus of regulators to avoid another consumer tragedy.

---

[1] https://www.consumerfinancemonitor.com/2022/07/28/director-chopra-goes-on-the-record-with-media/

The Governance of Markets: An Opportunity for Europe

In this period of crisis, the financial message has become political.

Whether by central banks or governments, the uncritical defense of alternative monetary and stimulus policies had only one objective: to reassure investors, especially the individuals who pounced on this windfall.

Nowhere was the White House's admiring chorus of delight at the slightest improvement in stock prices more evident than in the United States. Rumors of recessions were seen as coming from "lying democrats." Political parties outlined policies that ignored the limits created by the catastrophic state of the markets and the economy.

Do not the authorities have a fiduciary duty to tell the truth? Why should not parliamentarians or ministers be accountable for the information they have and use in the form of financial transactions where they are effectively "insiders"? The transgressions that lie behind their financial means and the tendency for their assets to cross borders are an abandonment of their fiduciary duties.

Developing a Robust European Financial Market

The ideology of American financial markets is not compatible with European values.

The globalization of financial markets has been dominated by the invasion of investors and market operators from across the Atlantic who have taken hold in Europe's London marketplace. Rethinking globalization and its limits

© The Author(s), under exclusive license to Springer Nature Switzerland AG 2023
G. Ugeux, *Wall Street's Assault on Democracy*, https://doi.org/10.1007/978-3-031-29094-7_32

and creating regional financial markets have become a priority. For Europe, this is a unique opportunity to define societal priorities that apply to markets.

The transformation of globalization opens up opportunities for Europe if it is prepared to take responsibility for them. Recent climate initiatives distinguish Europe from the rest of the world. With the election of Joe Biden and Kamala Harris, the United States' entry into the Paris Agreement provides a strong ally.

European financial markets have a unique opportunity to redefine the principles, values, and goals that do not match what is at the heart of the United States. This may be a benefit of Brexit, which will mitigate the City's influence on European regulations.

Establishing a European Model of Corporate Governance

The dogmatism of shareholder value, the financial valuation models, and the importance of investors responding to this model have created a form of iron law that has been imposed on companies.

This situation has created a handicap for the European markets. In addition to their fragmented liquidity, valuation is still largely national. For those parts of the world that consider companies to have a societal duty and cannot favor only shareholders, valuations have fallen.

But there is a serious lack of a European model of corporate valuation, which would seek a balance between respect for shareholders and respect for democracy as Europe understands it—participatory, multicultural, supportive, and fair.

Why do American banks trade at more than 20 times their profits on the stock market, while their European counterparts languish at around 10 times? Are they less professionally managed? Do they follow a different model than the American financial markets? These are the kinds of questions we need to ask ourselves.

How can we do this when a quarter of the capital of large companies is held outside Europe and mainly in the United States? Why is the European market dominated by BlackRock and not by European asset management firms?

The Regionalization of Globalization Is an Opportunity for Europe

Globalization Will Have to Evolve

Reactions to the abuses are being felt and are welcomes. In developed countries, the center of gravity of markets remains local or, more precisely, regional. The retreat of US moral and economic leadership under Donald Trump will not be adjusted easily by Joe Biden.

Protectionism is not absent—Brexit, for instance, was a painful revelation for Europe. The emergence of Chinese leadership with all its worrying aspects defines three new zones of influence: the United States, China, and Europe.

The financial markets will follow this redefined global economic model if it develops. This is the mistake the European Commission made when it forbade the takeover of Euronext by Deutsche Boerse. Euronext then took refuge in the arms of Uncle Sam, who ultimately rejected it, but not without having plundered it of its best assets: the derivatives market.

Antitrust legislation must evolve in the direction of regional centers. European companies must be allowed to build a base that, even if it seems exorbitant by European standards, allows them to compete with other global financial centers. After Brexit, this challenge is even more essential, and we must avoid sending the City of London back into the arms of the Americans or the Asians.

It is therefore becoming urgent to integrate the financial markets around these axes, creating an economic and social model that has its own liquidity and valuation capacity.

The European Capital Markets Union Is an Essential Ambition

The arrival of the euro was an opportunity for critical mass in the face of the neoliberal model. But the lack of progress of this currency as a reserve currency, and even more so as an integrator of fiscal policies, does not yet allow for the definition of a European regional market. The decline of the dollar as a reserve currency does, however, present an opportunity that the Eurozone can seize across its entire continent.

The Capital Markets Union initiative is undoubtedly a step in the right direction. But the way it is politicized and designed, and the lack of conversation with the city of London, unnecessarily complicates it.

Without this essential tool, Europe has no way to free itself from the American model. It is a matter of building a structure that makes transactions within the European Union transparent and free of administrative obstacles.

The time has come to leave the Olympus of high principles and to tackle the means of achieving these objectives in the concrete world of European systems and divergent political approaches.

Renewing the Threads of Trust in Finance: An Ethical Endeavor

In June 2022, the Rockefeller Foundation published a report on "the urgency of equity."[1]

Financial markets are confronted with an evolution whose complexity is indisputable, but they have abused it by venturing in directions that have increased inequalities and threaten democracy; these impacts are rarely an issue discussed around the board table. Societal responsibility is not on the agenda. Nor are ethics.

The loss of public confidence in the banking and financial sectors is justified. Trust will only be restored if the moral hazard and conflicts of interest are addressed, the OECD says.[2]

This journey will have allowed the reader to realize the difficulty of reconciling the two enemy sisters that are finance and democracy, in the context of financial markets that have become more important than financial intermediation by banks.

I am convinced that this is possible under certain conditions. Even if the measures put forward are likely to allow an adjustment of the influence of financial markets and their political, economic, and social power, they will not be enough without a profound change of mentality.

---

[1] https://www.rockefellerfoundation.org/matter-of-impact/the-urgency-of-equity/?utm_source=Rockefelle r+Foundation+eAlerts&utm_campaign=4539fd144a-EMAIL_CAMPAIGN_2022_06_29_MATTER_ OF_IMPACT_EQUITY&utm_medium=email&utm_term=0_6138ee88b7-4539fd144a-127873069& goal=0_6138ee88b7-4539fd144a-127873069&mc_cid=4539fd144a&mc_eid=92f2f74a67

[2] https://www.oecd.org/fr/finances/pour-une-finance-digne-de-confiance.htm

© The Author(s), under exclusive license to Springer Nature Switzerland AG 2023
G. Ugeux, *Wall Street's Assault on Democracy*, https://doi.org/10.1007/978-3-031-29094-7_33

Telling the Truth to Regain Confidence

The first condition for restoring trust is to recognize that the current characteristics of the financial markets increase inequalities in ways that are unsustainable for a democracy and feeds easy populism.

The abuse of financial power is a profound source of social and political instability. Whether it is the feeling that capitalism only benefits the rich, that corporations are rapacious, and that governments are corrupt or simply the experience of deep personal and family deprivation, there is a crisis of confidence in democracy.

Ignoring this crisis is the source of social movements, against which the elite is powerless. How can we avoid the reconstitution of a "center" where right-wing and left-wing populisms come together, and which collectively represent a growing fraction of the population of our Western countries? If the owners had the intelligence to understand that it is they who are at the origin of these sometimes-bloody protests, they would find in the menu mentioned here a catalog of measures that would reduce the social fracture.

Today, the population is deeply convinced that financial markets are a weapon of war directed against it. This is not false, even if it must be qualified. The succession of scandals, the drop in their purchasing power, or unemployment, all while the stock market soared in 2020, has definitively convinced them: the stock market is disconnected from the real economy, and everything is done to favor the shareholders.

It is urgent to tell the truth about the weakness of our public finances, the role played by central banks in the resurgence of stock prices, the economic recession, and the way in which the shareholder is favored over the employees.

Only by sharing this foundation of common truths will we rebuild credible communication and unbiased education. It is from this base of honesty that we will be able to obtain democratic support to rebuild a social and solidarity economy.

Disconnect the Remuneration System from the Stock Price

To regain trust, we need to change our mentality. This is perfectly possible, but it is not only individual measures that will change the operators of financial markets. How can we convince them that their interest lies precisely in credibility? If not, what rules should be imposed on them to prevent them from overrunning our democracies?

Tongue-in-cheek accountability has become the rule in finance. Certainly, there is a risk of legal proceedings in the event of an admission of responsibility by the financial institution. The American market regulator sentences perpetrators of fraud or irregularities to substantial fines, accepting that they agree to pay "without any admission of wrongdoing."

The need to regain trust requires a fundamental review of compensation inequalities. Corporate executives are not (all) mercenaries, and I know many who are willing to accept a "reasonable" compensation that would ensure greater trust with their staff, whatever the headhunters think.

This compensation inequality is truly intolerable. Limiting golden parachutes and taking the company's performance, not its stock market value, as a benchmark will ensure that competent managers are hired, rather than mercenaries who change companies every five years.

Do the beneficiaries of this bonanza realize that they are sawing off the branch on which they are sitting? Do they really believe that their self-interest will have no consequences?

Recognize the Politicization of Financial Markets

Democratic and citizen control is only possible if it becomes clear that it is the alliance of business and government that poses the profound problem of finance's politicization, particularly of financial markets:

- The astronomical sovereign indebtedness, the pharaonic support of central banks, and the conflict of value systems have led to an increasing politicization of financial markets.
- The lobbying of big business for privileges and subsidies leads to a form of collusion with the political world.
- The remuneration system and the governance of companies listed on the financial markets have become the most destructive factor when it comes to employment.

Financial markets have a particular duty: to ensure equity among investors, to open access to financing for medium-sized companies and emerging countries, and to support governance initiatives and climate risk. They play an essential role in these areas.

Will their shareholders allow them to do so?

Ex Aequo and Bono: The Need for Democratic Equity

Democracy implies a form of balance among parties. We are far from it. Finance does not seek to be equitable; it seeks its own interest, and the financial markets are a privileged place for this search. They encompass 10% of the population at most and 90% of the world's wealth.

All the recent categories of sustainable investing, such as ESG (environment, social, and governance) or SRI (socially responsible investment), have turned to aspects of finance that had been ignored: the societal impact. Achieving a form of equity, and even better, being perceived as equitable, seems today to be a Dantesque undertaking, as the distance between democracy and the practices of finance has become so great. It is a change of mentality that is needed, and at the center of it is an ethical backbone, which is painfully missing.

The financial markets have developed on the basis of an ideology—that of American financial capitalism. Founded on the advantage given to shareholder value, it has ignored the fact that a company cannot be run with the sole objective of the share price and the dividend. On the altar of this ideology, millions of jobs have been sacrificed, purchasing power has languished behind executive salaries, and financial wealth has reached record levels.

In line with this ideology, governments went into debt to maintain programs they could not afford at any cost, and central banks absorbed trillions of these debts. In doing so, they favored the borrowers, or the issuers of bonds, and indirectly supported a stock market rise that they refuse to reduce to its intrinsic value.

In the end, it is the citizen who, through direct or indirect taxation, suffers the consequences of these policies, which tax him twice: through taxes and through negative interest rates. The reform of financial markets cannot be done with a stroke of the pen—many adjustments to the financial system will be needed to recreate a balance between capital and labor. Failure to reform could lead to revolts by desperate populations.

2020 will have seen an explosion of world debt that will further aggravate a brutal economic recession. It will also have shown that this debt has not been directed toward health care or hospital structures, which are one of the most essential public and private services. As always, it will be the poorest who suffer the most.

There Is No Democratic Society Without Equity

The marketplace, by itself, cannot resolve every problem, however much we are asked to believe this dogma of neoliberal faith. Whatever the challenge, this impoverished and repetitive school of thought always offers the same recipes. Neoliberalism simply reproduces itself by resorting to the magic theories of "spillover" or "trickle"—without using the name—as the only solution to societal problems. There is little appreciation of the fact that the alleged "spillover" does not resolve the inequality that gives rise to new forms of violence threatening the fabric of society. It is imperative to have a proactive economic policy directed at "promoting an economy that favors productive diversity and business creativity" and makes it possible for jobs to be created and not cut. Financial speculation fundamentally aimed at quick profit continues to wreak havoc. Indeed, "without internal forms of solidarity and mutual trust, the market cannot completely fulfill its proper economic function. And today this trust has ceased to exist....we must put human dignity back at the center and on that pillar build the alternative social structures we need."

Pope Francis, Encyclical Lettre, Fratelli Tutti, October 2020

These Books Inspired Me

Jacques de la Rosière

Putting an End to Financial Illusion
2022 Odile Jacob Editions

Mohamed El-Erian

The Only Game in Town: Central Banks, Instability, and Recovering from Another Collapse
2019 Random House

Kathryn Judge

Direct: The Rise of the Middleman Economy and Power of Going to the Source
2022 Harper Business

Thomas Piketty

Capital and Ideology
2020 Harvard University Press

Katharina Pistor

The Code of Capital: How the Law Creates Wealth and Inequality
2019 Princeton University Press

© The Author(s), under exclusive license to Springer Nature Switzerland AG 2023
G. Ugeux, *Wall Street's Assault on Democracy*, https://doi.org/10.1007/978-3-031-29094-7_34

Raguram Rajan and Luigi Zingales

Saving Capitalism from the Capitalists: Unleashing the Power of Financial Markets to Create Wealth and Spread Opportunity
2004 Princeton University Press

Raguram Rajan

The Third Pillar: How Markets and the State Leave the Community Behind
2019 Penguin Press

Paul Sheard

The Power of Money: How Governments and Banks Create Money and Help Us All
2023 Prosper

Paul Tucker

Unelected Power: The Quest for Legitimacy in Central Banking and the Regulatory State
2018 Princeton University Press

9783031290930